Charlotte von Kirschbaum
and Karl Barth

**The Penn State Series
in Lived Religious Experience**

Judith Van Herik, General Editor

The series publishes books that interpret
religions by studying personal experience
in its historical, geographical, social, and
cultural settings.

Lee Hoinacki, *El Camino:
Walking to Santiago de Compostela*

Suzanne Selinger, *Charlotte von Kirschbaum
and Karl Barth: A Study in Biography and the
History of Theology*

Charlotte von Kirschbaum and Karl Barth

A STUDY IN

BIOGRAPHY AND

THE HISTORY

OF THEOLOGY

Suzanne Selinger

The Pennsylvania State University Press
University Park, Pennsylvania

The unpublished letters between Charlotte von Kirschbaum and Henriette Visser't Hooft-Boddaert are cited by courtesy and permission of the Karl Barth-Archiv, Basel, Switzerland.

Library of Congress Cataloging-in-Publication Data

Selinger, Suzanne.
    Charlotte von Kirschbaum and Karl Barth : a study in biography and the history of theology / Suzanne Selinger.
        p.   cm — (The Penn State studies in lived religious experience)
    Includes bibliographical references (p.   ) and index.
    ISBN 0-271-01824-0 (cloth)
    ISBN 0-271-01864-X (pbk.)
    1. Kirschbaum, Charlotte von, 1899–1975.   2. Theologians —Switzerland—Biography.   3. Barth, Karl, 1886–1968—Friends and associates.   I. Title.   II. Series.
BX4827.K55.S45   1998
230'.044'0922—dc21
[B]
                                                           98-16937
                                                           CIP

It is the policy of The Pennsylvania State University Press to use acid-free paper for the first printing of all clothbound books. Publications on uncoated stock satisfy the minimum requirements of American National Standard for Information Sciences—Permanence of Paper for Printed Library Materials, ANSI Z39.48-1992.

Contents

Acknowledgments

My first debt is easy to locate. This book owes its origin to a gift from a Drew student, Abraham Kwang Koh, in 1990. Upon completion of his doctoral work, he presented me with a copy of Renate Köbler's *In the Shadow of Karl Barth: Charlotte von Kirschbaum*. Very interesting, I thought; and, having begun another project, I put it in the back of my mind as a prospective research subject for someone else. A few years later, unsuccessful in giving away the subject, I realized it had taken possession of me. Then Janet Fishburn and Robin Lovin convinced me that it was a book, and the project was on its way.

My greatest debt is to Eberhard Busch, to whose densely rich biography everyone in Barth studies is obligated. Busch was Charlotte von Kirschbaum's successor as secretary to Karl Barth and now occupies the Chair in Reformed Theology at the University of Göttingen that Barth was the first to hold. He shared his recollections and responded to my multitudinous questions with answers that stimulated more questions. Corresponding with him has been one of the best experiences in my life.

I have also had the benefit of talking at length with John Hesselink, Neill Hamilton, Frederick Herzog, and John Godsey about Barth, their former teacher, and about von Kirschbaum, a memorable presence in their years at Basel. I was lucky enough to have exchanged several letters with Markus Barth before his death in 1994. I was also fortunate in corresponding with Esther Röthlisberger-Pestalozzi, who shared some of her mother's memories of Barth and von Kirschbaum with me.

I note with gratitude that my formal research began with an inquiry in 1992 to Hinrich Stoevesandt, director of the Karl Barth-Archiv, concerning access to correspondence in the Archiv, and ended in the last days before his *Emeritierung* in October 1997 with a flurry of faxes about the photographs that illustrate this book. Elisabeth Stoevesandt was part of this final service; there were many intermediate exchanges. The Stoevesandts were always as ready to help as they were cordial.

Daniel Migliore, Christopher Morse, and William Stroker generously found time to share important observations and information. Bruce McCormack and George Hunsinger provided information and were especially helpful in prodding me to examine and re-examine many aspects of my subject.

Drew University has been a wonderful place for work on this project. Donald Dayton gave the manuscript a knowledgeable reading and offered welcome encouragement. Donald Kent generously educated me about the medical conditions that correspond to von Kirschbaum's final illness. My student assistant, Matthias Beier, expedited some trans-Atlantic telephone calls; his lively interest in the subject of the calls was of further help. In ways less specifically related to von Kirschbaum or Barth but decisive nonetheless, the feminist community at Drew is part of this book. Especially I thank Catherine Keller for formative feminist dialogue and Virginia Burrus, who modeled feminist scholarship.

The Drew Library granted me a sabbatical in Spring 1994: this was an essential jump-start. I am additionally grateful to my library colleagues for all sorts of help. Linda Connors provided steady and crucial encouragement. Bruce Lancaster provided good leads in the history of technology. And Josepha Cook, CEO of Interlibrary Loan, handled every one of my obscure, elusive citations with grace and success.

It has been a pleasure to work with Penn State University Press. I thank Judith Van Herik, the Series editor, and I thank Philip Winsor and Cherene Holland, who took truly impressive care of the several drafts of this study. I also thank two anonymous readers for the Press who provided some excellent suggestions. After all these contributions, however, I remain responsible for the faults, omissions, and choices in this study.

And finally: I dedicate this book to my family—four generations!—with greatest gratitude for their sustaining faith and warmth.

Note on Quotations and Abbreviations

Generally, if a standard English translation of a German work exists, I quote from it in my text and refer to it by the translated title; the notes cite the English version and in parenthesis cite the original German. In certain instances, I have preferred my own translation, indicating it as such in the notes, occasionally with comment on the divergence. Where no English translation exists, the translation is my own. For quoted passages under close scrutiny, I provide the original German text in the notes.

The following abbreviations are used:

WF for Charlotte von Kirschbaum, *Die wirkliche Frau*

CD for Karl Barth, *Church Dogmatics* (*KD* for *Kirchliche Dogmatik*)

GD for Karl Barth, *Göttingen Dogmatics*

RGG for *Die Religion in Geschichte und Gegenwart*

PART 1 | # Questions

> *I should not like to conclude this Preface without expressly drawing the attention of readers of these seven volumes [of* Church Dogmatics*] to what they and I owe to the twenty years of work quietly accomplished at my side by Charlotte von Kirschbaum. She has devoted no less of her life and powers to the growth of this work than I have myself. Without her cooperation it could not have advanced from day to day, and I should hardly dare contemplate the future which may yet remain to me. I know what it really means to have a helper.*
>
> —Karl Barth, *Church Dogmatics* III/3: xii–xiii [1950]

1. Dramatis Personae

Charlotte von Kirschbaum was Karl Barth's secretary and theological assistant (Barth's term) for more than thirty-five years. So indispensable did her presence seem to Barth that he incorporated her into his household, which consisted of himself and his wife, Nelly, and five children; and she accompanied him, without Nelly, on lecture tours and on academic recesses in the mountain retreat owned by friends of his at Bergli. Most of the discussion of the two has consisted of value-laden speculation on their personal relationship: either they were or were not united in a romantic liaison. More recent attention has focused on von Kirschbaum's role in the evolution of the *Church Dogmatics*. This too

has taken the form of accusation and denial: to attribute anything substantive to von Kirschbaum seems to provoke a need to defend Barth's
authorial autonomy.

Barth and von Kirschbaum first met in 1924. He was thirty-eight and
she was twenty-five. He was Professor of Reformed Theology at the
University of Göttingen. His call to Göttingen from a pastorate in
Safenwil (in 1921) was the result of his immediately famous commentary,
The Epistle to the Romans. Lacking formal training at the doctoral level,
he was at first overwhelmed by the amount of preparatory work needed
for his lectures. His correspondence with Eduard Thurneysen, his
intimate friend and collaborator in the Safenwil years, makes clear—
sometimes with anguish, sometimes with humor—the full extent of his
sense of unpreparedness.[1] The lengthy letters also demonstrate Barth's
lifelong need for a dialogue partner, a theme to which we will return.
Barth felt further isolated by the Lutheran identity of the University of
Göttingen and its insistence that he specifically list his courses as
Reformed theology. At the end of the spring semester in 1925, he
accepted a professorship in dogmatics and New Testament exegesis at
the University of Münster. Here his relationship with von Kirschbaum
becomes more intensive and complex.

In 1924 Charlotte von Kirschbaum was a German Red Cross nurse in
Munich. Much about her early life and family, which included two
brothers, is unknown or unclear—she talked little about it. Her father was
a military officer; consequently, her childhood was largely a wandering
one. She was very close to her father, who recognized and encouraged
her intellectual gifts.[2] Charlotte completed a *Lyzeum* education, a course
that did not qualify for immediate entrance to a university, in 1915.[3] She

1. See especially Barth to Eduard Thurneysen, 26 March 1922, in *Revolutionary
Theology in the Making: Barth-Thurneysen Correspondence, 1914–1925,* trans. James D.
Smart (Richmond, Va.: John Knox, 1964), and the fuller German edition: *Karl Barth–
Eduard Thurneysen Briefwechsel, Bd. 2, 1921–30* ([Karl Barth, *Gesamtausgabe,* Bd. V.
Briefe], Zurich: Theologischer Verlag, 1974).
2. Renate Köbler, *In the Shadow of Karl Barth: Charlotte von Kirschbaum,* trans.
Keith Crim (Louisville, Ky.: Westminster/John Knox, 1989), 23–25; Inge Stephan, *Das
Schicksal der begabten Frau: Im Schatten berühmter Männer,* 6th ed. (Stuttgart: Kreuz
Verlag, 1991), 180–83.
3. Köbler, *In the Shadow,* 24. The *Lyzeum* was the higher secondary girls school
within the general secondary education system (established in 1908, lasting through
Weimar). Its curriculum was to be equal in value but not in kind to boys' schooling. It
emphasized modern languages, the arts, and needlework. See Ute Frevert, *Women in
German History: From Bourgeois Emancipation to Sexual Liberation,* trans. Stuart
McKinnon-Evans (Oxford: Berg Publishers, 1989 [orig. German, 1986]), 80.

worked for a brief time at an army office for mail censorship, and she seems to have intended, as the daughter of a military officer with the status of nobility, to join the Order of St. John, a military religious organization in the hospitaler tradition, devoted since its reorganization in 1852 to care of the sick.[4] Her father was killed in the Great War in 1916. At the end of the war she went to her mother's home and almost immediately left and entered training as a Red Cross nurse. The reasons for the change of plans are unknown; perhaps they are a combination of deteriorated relations with family that made immediate independence necessary and the palpable wartime health costs. The change seems institutional rather than vocational. The War had provided a test of women's efforts in the *Nationaler Hilfsdienst*.[5] The German Red Cross provided nurses' training to women (*Krankenschwestern*) in what seems to have been a more clearly religious framework than other branches of the international organization and (conversely) in a more practical program than the other pathways.[6] The deaconess movement, however, was the pervasive model for female care of the sick and needy in Germany. Founded in 1836 by Theodor Fliedner, the movement was inspired by eighteenth- and early nineteenth-century religious revivals in which prominent roles were assumed by women, largely in England. Although the German deaconess movement in turn stimulated the movement in U.S. Protestant churches,[7] its social, political, and indeed religious, ethos was vastly different from that in either England or America. With origins in the Wars of Liberation in the Napoleonic period, the deaconess movement was Christian (with Lutheran domination), nationalistic, and politically and socially conservative.[8] Its institutional

4. Köbler, *In the Shadow*, 24. On the Order of St. John, see *New Schaff-Herzog Encyclopedia of Religious Knowledge*, s.v. "John, Saint, Order of Hospitalers of." Köbler (*In the Shadow*, 142 n. 12) states that von Kirschbaum's nephew Wolf von Kirschbaum told her that Charlotte intended to become a deaconess; Eberhard Busch told her (on the basis of information from von Kirschbaum's friend, Lili Simon) that von Kirschbaum intended rather to join the Order of St. John.

5. *Die Religion in Geschichte und Gegenwart* (3rd ed., hereafter *RGG*), s.v. "Frau."

6. *Der Grosse Brockhaus* (18th ed.), s.v. "Rotes Kreuz." Local and loosely affiliated organizations existed since the mid-nineteenth century; a national organization was formed in 1921.

7. See Catherine M. Prelinger and Rosemary S. Keller, "The Function of Female Bonding: The Restored Diaconessate of the Nineteenth Century," in *Women in New Worlds*, ed. R. S. Keller, L. Queen, and H. F. Thomas (Nashville: Abingdon, 1982), 318–25.

8. Elisabeth Moltmann-Wendel, "The Women's Movement in Germany," *Lutheran World* 22 (1975): 122; and Catherine M. Prelinger, *Charity, Challenge, and Change: Religious Dimensions of the Nineteenth-Century Women's Movement in Germany* (Westport, Conn.: Greenwood Press, 1987).

trademark was the motherhouse diaconate, and it trained women to care for the sick, sinful people of the earthly city.[9] In the late nineteenth century, deaconess work was extended to other kinds of social need and was included in the *Innere Mission* organization of the Evangelical Churches.[10] It is the German deaconess movement that defined the character of the Women's Movement and early feminism in Germany—a subject with which we will be variously concerned.[11]

Von Kirschbaum had been interested in theology for a long time, and this interest deepened and flourished—and the horizons of her world widened—when she got to know Georg Merz, a Lutheran pastor, central figure in intellectual and cultural circles in Munich, theological consultant at Kaiser Verlag, and early champion of Barth's *Romans*. In 1922 Merz became editor of *Zwischen den Zeiten*, the journal founded by Barth, Thurneysen, and Friedrich Gogarten. Merz introduced von Kirschbaum to Barth's theology and then to Barth, probably first in a visit to the Bergli, the summer home of Ruedi and Gerty Pestalozzi that became "headquarters" for Barth, Thurneysen, and several other regulars for summer work and respites from the early 1920s to the 1950s. Published observations by these friends and colleagues constitute a principal source for this study.[12]

Von Kirschbaum and Gerty Pestalozzi became friends, and von Kirschbaum made a second, longer visit to Bergli in 1925, along with Merz. In this visit, she spent time with Thurneysen as well as with Barth. (Curiously, in light of the career ahead of her, her reason for the stay was a need for rest from the strenuous work of her nursing job.)[13] In August 1925 Thurneysen wrote to Barth that she ought to go to work for Kaiser, as Merz's secretary.[14] Barth regarded von Kirschbaum's summer visit of 1925 as memorably special: in a retrospective autobiographical chronology, he wrote for 1925, using the name by which all von Kirschbaum's friends knew her: "Bergli, Lollo!"[15] Apparently Barth, with financial support from the Pestalozzis—we don't know who initiated the idea— sent her to secretarial school in Munich, after which she left nursing and

9. Moltmann-Wendel, "The Women's Movement in Germany," 123–24.
10. Ibid., and *RGG*, s.v. "Frauenverbände."
11. See Moltmann-Wendel, "The Women's Movement in Germany," 122–30 passim.
12. On Merz's role in von Kirschbaum's life, see R. Köbler, *In the Shadow*, 25–27 and passim; Eberhard Busch, *Karl Barth: His Life from Letters and Autobiographical Texts*, trans. John Bowden (Philadelphia: Fortress Press, 1976), 158, 164.
13. Köbler, *In the Shadow*, 28.
14. Ibid., 29–30; ET to KB, 31 August 1925, *KB-ET Briefwechsel*.
15. Köbler, *In the Shadow*, 143 n. 13.

took a job as an industrial social worker at the Siemens Werke in Nürnberg.[16] By late 1926, it is clear that she was serving on a part-time basis as Barth's theological assistant, even if he does not yet use the term. She and Barth corresponded. Their letters are not yet accessible, but Barth describes the assistance she provided as manuscript critic in his letters to Thurneysen.[17]

Something else happened in 1925–26. The relationship of Barth and von Kirschbaum crystallized in February 1926 in Münster, where Barth lived without his family from late October to early March, awaiting final sale of the Göttingen house and purchase of a new house in Münster, when his family would rejoin him. Apparently intellectual rapport became personal attraction, and the two realized they loved each other. They confronted their situation directly and in letters, basing the discussion on two premises: that Barth's marriage must remain unbroken, and that Charlotte was not to be, or seem to be, Karl's mistress.[18] Barth's decision around 1926 was an extremely difficult one. Here we need to return to personal history; some threads from that history will stay with us throughout this study.

In the summer of 1907, when he was twenty-one and a student in Bern, Barth fell deeply in love with a young woman named Rösy Münger. We know very little about her. She looked like all the clichés for a beautiful and wholesome wife and mother, she was gentle, *and* Barth was teaching her to love theology. They knew with absolute certainty that they wanted to marry, but Barth's parents refused to accept the relationship, and Barth acquiesced in their intervention.[19] At a final meeting the two burned their letters. Barth never got over this love and kept a picture of Rösy till the end of his life. He saw her only once again, in an unplanned, fleeting encounter: she came to hear him preach at the cathedral in Berne around 1915. Rösy's life ended prematurely in 1925: she died of leukemia. Karl spent a day in his study grieving for her.[20]

16. Ibid., 31, 143 (n. 3 for chap. 4).

17. An edition of Barth–von Kirschbaum letters will eventually be published as part of the letter series in the *Gesamtausgabe*, but not in the immediate future (personal communication, Hinrich Stoevesandt, Director, Karl Barth-Archiv, 29 May 1992). See also pages 13 and 38–39 below on the project. The dates of the KB letters to ET on von Kirschbaum's assistance to him (discussed in Part 2 below): 8 November 1926, 19 November 1926, 26 December 1926. See also Busch, *Karl Barth*, 185f.

18. Eberhard Busch, personal communication, 19 July 1994 (letter).

19. Ibid. Rösy was the daughter of a liberal manufacturing family; perhaps there was some social snobbery here.

20. Busch has discussed the possible relationship between the breakup with Rösy at parental decree and Barth's conception of the divine vis-à-vis human will in *Epistle to the*

In 1913 Barth had married Nelly Hoffmann, and his marriage had been troubled and unhappy almost from the start.[21] Nelly (six years younger than he) was a member of his congregation and had been in one of his confirmation classes. The marriage was largely engineered by his mother, Anna. Nelly Barth and Anna Barth were similar in many ways— Barth once said they were all too similar. They were outspoken and hard-edged, domineering and "difficult." Nelly Barth ruled her kitchen helpers so harshly and arbitrarily that there was continual turnover: the workers found her intolerable. She behaved similarly toward Karl.[22] We will have occasion to return to Anna Barth as well as to the Anna-Nelly type (a formulation suggested by Eberhard Busch), which, I think, is very much like the women Barth depicts in his vitriolic remarks on feminism.

Charlotte was not the successor to either Nelly or Rösy. But Barth said that when he met her, his loneliness ended.[23] Loneliness, *Einsamkeit*, is a key word for Barth: he described hell as loneliness.[24] One of the striking characteristics of Barth's life is that he had an extraordinary number of close and lasting friendships, but at the same time (for example, even during his early, intimate friendship with Thurneysen), he could be deeply lonely. In 1925 that loneliness had deepened to a chasm. Then Charlotte came into his life. In April 1929 Barth wrote to Thurneysen from the Bergli describing the work on Augustine and Luther that he and Lollo were then doing. The letter opens with an unforgettable description of his contentment at Bergli:

The buds are already bursting out all round the Bergli; there are flowers on all the tables; the twins [Ursula and Franziska Pestalozzi] are already gamboling stark naked through the meadows in

Romans ("Theologie und Biographie: das Problem des Verhältnisses der beiden Grössen in Karl Barths Theologie," *Evangelische Theologie* 46 [1986]: 333).

21. E. Busch, personal communications, 16 December 1993 and 19 July 1994.

22. Barth made the Anna-Nelly comparison to Eberhard Busch (E. Busch, personal communication, 19 July 1994). Busch knew several of the kitchen workers.

23. E. Busch, personal communication, 16 December 1993.

24. Barth recounted a dream with this vision of hell; see discussion in Busch, "Memories of Karl Barth," [transcription of interview in November 1985 by Donald K. McKim] in *How Karl Barth Changed My Mind*, ed. Donald K. McKim (Grand Rapids, Mich.: Wm. B. Eerdmans, 1986), 13–14, and in Busch, "Gelebte theologische Existenz bei Karl Barth," in *Theologie als Christologie: Zum Werk und Leben Karl Barths. Ein Symposium*, ed. Heidelore Köckert and Wolf Krötke (Berlin: Evangelische Verlagsanstalt, 1988), 190–91.

the sunshine, we are already eating lunch in that memorable corner behind the house with its marvelous views, and all the indications are that things will get better and better—indeed almost better than our doctrine allows us to expect in this earthly life.[25]

Why did Barth not divorce Nelly and marry the woman who changed his life so radically, with whom he wanted to live his life, in the late 1920s? On the one hand, divorce would have been difficult. It was uncommon, and among clergy it could be an extreme liability.[26] Five children would have been affected by it. Nelly, who married Karl at the age of nineteen, could have been supported financially but would have been abandoned with no survival skills whatsoever in a patriarchal society. Barth's theology of marriage, which we must listen to literally even if we find it multilayered, proclaimed God's grace for marriage in all its human imperfections. On the other hand, Barth was unconventional. Not only was he the red pastor of Safenwil; Bergli society contained a streak of Weimar by way of Zürich; it was a commune of new ideas and gender-integrated conviviality, of health food and sleeping in open air under the trees. Gerty Pestalozzi, the "mother" of the Bergli regulars, seems to have embodied a lively engagement with new trends and ideas and a contagious spirituality of peace and love.[27]

Perhaps the decisive factor against divorce in the 1920s was family pressure. Barth's mother (his father had died in 1912) and brothers strongly disapproved of his increasing closeness to Charlotte von Kirschbaum. His mother and his brother Heinrich especially rejected her. In early May of 1928 Barth had a terrible quarrel with his brothers in their mother's home. It is probable that the subject of von Kirschbaum was a major part of this quarrel and that it was also a major reason for his mother's visit a few weeks later to Karl's home in Münster, contrary to his wishes, while Nelly and their children were visiting in Switzerland.[28]

25. E. Busch, *Karl Barth*, 184 (full text in *ET-KB Briefwechsel*, 659–60: 29 April 1929).
26. Pieter De Jong, personal conversation, 1994.
27. E. Busch, personal communication, 19 July 1994; and recollections of Esther Röthlisberger-Pestalozzi, personal communication, September 1994 (letter). See also Busch, *Karl Barth*, 74–75.
28. E. Busch, personal communication, 19 July 1994. Wolfgang Schildmann discusses the quarrel and the visit (*Was sind das für Zeichen? Karl Barths Träume im Kontext von Leben und Lehre* [Munich: Chr. Kaiser Verlag, 1991], 110–11 and 143f.). Recognition of the matter of von Kirschbaum would make his interpretation considerably more complex and accurate; see below, page 41, on his omission of her as a subject.

Barth did decide and attempt to bring about divorce and remarriage once, in 1933. He wrote to Nelly requesting a divorce under the following terms: that they mutually and peaceably agree to part, in humble recognition that their marriage had been a mistake from the start. Nelly did not acquiesce, and Karl dropped the plan and did not propose it again.[29]

Barth's action and his acceptance of Nelly's position are consistent with German law. From 1900 through the 1950s, divorce law required the acquiescence of both parties. (The Nazi period is an exception. Nazi divorce laws were loosened so that one party alone could sue for divorce.)[30] Barth's acceptance of Nelly's position was probably reinforced, perhaps decisively, by the disapproval of the German *Bekennende Kirche* (Confessing Church)[31] with regard to his plan. Its disapproval seems to have played a role in the growing separation between Barth and the group, a separation which contributed to his return to Switzerland.[32] But one may still think that Barth's acceptance of Nelly's decision without—as far as we know—challenge or attempt at persuasion demonstrates a less than wholehearted will to carry through his plan. I think there were more than legal and ecclesiastical considerations at work. In 1933, and in 1926 and 1928 also, Barth seems to reveal a strong streak of fatalism with regard to his personal life, which may be closely connected with the whole course of his love for Rösy Münger. I also wonder if the timing of his initiative—1933, a year of urgent political developments that were to claim and transform all of Barth's activities, as distinct from the less chaotic time of the late 1920s—indicates an unconscious attempt to make the initiative fail.

29. E. Busch, personal communication, 19 July 1994. Barth recounted this story to Busch.

30. See Frevert, *Women in German History*, 285–86. On Nazism: Frevert, 236–38: the divorce laws were changed in order to help assure the propagation of the Aryan race.

31. The *Bekennende Kirche* was the collective term for German Protestants in resistance, overtly or covertly, to the Nazi "reorganization" of the German churches. The term will always be associated with the "Theological Declaration" composed at the first Confessing Synod at Barmen in 1934 and largely written by Barth.

32. E. Busch, personal communication, 19 July 1994. Note that there is a rumor alive—I encountered it twice, once in conversation at Union Theological Seminary and once at Princeton Theological Seminary—that Thurneysen persuaded Barth not to divorce because it would cause a scandal in the Swiss Reformed church and thus undermine their theological cause. Both parts of this seem to be inaccurate: Thurneysen supported the idea of divorce (which seems commendable insofar as it surely would have threatened his own intimacy with Barth), and I have found no evidence that the Swiss church had any reaction at all to the proposed divorce (ibid.).

Between late 1925 and 1928, Barth, with von Kirschbaum's help and assent, carved out an arrangement for collaboration. Charlotte got secretarial training at a business school for women in Munich and a kind of pedigree: Pygmalion-like, Barth ghost-wrote the written work needed for graduation from a preparatory school for university admission in Berlin.[33] (This is one of many moments at which I think things could have been otherwise. She should have been expected to write her own exam and given time to do it.) Initially the arrangement was part secretary and part research assistant on the model of German university practice, which traditionally demanded a huge, almost punishing, amount of work.[34] It was theological assistant as described in Barth's letters to Thurneysen and as described to me by Frederick Herzog, Barth's live-in student in 1947–48, and by Eberhard Busch, von Kirschbaum's successor (after the onset, in 1962, of an ultimately fatal illness).

We will examine details of her role, as it came to include more and still more, in Part 2. In this study I will deal with the question of her contributions to the *Church Dogmatics* as well as with the wonderful harmony, described by friends, that was at the core of their collaboration, and with the exploitation that has not been confronted by their biographers. Their arrangement also mirrored a less common European tradition: the great man and his muse or *femme inspiratrice*.[35] Von Kirschbaum was working full-time for Barth by 1929.

Besides the question of whether Karl intended to marry von Kirschbaum, one may wonder whether von Kirschbaum expected such a marriage. These are two different questions, and they become relevant to a biographer when the final development in their arrangement took place. Barth decided von Kirschbaum's full-time presence was indispensable to his work, and in October of 1929 she moved into the Barth household in Münster. She continued to live with the Barth family, in Münster and their successive homes in Bonn and Basel, until 1966.

From 1962 (at age sixty-three) to 1965, von Kirschbaum gradually succumbed to a debilitating mental disorder and was finally, in January

33. Busch, *Karl Barth*, 185; and Köbler, *In the Shadow*, 31, 33.
34. Neill Hamilton, personal conversation, November 1992. Hamilton was a doctoral student of O. Cullmann; he also studied with Barth.
35. Charles Courtney made this connection in a personal conversation, September 1992. See studies of the phenomenon in Phyllis Rose, *Parallel Lives: Five Victorian Marriages* (New York: Random House, 1983), and Inge Stephan, *Das Schicksal*, 7–20 and passim.

1966, placed in the Sonnenhalde Sanatorium (in Riehen, outside of Basel) where she remained until her death in 1975. In the early stages she lost powers of attention and memory and suffered tremendously from insomnia; after hospitalization she withdrew further and further from reality, lost most of her capacity for speech, and regressed to a childlike state. Speculative diagnoses have included Alzheimer's disease (which may be genetic), viral infection, and an inherited brain disease— not further identified—which her mother is reported to have had.[36] Barth visited her every Sunday until his death in 1968. While communication was barely possible, he sang chorales for her. After Barth's death, his son-in-law, Max Zellweger, continued the Sunday visits. Nelly Barth and other family members sometimes visited also.[37] Von Kirschbaum died in 1975 and is buried in the Barth family tomb.

Many have wondered—as I did—if three decades of almost ceaseless overwork contributed to von Kirschbaum's illness.[38] Von Kirschbaum herself made this association to Eberhard Busch.[39] But there is medical consensus that exhaustion and stress are not risk factors and have no causal relation to Alzheimer's or similar kinds of dementia; nor do they accelerate the course of such diseases.[40] There is always a relationship of sorts, a tempering, "a delicate dance" (in Donald Kent's phrase) between an illness and the patient's premorbid psychological makeup. In the instance of von Kirschbaum, it seems to have been the illness that

36. Köbler, *In the Shadow*, 70–73; E. Busch, personal communication, 16 December 1993. To my Drew colleague Donald Kent (M.D., Ph.D.), her symptoms describe a profound dementia, an organic disease. It might well have been Alzheimer's, which can only be diagnosed posthumously by autopsy of brain tissue and elimination of other possibilities (personal conversations, September 1997).

37. Köbler, *In the Shadow*, 70–75.

38. Ibid., 71–73.

39. In 1965, when she was confronting her full decline, she told Busch, in despair, that she had come to the end of her powers because she had consumed herself and worn herself out in her work for Barth. (In Busch's report: "Sie sei am Ende ihrer Kraft, weil sie sich für ihre Arbeit bei KB 'verzehrt und verbraucht' habe.") E. Busch, personal communication, 16 December 1993.

40. Personal conversation with Donald Kent. The consensus is long-standing. When Eberhard Busch told Barth about the moving moment in which von Kirschbaum had connected her illness and her all but ceaseless work, Barth consulted a physician on the subject. The physician told him there was no connection between the two phenomena; von Kirschbaum had apparently inherited the disease from her mother (E. Busch, personal communication, 16 December 1993). See also the helpful review in Margaret Gatz et al., "Dementia: Not Just a Search for the Gene," *The Gerontologist* 34:2 (1994): 251–55. Eleanor Jackson reached the same conclusion in her "Introduction" to *The Question of Woman: The Collected Writings of Charlotte von Kirschbaum*, trans. John Shepherd, ed. Eleanor Jackson (Grand Rapids, Mich.: Wm. B. Eerdmans, 1996), 137.

affected her psychological state.[41] Von Kirschbaum was distressed and depressed at the mounting impact of her illness. One can probably assume that her depression was compounded by guilt for failing Barth and panic about where in the world she now belonged.

Von Kirschbaum's life with Barth contained its own pathos, even though that is not its major tone. It is insufficient to say that the incorporation of Lollo in the Barth household had some unfortunate effects or even that it created serious problems. While Barth took the "responsibility and blame" for all that followed, he felt that all three—he, Nelly, and Lollo—had no choice but to tolerate it. In Eberhard Busch's description, the three "bore a burden which caused them unspeakably deep suffering. Tensions arose which shook them to the core."[42] The children were also affected, though in varying degrees. It was most difficult for Matthias and Hans-Jacob; Christoph and Markus were able to accept it. And later Markus's wife, Rose Marie, became a close friend of von Kirschbaum. It was Franziska's husband (Max Zellweger) who continued to visit von Kirschbaum in the sanatorium after Barth's death.[43] Close friends were well aware of the situation and tried to ease it in various ways. Gerty Pestalozzi, who knew Nelly as a guest at the Bergli (Karl at first visited with his family), maintained friendships with both Nelly and Lollo and corresponded with Nelly throughout her life and with Lollo until her illness made it impossible. Gerty, and also Thurneysen, were deliberately inclusive in letters to Karl: he was to convey warmest greetings to Nelly and Lollo both.[44]

The most frequently asked question about Barth and von Kirschbaum—asked by Barth's theological enemies in Catholic and Protestant circles, asked in Protestant universities in Europe in the 1930s and 40s and 50s and 60s, and asked by theological students in the United States then and still today—is whether they were lovers. Throughout their time together a great many people, including Barth's detractors and a large

---

41. Suggestion made by Donald Kent in personal conversation. On the likely measure of its effects, Kent said "she was carrying a millstone around her neck."

42. E. Busch, *Karl Barth*, 186. It seems certain that this situation is part of an unforgettable allusion Barth made late in life to his peculiar need for God's mercy (Eberhard Busch, *Glaubensheiterkeit: Karl Barth: Erfahrungen und Begegnungen* [Neukirchen-Vluyn: Neukirchener Verlag, 1985], 85).

43. E. Busch, personal communication, 19 July 1994.

44. Information on G. Pestalozzi letters in personal communication from Esther Röthlisberger-Pestalozzi, 23 September 1994. See many such letters from Thurneysen in *KB-ET Briefwechsel*, e.g., 12 January 1930.

number of his loyal students, assumed they were.[45] And many of their friends and many of Barth's students think they were not.[46]

When students came to Barth's Basel home for evening discussion sessions, Nelly opened the outside door and Lollo met them at the second-floor landing. Von Kirschbaum's room in the Barth household was separate from family quarters: it was next to Barth's study and could only be entered or exited through the study (fig. 13). At first she did not share meals with the family, but she was soon included, and she was called "Tante Lollo" by the Barth children. In the first years of their relationship, Barth apparently tried to integrate her more fully into the household, just as he sometimes tried to include Nelly and Lollo both in discussions of his professional life.[47]

In August 1927, von Kirschbaum was with the whole Barth family at Nöschenrode in the Harz. There she and Barth worked on the *Christliche Dogmatik* manuscript. But a few weeks after Barth reports this to Thurneysen, von Kirschbaum and he have gone on a two-day trip to the *Niederrhein*.[48] As Barth grew increasingly famous, the two often traveled together on lecture tours—often, it should be noted, with a third or several friends. The two often took advantage of a good location for long walks, which Barth could describe in wonderment.[49] It was at least in part to relieve tensions in the household that the two spent vacation times and academic recesses at Bergli.[50] In a review of his career in an article in *Christian Century*, Barth reports that, accompanied by his "faithful assistant Charlotte von Kirschbaum," he was guest professor for the postwar summer semesters of 1946 and 1947 at his former University in Bonn.[51] In the U.S. tour in 1962, they shared the same room at Princeton Theological Seminary. A measure of the scandal she represented occurred in 1960 when the University of Basel celebrated its five-hundredth anniversary. Barth, who had long been a faculty "star," was

45. William Stroker told me about a discussion among a group of his fellow-U.S. students in Basel. They were absolutely certain that the two were lovers.

46. John Hesselink, personal conversation, October 1990.

47. He told Thurneysen that, besides him, only Nelly and Lollo knew about a very unpleasant exchange of letters he and Brunner were having in the fall of 1929 (*KB-ET Briefwechsel*, 16 November 1929).

48. *KB-ET Briefwechsel*, 21 August 1927 and 17 September 1927.

49. E.g., his description of walking in the "paradise" of upper Franconia in October 1927. Busch, *Karl Barth*, 178.

50. Busch, *Karl Barth*, 186.

51. Karl Barth, *How I Changed My Mind* [the collected articles from the *Christian Century* series] (Richmond, Va.: John Knox Press, 1966), 56.

invited to speak on the occasion. When he requested von Kirschbaum's presence at the ceremony, the request was denied. Barth boycotted the celebration and had a good time instead with Lollo, Georges Casalis, and Heinrich Vogel.[52]

Markus Barth decided to publish the extant letters of Barth and von Kirschbaum in part to dispel the notion that von Kirschbaum was Barth's mistress.[53] In their life together, Karl Barth did little to dispel the rumors: this, however, can be interpreted in totally different ways. In the early stages of this study, I felt certain that the two were lovers and that anyone who doubted it was painfully naïve. Further inquiry and review led to diminished certainty. I think one must be careful not to think one can know.

A wide range of possibilities exist, including sexual relations rarely, or only in the early years. Münster in 1926 seems like a good guess, but it can only be a guess. We are dealing with sexual and marital mores before divorce became common and before birth control was absolutely reliable. We are also dealing with a citizen of Basel many decades ago. We hear that citizen in the stiff, unfocused set of pages in *Church Dogmatics* in which Barth discusses birth control.[54] It may be permissible in some circumstances, he agrees, but even then it would be natural to feel, in all the available methods, "a kind of instinctive, even aesthetic repugnance [*Abscheu*]," and they are also not always reliable. A view shared by several of Barth's contemporaries in the United States is, I think, piercingly correct. They maintain that the question of consummation is unnecessary and beside the point, because any married man who devoted as much time and attention to another woman as Karl Barth did to Charlotte von Kirschbaum *was* committing adultery.[55] I would only add that von Kirschbaum too is involved in this charge and all that it meant to Nelly and the Barth children, though to a lesser

52. Casalis letter in Köbler, *In the Shadow*, 137. But Busch gives a different account in *Karl Barth*, 442: the issue was that Basel would not invite any universities from behind the Iron Curtain. I have two sources for the Princeton information, who want to remain anonymous. (See last note to this part.)

53. He also hoped to dispel the notion that von Kirschbaum "wrote" the Dogmatics or major parts of it (conversation of Markus and Rose Marie Barth with Bruce McCormack in Riehen, related to me by McCormack in personal conversation [telephone], May 1992).

54. *CD* III/4:268–76, esp. 274–75; *KD* III/4:301–10, esp. 308–9.

55. Christopher Morse (personal conversation, January 1992) attributed it to Paul Lehmann. Nancy Duff (personal conversation, November 1994) thinks, rather, that the interpretation was shared by several people in Union Theological Seminary circles who discussed the question around the time of Barth's visit to the United States.

extent and with much of the blame on Barth. I think this is all anyone can do with this question and all that needs to be done.

Eberhard Busch, the only Barth scholar to confront von Kirschbaum's place in Barth's life, has commented on von Kirschbaum's special vulnerability in the arrangement: single women did not do such things without the cost of their world's respect.[56] Von Kirschbaum crossed the Rubicon when she moved into Karl Barth's home; and she did this all the more definitively some five years later, in 1935, when Barth was forced to leave Germany and return to Switzerland, and she left her country to remain with him. I would add that she embarked on a life of dependence on one man and control by him. She did not receive a salary. Instead, her expenses were paid by Barth, as he paid those of any member of his family, and she received a small monthly allowance.[57]

An immediate question is why she agreed to this arrangement. The cost for her was a break with her family and scandal—these, besides the everyday tensions, embarrassments, frustrations, and hurts. And guilt, despite Barth's assumption of responsibility, as the cause of unhappiness to Nelly and discomfort to their children. Her mother never forgave her, and her brothers were effectively alienated, though she tried to maintain contact with them. Georg Merz said he regretted all his life that he had introduced her to Barth.[58] Was there a promise or suggestion from Barth that the situation would, or might, be turned into marriage as soon as possible or when the right moment came? The possibilities here range from genuine intention, to deception, to self-deception. I suspect that von Kirschbaum, through the 1930s, thought Barth was going to marry her.

Within the horizon of possible union, she had many reasons to concur in the arrangement, and they would have grown stronger with time. First, there was her response to Barth's theology. Like Thurneysen, like Busch, like Merz, and like Gertrud Staewen (a friend and Bergli "regular"), she said, in effect, "That's it!"[59] It was a core response to a theology that was fascinating and transfixing, that the world needed, and that gave sense and purpose to her life—a life that was, after all, nomadic and rootless.

Another reason, one of the strongest, was that she was convinced that it was her calling to follow Barth and serve his theology. She said

56. Busch on von Kirschbaum's vulnerability: *Karl Barth*, 185.
57. Köbler, *In the Shadow*, 44.
58. Ibid., 38–39.
59. Busch, personal communication, 16 December 1993.

many times, "He called me."[60] An American student assistant who lived in the household for several years described her as "a deaconess type."[61] Friends at the Bergli characterized her as one who always chose the difficult—the intellectually arduous, the imperative to apply theology to worldly issues.[62] Her life was one of service to the church. Her work could be described as nurturing the *Church Dogmatics*. And another reason, which may be the strongest: in the work she grew as a theologian, and this meant an increase in her contribution to Barth's theology as well as her appreciation and joy in its evolution. She wrote to Helmut Gollwitzer (an early student of Barth and intimate and blessed friend of both, who gave her funeral oration) that it is "a breathtaking affair to see how such a chunk of rock evolved by almost imperceptible degrees through his constant concentration on innumerable and tireless efforts at chiseling and shaping."[63]

Barth was von Kirschbaum's mentor and tutor; they enjoyed an extraordinary rapport together; she was respected by many theologians, one of whom called her "a theological blue-stocking."[64] After World War II she delivered a lecture series and published a collection of the lectures (and other material) entitled *Die wirkliche Frau* (The Real Woman), a formulation of a Protestant doctrine of women, in 1949. (She presented the lecture material to several new audiences in Germany and Switzerland in the early 1950s.) *Die wirkliche Frau* is cited in Markus Barth's commentary on Ephesians and in Karl Barth's *Church Dogmatics*—and in the article "Anthropologie" in the standard reference set *RGG*.[65]

This work was the product of a long-standing and active interest in the subject. Von Kirschbaum was a respected expert on the doctrine of women in church circles beyond Basel. Henriette Visser't Hooft Boddaert, introduced to Barth and von Kirschbaum as the wife of Willem Visser't Hooft, the ecumenist and friend of Barth, carried on a brisk correspondence with von Kirschbaum—a correspondence to which we will later return—between 1935 and 1952. Visser't Hooft Boddaert also wrote and

60. See prologue by Rose Marie Barth in Köbler, *In the Shadow*, 16.
61. Frederick Herzog, personal conversation, November 1992.
62. Esther Röthlisberger-Pestalozzi, personal communication, September 1994 (letter).
63. Quoted in Busch, *Karl Barth*, 374.
64. Reported by Karl Handrich in Köbler, *In the Shadow*, 133; Köbler's book ends with an epilogue (125–40) containing several tributes to her, most notably those of Hans Prolingheuer and Georges Casalis.
65. Charlotte von Kirschbaum, *Die wirkliche Frau* (Zollikon-Zurich: Evangelischer Verlag, 1949); Busch, *Karl Barth*, 402. (*RGG=Die Religion in Geschichte und Gegenwart*).

spoke on the subject of women in the church. She sent articles and essays to von Kirschbaum for criticism; she quoted von Kirschbaum in various women's church organizations and related discussion groups, and once conveyed an invitation to speak on women in the early Christian church. She particularly looked to von Kirschbaum for theological criticism of her work. Always, Visser't Hooft Boddaert wanted to be kept up to date on the progress of von Kirschbaum's studies in this subject area.[66]

There is a fierce loyalty to von Kirschbaum and Barth among friends who were close to both and a consensus (though here I think we have some evasion) that von Kirschbaum was happy and felt fulfilled in the relationship, even if overworked, even if used. The most frequent and, I gather, universally accepted characterization of von Kirschbaum is that she was a genuinely charming person and a fine person, warm, caring, and helpful. Neill Hamilton remembers her as "always sunny." Many of Barth's students revered her: she played (and surely this means enjoyed) a somewhat maternal role for some.[67]

The pattern of comments on the person of Karl Barth is more complex and somewhat less uniform. Friends and disciples recognize his infamous stubbornness, fierceness in combat, and impatience—some call this set of characteristics arrogance. But there is a very wide consensus that he was also a wonderful and psychologically healthy man. He was gregarious, hearty, generous, an extraordinarily good listener to whom students as well as friends and a congregation as big as the world repeatedly turned for advice. Eberhard Busch said that Barth became, in the best sense of the word, his fatherly friend. His sense of humor, which could be used self-critically, is famous too.[68]

Several dissenting observations are relevant for this study of Barth and von Kirschbaum: one is by Barth himself, and another, by Hans

66. Their letters were made available to me by courtesy of the director of the Barth Archiv, Hinrich Stoevesandt. Here I have drawn upon the following: CvK to HVH, 20 November 1941; HVH to CvK, 22 October 1942; and the speaking invitation in HVH's (undated) response to von Kirschbaum's letter of 20 November 1941. (It is not clear whether she accepted the invitation.)

67. N. Hamilton, personal conversation, May 1996. On the maternal role: Markus Barth, speaking of Frederick Herzog in personal communication (letter), 19 June 1992; Busch, personal communication, 16 December 1993.

68. See, inter alia, John Hesselink, "The Humanity (*Menschlichkeit*) of Karl Barth," *Reformed Review* 42 (1988): 140–45. In his funeral address for Barth, Helmut Gollwitzer evokes Elisha calling after Elijah (*Karl Barth: 1886–1968. Gedenkfeier im Basler Münster* [Theologische Studien 100]; Zurich: EVZ-Verlag, 1969). E. Busch on relationship with Barth: personal communication, 16 December 1993; his *Karl Barth* records the camaraderie in a great number of friendships.

Frei, proceeds from Barth's self-characterization. They may both correlate with the fact that Barth—the theologian of church proclamation and the fighter for workers' rights—was not comfortable as pastor at Safenwil.[69] Barth was aware that his uncompromising, forceful personality could be overwhelming, and he noted a "centrifugal effect" that sometimes cost him valued friendships, even though they were often quickly replaced by other friendships.[70] Hans Frei thinks his relationships with others were "forged through a sense of common vocation and common moral tasks, rather than through the art of mutual personal cultivation or direct in-depth 'encounter.'"[71] And he sees Barth's "intimate relation with his long-time assistant, Charlotte von Kirschbaum," as the major instance of the first kind and his "sad misrelation to his wife" as his "paradigmatic failure in the other kind."[72] Frei also suggests perspicaciously that Barth would not have been a very patient subject in psychoanalysis. A recent study by the psychoanalyst Wolfgang Schildmann documents Barth's frequently expressed distrust of, and annoyance with, psychology.[73] Barth's letters are not introspective; he does not seem habitually to practice self-examination. Part of this is due to personality type, and part is due to his probably healthy, if not thoroughly accurate, association of introspection with Liberal Protestant self-centering.[74]

69. He was especially uncomfortable with children: Schildmann, *Was sind das für Zeichen?* 100. See Busch, *Karl Barth*, 63–64, for his regret (and frustration) in not finding himself in rapport with the congregation.

70. Busch, *Karl Barth*, 249.

71. Hans Frei, "Eberhard Busch's Biography of Karl Barth," in his *Types of Christian Theology*, ed. George Hunsinger and William C. Placher (New Haven: Yale University Press, 1992), 150.

72. Ibid.

73. W. Schildmann, *Was sind das für Zeichen?* 15 and chap. 1 ("Karl Barth und die Tiefenpsychologie," 8–18), passim.

74. Barth often uses the classic characterization of the sinner as "homo incurvatus in se" (e.g., *CD* III/4:473). See Schildmann (*Was sind das für Zeichen?* 13ff. and chap. 1, passim) on Barth as extroverted intellectual. Barth had "the extrovert's life-ideal" of psychological well-being as an outward move to community and the intellectual's distrust of feeling. Schildmann correlates these "givens" with disturbances he finds in Barth's inner life; together they produced a significant amount of repression, reflected in the dreams that Barth recounted to friends. I think Schildmann overestimates by far Barth's negativity about the sphere of human impulses per se. For example, a major prooftext for him is *CD* III/4:344–49 (*KD* III/4:391–96) in which Barth speaks of the "lower drives" that are so "terribly energetic" and that "undoubtedly belong to the animal element in human life." But Barth's guiding perspective is that the human being, certainly a creature among other creatures, has also been visited by grace, in creation and in salvation. For this reason, Barth continues, everything in human life has dignity and merits respectful attention.

Late in his life, Barth attempted without success to write a formal autobiography. Though he began it (in January 1966) enthusiastically, it proved increasingly difficult to return to it following interruptions. The task was a little frightening, he told Busch in November 1966.[75] On another day (February 1967) he found that certainly "the most gripping [*spannendste*] chapter" would be that on women. Here there would be a full-scale drama to relate. But it would be difficult, within the boundaries of proper reticence, to be entirely open in such a chapter. And if he could not do so, he'd rather not write any autobiography at all. Finally (March 1967), he gave up the project: God should not find him engaged in trivia when the time to meet Him finally came.[76]

Women somehow were a charged subject for Barth, and his relations with women may contain an unusual portion of irrationality. Schildmann has convincingly argued that Barth's less-than-satisfactory relationship with his mother had major effects on his life and work. He finds evidence for his argument in Barth's report of a recurring dream in which (first in 1920) he found himself in a grave, being buried. He protested that he was not really dead. His mother, in a friendly manner, counseled that the grave preparation should continue, then Karl would be "fully" dead. He succeeded in breaking out and ran back to life. The dream recurred in 1928—as Barth's mother was on her way to Münster to visit and keep house for her son, against his wishes. Schildmann's analytic framework is the archetypal psychology of Erich Neumann, specifically his work on the *Todesmutter*, the "Terrible Mother" of death and the underworld, as the dark side of the feminine.[77] Thus Schildmann stresses the striking disparity between Anna's friendly demeanor and her murderous intention in the dream.[78]

Schildmann plausibly correlates Barth's craving for directness and trustworthiness with the God of his theology and suggests that Barth's mistrust of parental authority may be part—a hidden part!—of his doctrine of the hidden God.[79] In human relations, a craving for the polar

75. I am following Busch's account from his journal entries in "Gelebte theologische Existenz bei Karl Barth."

76. Ibid., 177–78.

77. The dream is the subject of chap. 6, "Flucht vor der 'Todesmutter,'" Schildmann, *Was sind das für Zeichen?* 93–117.

78. Ibid., 108ff. Though on the whole Barth thinks he had a healthy childhood, his recollection of his mother lends credence to the dream picture. He said she advocated kindness but insisted constantly on strict obedience to the rules she issued. See report in Busch, *Karl Barth*, 12.

79. Schildmann, *Was sind das für Zeichen?* 114–15.

opposite of the *Todesmutter* might explain both his insistence on total loyalty among his friends and his non-negotiable need to have Charlotte always accessible. When von Kirschbaum's illness progressed so far that she was placed in the sanatorium, Barth (at the age of eighty) surprised many people by entering into two new, intense relationships, one proudly and happily, and the other largely an embarrassment: these are the friendships with the literary figure Carl Zuckmayer and with a Roman Catholic nurse who cared for him from 1965 until her marriage a short time before his death. To a student of the Barth–von Kirschbaum relationship, they may seem patently attempts to find a substitute for her.[80]

Schildmann's study provides sufficient material to think of von Kirschbaum in relation to Barth's mother in other ways. Barth's incorporation of von Kirschbaum into his household was a (finally) successful defiance of his mother, and apparently she realized in the early 1930s that the marriage with Nelly had been a mistake.[81] If Schildmann is correct that Barth's terror of loneliness is related to the absence in his childhood of a foundational relationship of trust with his mother,[82] von Kirschbaum's role was all the more beyond reasoned discussion for everyone in the Barth family. And it was a relationship in which Barth wielded enormous power and did not dwell upon its costs to the other person.

I think this psychological dimension is a presence in Barth's relations with women, in his anthropology of gender, and in his theological

80. On the friendship with Zuckmayer, see *A Late Friendship: The Letters of Karl Barth and Carl Zuckmayer*, trans. Geoffrey W. Bromiley (Grand Rapids, Mich.: Wm. B. Eerdmans, 1982). On the nurse, see Busch, "Deciding Moments in the Life and Work of Karl Barth," trans. Martin Rumscheidt and Barbara Rumscheidt, *Grail* 2 (1986): 66; amplified in personal communication, 19 June 1994. There is a curious literalness in the way they do correspond. Zuckmayer was like and unlike Barth: he was an intellectual peer with whom Barth could really talk, but he was an artist. And he was in awe of Karl Barth: Barth was in control of this relationship too. Barth initiated the friendship with a statement of admiration. Then he took control of the discussion with queries on Zuckmayer's faith and lectures to correct certain weaknesses therein (KB to CZ, 16 May 1967 and 12 September 1967, in Zuckmayer, *A Late Friendship*). Of the Catholic nurse, very little is known, but we should remember that von Kirschbaum was a nurse when Barth met her and Barth may well have called upon that training as he grew older. Busch disagrees with me: noting that the nurse's name was Rösy (nickname for Rose-Marie), he thinks there is a substitutional analogy, not with von Kirschbaum, but with his early love. Maybe it is both.

81. E. Busch, personal communication, 19 July 1994, on Anna's reassessment of the marriage.

82. Schildmann, *Was sind das für Zeichen?* 179.

condemnation of the solitary life and it should be remembered. But it also should not be exaggerated. Barth possessed a generally level-headed healthiness. We would similarly be mistaken if our only concern was to fathom the personal relationship of Barth and von Kirschbaum. That is fascinating—and necessarily speculative.

Just as speculative is discussion of the second most frequently raised question about Charlotte von Kirschbaum: How much did she contribute to the writing of *Church Dogmatics*? Here the focus of discussion has been quantitative as well as evaluative. People have wondered what parts of the text she wrote or how much she wrote. There is a persistent rumor (which lives on as part of U.S. seminary lore) that she wrote the notes—the lengthy, small-print discussions of sources and interpretations that run throughout *CD*. This proposition, we will see, is rooted in reality but misleading in formulation. We will indeed examine her contributions to the Dogmatics. But I think our focus should not be on measuring the amount she contributed or on evaluating her ideas vis-à-vis Barth's. It should be on finding her voice. This is not only a voice that can speak to us, but it is also the voice that Barth engaged in dialogue. The real subject for scholarly inquiry into the Barth–von Kirschbaum relationship is their collaboration. This seems to call for something akin to thick description. We need to move outward as much as inward, to its many-dimensioned historical contexts. To move toward the external is not to move away from the personal. For example, an immediate result of contextualization is to see a new question about their relationship: What were the alternatives?

2. Texts and Contexts

We can begin our study of the Barth–von Kirschbaum collaboration by looking at the source material each has provided. *Die wirkliche Frau* is one of our primary sources. Its subject is the Protestant woman in the context of the male-female relationship, which is seen as the realization of the image of God in humankind. Von Kirschbaum's commentary on the male-female relationship is highly relevant for a study of the relationship of Charlotte von Kirschbaum and Karl Barth. Barth wrote a parallel text: the male-female relationship is discussed in III/1, III/2, and III/4 of the *Church Dogmatics*. Like von Kirschbaum's work, it seems to serve also as a commentary on the relationship that we are studying. Furthermore, each writer comments on the work of the other—a rare record of a collaboration as it occurs.

Finally, in their combined texts we have material for a contribution to the history of the anthropology of gender, which this study also intends to be. The subject needs attention: Barth's doctrine of women is notoriously hierarchical and antifeminist, and von Kirschbaum's could be seen as another version of the same. Barth's doctrine has been seen by feminists as a barrier to accessing his thought or as an excuse for rejecting it and has been largely ignored or dismissed as a "detachable" anachronism by liberal Barthians.[83] A more constructive trend has emerged in the last decade, finding important "redeeming" material in Barth's theology and sometimes "using Barth to correct Barth" (in the phrase of Hannelore Erhart and Leonore Siegele-Wenschkewitz).[84]

83. The major points in feminist criticism of Barth's doctrine of women—to which I shall return in Part 3—are that it affirms the subordination of women, that it affirms passivity, and that it justifies the presumption of qualitative difference and inferiority. A recurring critical theme is that Barth's theology is dualistic and nowhere more so than in his thinking about male-female relations. In U.S. feminist theology courses, Barth is a very convenient prooftext of patriarchalism (see, for example, *Women and Religion: A Feminist Sourcebook of Christian Thought*, ed. Elizabeth Clark and Herbert Richardson, chap. 19, "The Triumph of Patriarchalism in the Theology of Karl Barth" [New York: Harper & Row, 1977], 239–58). In a widely read study ("The Protestant Principle: A Woman's-Eye View of Barth and Tillich," in *Religion and Sexism: Images of Woman in the Jewish and Christian Traditions*, ed. Rosemary Radford Ruether [New York: Simon & Schuster, 1974], 314–41, esp. 321–29, 337), Joan Romero has focused on the pervasive structures of superiority and dominance in Barth's theology. The Dutch theologians Marga Baas and Heleen Zordranger ("Freiheit aus zweiter Hand: Feministischer Anfrage an die Stellung der Frau in Karl Barths Theologie," *Zeitschrift für dialektische Theologie* 3 [1987]: 131–51) summarize criticism of Barth's doctrine of women and engage Romero in sympathetic debate. In a perspicacious critique, Hannelore Erhart and Leonore Siegele-Wenschkewitz ("'Vierfache Stufenleiter abwärts . . . : Gott, Christus, der Mann, das Weib': Karl Barth und die Solidarität und Kritik von Henriette Visser't Hooft," *Wie Theologen Frauen sehen—von der Macht der Bilder*, ed. Renate Jost and Ursula Kubera [Freiburg: Herder, 1993], 145–51) observe that Barth's anthropology is grounded, not in the doctrine of creation, but in Christology—hence the analogy of Christ and the church can become absolute and all-pervasive for the male-female relationship.

84. Erhart and Siegele-Wenschkewitz, "Vierfache Stufenleiter abwärts," 155. It should be noted that an early and trenchant example of such usage of Barth was conveyed directly to him by Henriette Visser't Hooft Boddaert. In a letter of May 1934, a few weeks before the drafting of the Barmen declaration, she told Barth that traditional acceptance of male domination had as one result the madness abounding before their eyes in Germany. Idolatry breeds idolatry. But Barth did not respond to this letter—or carry its message to Barmen (ibid., 152–54). The letter is published in *Eva, wo bist du? Frauen in internationalen Organisationen der Ökumene: eine Dokumentation*, ed. Gudrun Kaper et al. (Gelnhausen: Burckhardthaus-Laetere Verlag, 1981), 17–19. Barth had already dismissed an earlier letter from her with great condescension (ibid., 14–17).

Increasingly, feminist theologians make positive use of Barth's insistently relational anthropology.[85] Alexander McKelway and Elizabeth Frykberg have emphasized the unmistakably perichoretic quality in Barth's view of the male-female relationship, and Frykberg has suggested a plausible correction of its weakness. She would locate superordinate and subordinate existence in the realm of parent-child relations.[86] One may welcome her revisionist critique, and that of others, but still find them incomplete. The problem of gender inequality cannot be "fixed" unless one confronts its multidimensional nature in Barth's thought.

It is especially in regard to the anthropology of gender that we need to contextualize our sources, to inquire into the history and contemporary state of the question Barth and von Kirschbaum deal with and into what is going on around them as they write. In relation to their collaboration, we also need to consider influence as a two-way exchange. And we need to consider the possibility of common sources—material available to both of them.

The historical context of any study of the mature Karl Barth (and of Charlotte von Kirschbaum) is the rise of Nazi Germany and World War II and its aftermath. In unexpected ways, we will see, this is reflected in their anthropology. But another historical context is more directly important for the study of the Barth–von Kirschbaum collaboration and for their thinking about gender and also for their human relationship: the cultural context of early European feminism. I was prompted to use this perspective as I encountered von Kirschbaum's references to Barth (several times in *Die wirkliche Frau* and in her "Address for the Movement 'Free Germany' [*die Bewegung 'Freies Deutschland'*]," in which she

85. E.g., Rebecca S. Chopp, *The Power to Speak: Feminism, Language, God* (New York: Crossroad, 1991), 8–9, 73, 84–85. In the same path, though more defensively, see Baas and Zordranger, "Freiheit aus zweiter Hand," 142ff.
86. Alexander J. McKelway, "Perichoretic Possibilities in Barth's Doctrine of Male and Female," *Princeton Seminary Bulletin* 7 (1986): 231–43; Elizabeth Frykberg, *Karl Barth's Theological Anthropology: An Analogical Critique Regarding Gender Relations*, Studies in Reformed Theology and History (Princeton: Princeton Theological Seminary, 1993), 1–54. Frykberg notes that her revision also supplements Barth's anthropology by providing—in the unit of man, woman, and child—a truer analogatum for the trinitarian nature of God. This part of her argument seems to achieve neatness at the expense of plurality in Christian life. Paul Fiddes offers another conservatively open review of Barth's doctrine in "The Status of Woman in the Thought of Karl Barth," in *After Eve: Women, Theology and the Christian Tradition*, ed. Janet Martin Soskice (London: Marshall Pickering, 1990), 138–55. He argues that the covenantal nature of the male-female relationship could serve as a guide for revising the doctrine to exclude subordination while affirming difference. As Baas and Zordranger ("Freiheit aus zweiter Hand," 144–45) have observed, however, it is only the male who makes the self-determining decision for fellow-humanity.

quotes extensively from pamphlets by "Professor K. Barth").[87] Annoyed
by the tone of reverence before a Great Man, I suddenly remembered the
same reverence, and my same reaction, in Simone de Beauvoir's references to Sartre in her autobiography. Von Kirschbaum engaged Beauvoir
in debate; they had more in common than she realized.

More particularly, the cultural context of Barth's and von Kirschbaum's
doctrines of women (and more) is early and mid–twentieth-century
German feminism. What happens when we see this is quite exciting. The
feminist context sheds great light on the difficult paradoxes that, as we
will see, are part of Barth's and von Kirschbaum's thinking about
women. It also enables us to review von Kirschbaum's life and its own
seeming paradoxes—of self-suppression, of willing bondage—in relation
to the actual (*wirklich!*) options and standards of the time and place in
which she lived. And, conversely, the Barth–Von Kirschbaum relationship and the Barth–von Kirschbaum collaboration offer a particularly
clear vista on German and, in fact, European feminism and on male-
female communication in their time.

Von Kirschbaum did comment and shed light on her situation in
exegesis of Genesis 2:18. I agree with Markus Barth and Renate Köbler
that *Die wirkliche Frau* is "'her scholarly based self-confession,' her
'statement of accountability before God and man.'"[88] There she discusses
the male-female I-Thou relationship as the image of God, a fulfillment of
the divine plan. She suggests that "it may well be that the single man or
single woman lives more strongly in encounters than many a man or
woman in marriage."[89] In a less directly autobiographical way, she also
suggests, of Isaiah 54:1, that there is "a motherly existence which vies
with [*übergreift*] biological motherhood. There are prophetic women
who become spiritual mothers."[90]

Barth concurs and adapts von Kirschbaum's statement in the *CD* discussion of the fellowship of man and woman. He affirms that the married
man in genuine encounter with the unmarried woman is no less a man
than he is in his marriage, that he lives no less in fellowship with the

---

87. Further discussion of the passages in Parts 2 and 3 below. (The text of the
address is in Köbler, *In the Shadow*, 81–92.)
88. Markus Barth, quoted in Köbler, *In the Shadow*, 64.
89. Von Kirschbaum, *Die Wirkliche Frau*, 16 (*The Question of Woman*, trans. J.
Shepherd, 68). Cf. also ibid., 37 (Shepherd: 94): The single woman who does live in
encounter "can thereby be a pointer to the limits of all earthly ordering and to their
fulfillment in the kingdom of God."
90. Ibid., 63 (Shepherd: 128).

24 | Questions

unmarried woman than with his wife.[91] And he seems to present his own self-confession and statement of accountability with respect to both his family and von Kirschbaum when, in discussion of marriage, he states:

> [I]f there is no perfect marriage, there are marriages which for all their imperfection can be and are maintained and carried through, and in the last resort not without promise and joyfulness, arising with a certain necessity, and fragmentarily, at least, undertaken in all sincerity as a work of free life-fellowship. There is also loyalty even in the midst of disloyalty and constancy amid open inconstancy. And, let it not be forgotten, there is genuine, strong and whole-hearted love even in relationships which cannot flower in regular marriage, but which in all their fragmentariness are not mere sin and shame, and do not wholly lack the character of marriage.[92]

This is also self-exculpatory theology, and I will have occasion to return to it as such in Part 3 below. However, as always in this complex relationship, we have to consider whether von Kirschbaum or Barth might mean exactly what they are saying to a much greater extent than our own reading allows or that they may be signifying something other than what our reading sees. In the 1990s we are half a century removed from their moral, cultural, and social worlds.

Happily, von Kirschbaum's work has recently become more available than hitherto. Köbler's book includes two of von Kirschbaum's lectures: "Address for the Movement 'Free Germany,'" delivered in 1945, and "The Role of Women in the Proclamation of the Word," in 1951. The latter (which was separately published as no. 31 [1951] in the *Theologische Studien* series that Barth edited) is an adaptation and elaboration of the third lecture in the series of four given at a conference in Bièvres (near Paris) in the spring of 1949. The original four lectures were revised and published with additional material as a book in 1949 under the title *Die wirkliche Frau*. Finally, as this study was being completed, Wm. B. Eerdmans issued an English translation of all the writings on women.[93]

91. *CD* III/4:165 (*KD* III/4:183–84).
92. *CD* III/4:239 (*KD* III/4:268).
93. Von Kirschbaum, *The Question of Woman*: see note 89 above. I will continue to use my translation, which is generally more literal (and, for the same reason, I will use the translation of Keith Crim for the lecture included in Köbler, *In the Shadow*). In all cases, however, I will include page references to the Shepherd translation.

We therefore have a total of approximately 135 pages of text (150 in the Eerdmans volume) from von Kirschbaum. The conference at Bièvres followed by a year the first Assembly of the World Council of Churches in Amsterdam, in which Barth was an active participant. One of his duties was chairing a committee on "The Life and Work of Women in the Church," and he registered some exasperation that the female attendees forgot that Paul wrote more on women than Galatians 3:28.[94] Von Kirschbaum sympathized with both sides. The primary effect of the committee reports, however, was to convince her not only of the lack of agreement on the subject among the churches but also of the lack of any theological foundation for agreement. Her work is intended to begin the building of such a foundation.[95] Because the book has only recently become available in translation, a survey of its content may be useful here.

The common theme of the four lectures or essays in *Die wirkliche Frau* is the biblical witness on women. The first lecture, "Jesus Christus und die Gemeinde—Mann und Frau" (Jesus Christ and the Community—Man and Woman), and the second, "Die Frau in der Lebensordnung des neuen Bundes" (Woman in the Ordering of Life Under the New Covenant), discuss the situation of women in male-female encounter; this is von Kirschbaum's view of the ordered, communal existence of women in relation to men. The first concentrates on the correspondence of the male-female duality to the non-aloneness of God. The second concentrates on New Testament women in encounter with Jesus. There is a practical application in the first: that marriages would be strengthened and divorces fewer if the correspondence were better understood. In the second, the application is to present the true Christian existence of women as an alternative to "the women's emancipation movement." The third lecture, "Der Dienst der Frau in der Wortverkündigung" (The Role of Women in the Proclamation of the Word), focuses on the different gifts men and women can bring to the service of the Word. A response to the wartime situation in which women often had to assume the duties of the male pastor, it argues that women should be involved in this service not only in emergencies. The fourth lecture, "Die 'Mutter der Lebendigen'" (The Mother of All Living), discusses motherhood in the Old and New Testaments as fully human and, in all its creaturely limits, more relevant

94. See Busch, *Karl Barth*, 357–60.
95. See her opening remarks on the committee in the 1951 version of "The Role of Women in the Proclamation of the Word," in Köbler, *In the Shadow*, 93–94 (Shepherd: 173–74).

to us than the Roman Catholic apotheosis of Mary. (This essay is followed by a brief excursus on Mary in current mariological discussion.) In an important fifth essay in the book, "Kritische Ausblicke" (Critical Views), von Kirschbaum charts her course between Gertrud von Le Fort's *Die ewige Frau* and Simone de Beauvoir's *Le deuxième sexe*. The two are occasional reference points in the preceding essays, just as the themes of the preceding essays are test cases for the Catholic and feminist-existential views of women.

In a separate lecture delivered in 1945 (in St. Gallen, Geneva, and Montreaux), the address for the Free Germany (*Freies Deutschland*) movement, von Kirschbaum speaks as a German confronting the collapse of the Nazi state and as a Protestant pondering the role of the church in the war years and in a new beginning. The present and the future require recognition of guilt and rejection of hopelessness.[96] Her audience is female. It is at first startling that she presents a plan for sewing and mending used clothing, until she asks the question in her reader's mind: "'Confessing Church' and 'Free Germany': Have we abandoned our theme and ended up in a sewing and mending circle?"[97] Her answer is that concern "with such little things" demonstrates that we understand shared responsibility and the need to move forward. That is her main concern.

Lecture V makes it particularly clear that von Kirschbaum and Barth are in different intellectual or dialogical situations. Von Kirschbaum's way is to seek, between Catholicism and feminism, "an evangelical [Protestant] doctrine of woman."[98] Although Barth discusses all the subjects she treats, including Catholic Mariology and Beauvoir's feminism, in *CD* III, his dialogical situation is as ever between Liberal or Neo-Protestantism on the one hand, and Roman Catholic theology (and sometimes conservative Protestant theology) on the other. Yet even with this essential difference, the title of von Kirschbaum's book tells her readers that it is written with reference to Barth's theology too. "Die wirkliche Frau" points to the "ewige Frau" (the Eternal Feminine) of Catholic doctrine (and beyond, to the cultural archetype), and just as identifiably points to the "wirkliche Mensch," a theme of Barth's and the title of a section of Par. 44 in *CD* III/2 (1948). There is a reference and a difference. One result of my study has been to find deep similarities in the thought of the two as well as unanticipated differences, even

96. Von Kirschbaum, "Address for the Movement 'Free Germany,'" passim, esp. 90.
97. Ibid., 91.
98. *Die wirkliche Frau*, Vorwort.

disagreements. Barth and von Kirschbaum are collaborators and independent agents. Thus I will be interested throughout in exchange and appropriation.

As the daughter of a military officer and a young woman with an early inclination toward religious life that was channeled into the German Red Cross, Charlotte von Kirschbaum probably knew little about the women's movement or feminism before the 1920s. She encountered them directly during her study at the preparatory college for women in Berlin to which she was sent by Barth, and she was keenly interested in the movement from that time onward.[99] Köbler describes interest in the women's movement as a bond among the women who gathered at Bergli.[100]

As Elisabeth Moltmann-Wendel has reminded feminists and students of women's history in the United States, the *Frauenbewegung* (Women's Movement), *Frauenfrage* (the debate on women especially in regard to women's rights), and feminism in Germany have been, since their origins in the nineteenth century, distinctly conservative. The motherhouse diaconate—which we have encountered in our discussion of the young Charlotte von Kirschbaum—is Germany's major contribution to the *Frauenbewegung*.[101] Characterized by authority rather than sisterhood, it had as its purpose alleviating suffering and guilt. Its ethos (in Moltmann-Wendel's summary) was one in which "the world was regarded as a hospital full of sick and sinful people. The number of wounded was increasing. Women were needed to heal them, and they were trained to do so. But no one inquired how many of those wounds had been

99. Köbler, *In the Shadow*, 33, 36–37, 144 (n. 11 for chap. 5). It is probably here, too, that she became a close friend of Gertrud Staewen (ibid., 144, n. 15 to chap. 4). John Hesselink, who began study with Barth in 1958, told me he remembers seeing feminist pamphlets on her desk.

100. Ibid., 36–37.

101. Moltmann-Wendel, "Women's Movement in Germany," 123. C. M. Prelinger and R. S. Keller have contrasted the institutions of the German and U.S. deaconess movements, the latter in the late nineteenth-century Methodist form that succeeded in the United States (as distinct from earlier direct imitations of the German Motherhouse design of Fliedner). Both the German and the U.S. kind highlighted the ideal of motherly care for those unable to care for themselves. But Fliedner stipulated adherence to male direction and precedence "by human and divine right" (Prelinger and Keller, "Function of Female Bonding," 320). The U.S. model (first tried in Chicago, where the Chicago settlement house and training school of Lucy Rider Meyer paralleled the secular Hull settlement house) moved the mothering into the "public rather than solely private sphere" (ibid., 337); it stressed sisterly solidarity under female leadership (reaching into the churches to involve parish women as co-workers and financial supporters) and refused to define and delimit the ways in which women could serve (ibid., esp. 334ff.).

inflicted by the state."[102] A parallel secular women's movement in Germany did not—like movements in Western Europe and the United States— look back to the human rights tradition of the Enlightenment. Rather, liberation meant "inner" liberation, in the tradition of German Idealism. Efforts inspired by the revolutions of 1848—for the education of women, for enabling the needy to help themselves—failed: "The state church retained its monopoly over Christian life."[103]

Some important gains were visible in the late nineteenth century. Female teachers, led by Helene Lange, had their own organization and newsletter; by the turn of the century the first universities—Marburg, Heidelberg, Berlin—had opened study in all faculties to women, finally catching up with policies instituted in universities in other Western countries much earlier in the century.[104] But these were qualified gains. Teacher training was separate for women. Female teachers were both outnumbered and confined—that inevitable word in women's history— to appropriately modest niches and levels in elementary and higher girls' schools. In 1900 women constituted just under 20 percent of German elementary school teachers. (In Sweden it was 60 percent in 1900; in England, 75 percent by 1914, and a majority in France in 1909.) As for the universities—which were state institutions—admission to lectures was not the same as progression from matriculation to examination to graduation. Obstructionism was greater in some fields than others. Not until 1919 could a female student in Germany take the regular, church-administered (i.e., established church) examination in theology as the formal conclusion of her study.[105] Furthermore, the Christian and secular women's movements worked in isolation from each other until well after World War II, and legislation was achieved in piecemeal fashion. One could add that the focus in German Romanticism on inner forces and

102. Moltmann-Wendel, "Women's Movement in Germany," 124.

103. Ibid., 125. (Since the Reformation, German Evangelical churches were governed by their territorial or state rulers.) See also the classic study by Leonard Krieger on German idealism and quietism: *The German Idea of Freedom* (Boston: Beacon Press, 1957).

104. Cf. U.S.: since 1833; France: 1863 (excluding theology faculties); Switzerland: 1865; England: 1869; Russia (medicine faculty): 1872. Dagmar Henze, "Die Anfänge des Frauenstudiums in Deutschland," in 'Darum wagt es, Schwestern . . .': zur Geschichte evangelischer Theologinnen in Deutschland, Frauenforschungsprojekt zur Geschichte evangelischer Theologinnen in Deutschland [Göttingen]. (Neukirchen-Vluyn: Neukirchener Verlag, 1994), 20.

105. Bonnie G. Smith, *Changing Lives: Women in European History Since 1700* (Lexington, Mass.: D. C. Heath, 1989), 299; Frevert, *Women in German History*, 120–22; Henze, "Anfänge des Frauenstudiums," 33–34.

depths beyond the range of reason and its particular association of these with women (a subject to which we will return) is part of the orientation of the German Women's Movement. Von Kirschbaum was correct in 1949 when she chose to debate the Frenchwoman Simone de Beauvoir as the representative of something new.

The German Women's Movement that von Kirschbaum came to know in the 1920s was nevertheless a sister, if the odd one, in the larger women's movement, and it was part of a culture—Weimar—that conferred upon it a generational identity. In Germany, as in England and other countries of Western Europe and North America, the arena of the women's movement was legal reform, health care, and of course suffrage. It was a cultural as well as a social and political phenomenon. In Germany changes in property and divorce laws were part of the *Frauenfrage* well before World War I.[106] Novels before and after the war portrayed the "New Woman" as adventurous and iconoclastic, a free spirit who was taking control of her destiny.[107]

The postwar New Woman was nowhere entirely self-defined. She was the woman in Europe and the United States whose path had been diverted by World War I. During the war women in Germany, like those elsewhere, demonstrated patriotism and resourcefulness and assumed jobs previously held by men.[108] After the war many continued to work for several reasons. Besides stark economic necessity, they knew that options other than marriage existed. Furthermore, the massive loss of male lives at the front in World War I ensured that marriage did not seem to be waiting for everyone.[109]

The Weimar Republic was born of revolution; in the course of the revolution, women received the right to vote.[110] The Weimar Constitution

106. Smith, *Changing Lives*, 319, 321. (The social legislation initiated by Bismarck was largely a preemptive strategy against the tide of democracy and socialism.)

107. Ibid., chap. 8, "The New Woman."

108. The National Women's Service (Nationaler Frauendienst, known as NFD), formally established by the Prussian government, included the Federation of German Women's Associations (Bund Deutscher Frauenvereine, known as BDF), an umbrella group of charitable and other women's organizations, including, prominently, church groups such as the German-Evangelical Women's Federation (Deutsch-Evangelischer Frauenbund) and patriotic associations. See Frevert, *Women in German History*, 161 and passim.

109. Smith, *Changing Lives*, 395–96

110. Germany is in line with England and the United States on women's suffrage: cf. England, 1918 (though with some restrictions); the United States, 1920. France and Italy did not introduce it until just after World War II. Switzerland is the special case in suffrage history. Partly to preserve cantonal rights, Swiss women did not get the vote until

included sexual equality as a basic right—though as in the education system, equality really meant equivalency.[111] Middle-class women sometimes used the term "motherly politics" (*mütterliche Politik*) in advocating policies that would strengthen and aid the welfare of the family. Women in the Social Democratic party and in socialist trade unions were not so far from this orientation, particularly as the high hopes of the new republic gave way to grim economic realities and successive political crises: the 1923 inflation is a signpost of Germany's special vulnerability after the war settlement. The majority of German women sided with avowedly Christian political parties.[112]

The female work force did grow dramatically in numbers, and it changed in kind. The New Women (who were sometimes called women of the New Objectivity [*Neue Sachlichkeit*]) were urban and white-collar workers, in contrast to the pre–World War I majority in agrarian and domestic service.[113] Yet the New Woman in Berlin and other German cities of Weimar Germany was neither a feminist engaged in self-realization nor an activist against patriarchal institutions. She was a product of the *Frauenbewegung* in a new environment. The post–World War I economy, under great international pressure, became an office and factory economy run on principles learned in wartime assembly lines and from American Taylorization: a system of routinization, rationalized tasking, regulated time and motion. This work required an efficient and docile workforce. The work that thousands of women assumed was underpaid, repetitive, and tiring. Ute Frevert has drawn a vivid portrait of the prototype of the New Woman in Weimar. She was a clerical worker who did unskilled or semi-skilled work for less pay (this is official policy) than male workers but was proud of her white-collar status.[114] She was blocked from advancement to a managerial level because the postwar German economy was organized into gender-stereotypic parts. She probably did not mind a great deal because women's employment was regarded by most people, including "progressive" socialists and women's organizations, as temporary: an intermediate stage between schooling

---

1971 (and some cantons and small communes still exclude women from voting on local issues). See entries for each country in the current *Europa Yearbook*.

111. Frevert, *Women in German History*, 168–70, 179–80.

112. Ibid., 170–71, 174–75. The term *mütterliche Politik* originates with Helene Lange (1914).

113. Ibid., 177.

114. Frevert reports the imaginative rationale for the pay difference: because women could knit and sew and cook, their clothing and living expenses were lower (ibid., 179).

and married life. While in reality one out of five female industrial workers was married, female employment was not generally accepted in Weimar. As Frevert observes, it was encouraged when the economy needed it and discouraged when the economy did not need it or when unemployed male workers needed the jobs more.[115] The Weimar cinema, besides its famous avant-garde products, provided for the New Woman story after story of the secretary or shop-girl who won the heart of her rich, handsome boss and married him.[116]

These are not subversive women. But if the New Women had neither time nor interest in social change, they constituted, in their nondomestic and arguably nonfeminine role, a new entity; therefore—like the women's movement everywhere—they were inherently anxiety-provoking.[117] The normality of marriage was challenged de facto in Germany and the rest of the Western world in the 1920s. The social and, notably in Germany, the political right responded to the challenge by exploiting the anxieties it provoked. Women were to be restored to their place: domesticity in a male-dominated world. The raising of children was both proper and urgently necessary, not just to restore the war losses but because the birthrate in Europe had been dropping since the mid-nineteenth century.[118] The feminist "threat" elicited exaggerated defenses and loyalties to the traditional male-female ordering and family, and not only among right-wing observers.

The iconoclasm inherent in the New Woman phenomenon would have been amplified by Weimar culture, which was unconventional above all.[119] Berlin—which Karl Barth knew directly from the semester he spent there in 1906–7 and through many other contacts—was the cultural as well as the political capital of Weimar. Besides expressionist art, its dazzling and often shocking forms of expression, deliberately overriding the traditional borders of life and art, included political and social satire,

115. Ibid., 184–85.
116. Ibid., chap. 14 passim, esp. 176–79, 181–85, 200.
117. Atina Grossmann, "*Girlkultur* or Thoroughly Rationalized Female: A New Woman in Weimar Germany?" in *Women in Culture and Politics: A Century of Change*, trans. from the French and ed. Judith Friedlander et al. (Bloomington: Indiana University Press, 1986), 64, 76. See also Frevert, *Women in German History*, 178–79.
118. Frevert, *Women in German History*, 159; Smith, *Changing Lives*, 345f.
119. See Peter Gay, *Weimar Culture: The Outsider as Insider* (New York: Harper & Row, 1968), and Modris Eksteins, *Rites of Spring: The Great War and the Birth of the Modern Age* (Boston: Houghton Mifflin, 1989), which stresses affinities in Left and Right in their rejection of bourgeois civilization—though the Right did not, we need to remember, reject the bourgeois ideal of family.

nihilism, and transvestitism.[120] It seems likely that von Kirschbaum and Barth (the latter as a theology student in Germany with a Swiss Reformed Church background) went through similar culture shock—and that they embraced many aspects of Weimar while still maintaining some detachment.[121] Conversations about books and other cultural phenomena were part of Bergli society, as they are part of Barth's letters to Thurneysen in the 1920s. Switzerland was affected by the postwar cultural explosion. Even before the 1920s Dada, an artistic movement of total protest against European civilization, had been founded in Zürich.[122]

Late in Barth's life he may have looked back to Weimar when he initiated his friendship with its well-known playwright Carl Zuckmayer. However, within this culture, Barth never gave the Women's Movement a chance: he felt it as an annoyance from the start, and it set off an increasingly hostile reaction. I think his hostility is overdetermined insofar as his descriptions of feminists bear an intriguingly close resemblance to the female type he saw in Anna and Nelly. It is von Kirschbaum who takes the women's movement and feminism seriously. In its radical form—Simone de Beauvoir's feminism—it is dangerous and partly correct, and for both reasons von Kirschbaum engages with it.

When Charlotte von Kirschbaum said that she followed Karl Barth because he called her, it is technically true that she had no other options: she was making a statement of religious conviction.[123] But her statement about calling also means that she saw no alternatives. The New Woman of Weimar may have been less challenging than nursing. But there were, in fact, viable options: the professions that were closed to the majority of women, but not to the exceptional woman. On the eve of World War I, women constituted 6.3 percent of the German university student population.[124] A career in university teaching was virtually inconceivable.[125]

120. Gay, *Weimar Culture*, esp. 69, 128–29.
121. One might note that Karl and Nelly Barth's Swiss Reformed social conservatism is reflected in the fact that they had five children: the norm in Weimar Germany, for couples marrying in the early 1920s, was 2.27 and declined to 1.98 for marriages between 1925 and 1929 (Frevert, *Women in German History*, 186).
122. Eksteins, *Rites of Spring*, 210. Busch ("God Is God: The Meaning of a Controversial Formula and the Fundamental Problem of Speaking About God," *Princeton Seminary Bulletin* n.s. 7 [1986]: 103) sees a possible connection between Ragaz, the religious socialist (of importance to Barth), and the Dadaists.
123. It would be similarly accurate to say that the Beauvoir-Sartre model did not exist for her or for Barth. They were confessional Christians; marriage was a scripturally mandated institution.
124. Frevert, *Women in German History*, 122.
125. Italy was the only European country in which women were, though with extreme rarity, able to teach in universities (Smith, *Changing Lives*, 323).

The academic progression and career of an Ursula Keppel-Compton Niebuhr (at Oxford and Union Theological Seminary; then to the faculty at Barnard College) would have been outside von Kirschbaum's considering. But a career as *Theologin*—the word for female theologian in a gender-inflected language—was possible. The "Verband evangelischer Theologinnen Deutschlands" was formally constituted by thirty female students in Marburg—they were largely philologists specializing in religion—in 1925. By 1929 membership was about 70, by 1930 it was 107, by 1935 it was 250, and by 1942 it was 284 (fig. 2).[126]

Theologin had more general connotations than we are accustomed to. The *Verband* was concerned with the full range of professional roles in the church, from teaching to pastoral duties. Much of its activity in the 1920s was directed to defining a course between a resistant church officialdom and the secular women's movement. It was not itself united on the subject of women in the actual office of parish minister (*Pfarramt*). The majority in the *Verband* accepted the incremental goal of working toward official recognition by church authorities of a specific office to be held *by* women to fill the needs *of* women in the church. For the time being, a wider range of pastoral duties would be justified only in exceptional circumstances. In 1928 a small, radical group that called for full equality in the office of pastor broke away from the *Verband* and constituted itself as the "Vereinigung evangelischer Theologinnen." It lasted only until 1933, when the new political situation silenced even the most moderate feminist organization.[127]

The teachers in the *Verband* were catechists within the church or Bible teachers in private and state schools.[128] The association held

126. Dagmar Henze, "Die Konflikte zwischen dem 'Verband evangelischer Theologinnen Deutschlands' und der 'Vereinigung evangelischer Theologinnen' um die Frage des vollten Pfarramtes für die Frau," in *'Darum wagt es, Schwestern,'* 132. The membership figures are in the same essay, 132 n. 13. Henze observes that her source (an Erlangen dissertation that she frequently cites) doesn't state where it found these figures, but she located an alternative archival list for 1929, which names 64 "ordentlichen" members and 37 "ausserordentlichen" members. The photograph in figure 2, taken at one of the first Tagungen, shows 30 women (and a few male guests). So the numbers are probably accurate, with some approximating in round numbers.

127. Henze, "Die Konflikte," 129–50.

128. *RGG*, s.v. "Frau," esp. sections III–V; and the following essays in *Darum wagt es, Schwestern*: Hannelore Erhart, "Der 'Verband evangelischer Theologinnen Deutschlands' zwischen Frauenbewegung und Kirche in der Zeit der Weimarer Republik," 151–57; Henze, "Die Konflikte," 129–50; idem, "Schule als Arbeitsfeld für Theologinnen in der Zeit bis 1933," 191–209; Petra Kurtz, "Der 'Verband evangelischer Theologinnen Deutschlands'

annual conferences (*Tagungen*) and published its first proceedings (*Mitteilungen*) in 1930.[129] Karl Barth was acquainted with the proceedings. He referred to them in an exchange of letters in the Swiss *Reformierte Kirchenzeitung* in 1932 on the subject of the office of parish minister for women—which he considered a possibility though not a normative one. He could not agree with everything he read in the *Mitteilungen*—"How could it be otherwise?"—but he recognized and respected the seriousness of the writers.[130] Charlotte von Kirschbaum cited the *Reformierte Kirchenzeitung* letters in her writing on the role of women in church proclamation.[131] Barth, von Kirschbaum, and many of the *Theologinnen* were on the same side in regard to Nazism. It is of interest to learn that many of the *Theologinnen* were Barthians in more fundamental ways— and it seems consistent that they should feel strengthened by his theological scorn for human authority or any linkage between theology and culture. Liselotte Lawerenz, who studied with Barth in Switzerland, said she valued in him the combining of clear political analysis with concentration on the Word of God.[132]

A close contemporary of von Kirschbaum, Anna Paulsen (1893–1981), combined ability with a life-long determination to become a *Theologin*. Stimulated in childhood to live in the intellectual world of her father, a pastor with special interest in Kierkegaard, she overcame the many obstacles to completion of university work and in 1924 became the first female licentiate with high honors at Kiel. She went on to teach and direct a Bible School (at the Burckhardthaus in Berlin-Dahlen) for young women preparing to be parish assistants (*Gemeindehelferinnen*). Her teaching made her financially independent; she remained single

---

im Spiegel seiner 'Mitteilungen' in der Zeit der Weimarer Republik," 175–90. ('*Darum wagt es, Schwestern*' is a very rich collection of essays focusing especially on the Weimar and Nazi periods by the Frauenforschungsprojekt zur Geschichte der Theologinnen, Göttingen. Another collection from the Frauenforschungsprojekt, *Querdenken*, is cited below.)

129. Petra Kurtz, "Der 'Verband,'" 175.

130. *Reformierte Kirchenzeitung*, no. 28 (1932), 220–21.

131. Von Kirschbaum, "Role of Women in the Proclamation of the Word," in Köbler, *In the Shadow*, 103 (Shepherd: 183). This is the closest I can come to the question of her relationship, if any, with the *Verband* and the kind of support network it represents. Did she bring its existence (and publications) to Karl's attention? Did she have any other contact with it? Did she shy away from it as a potential temptation? Or did she prefer dialogical situations to the mix of individual and group life of the Verband? What would the Verband have thought of her after she cast her lot with Barth? We can wish for evidence on some of these questions and only wonder on others.

132. Gerdi Nützel, "Jugendarbeit als Arbeitsfeld für Theologinnen in der Zeit des Nationalsozialismus," 436.

through her long life. She wrote books on women in Scripture (in 1935, with a revised edition in 1960), on Kierkegaard, and on the roots of the *Frauenbewegung* in the nineteenth century. She also prepared reports for the Evangelischen Kirche Deutschlands on the situation and roles of women in the church.[133]

Anna Paulsen and Charlotte von Kirschbaum had many of the same interests and some important affinities; they also thought differently about many things.[134] We don't know whether or in what combination their different life patterns were the result of chance, biographical contingencies, or choice.[135] What Paulsen's life demonstrates is the possibility of a professional and scholarly career in religion for a woman in early twentieth-century Germany.

Even without the *Verband*, such a possibility would not have been an alien notion to Barth. His mother, Anna, had some involvement in the *Frauenbewegung* in Bern and, after 1918, as a committee member in a Women's Aid Group.[136] In 1902 his father, Fritz, spoke in firm (and courageous) support of independence and emancipation of women in his "Die Frauenfrage und das Christentum"—von Kirschbaum quotes

---

133. See Almut Witt, "Anna Paulsen—Lebensbild einer Theologin," in *Querdenken: Beiträge zur feministisch-befreiungstheologischen Diskussion*, 2nd ed., Frauenforschungs-projekt zur Geschichte der Theologinnen (Pfaffenweiler: Centaurus-Verlagsgesellschaft, 1993), 268–89.

134. Paulsen drew on the early work of Barth and dialectical theology for her inaugural dissertation (on the relationship between revelation and history). In *Geschlecht und Person*, her 1960 revision of *Mutter und Magd* (on women in the Bible), she cited the two volumes (III/1 and III/4) of *KD* that—as we will see in Part 3—Barth and von Kirschbaum collaborated on most visibly. (She does not refer to von Kirschbaum, and neither von Kirschbaum nor Barth cites her.) She found in scripture legitimation for the unmarried as well as married state for women (an intentional critique of the ideology of Motherhood in Nazism). In the Nazi period she continued her teaching work at the Burckhardthaus while being a member—though not active—of the Confessing Church and a friend of Martin Niemöller. Intellectually, Paulsen's guiding principle as a Kierke-gaardian, in biblical exegesis, theology, and history, was the personal relationship of the individual believer—female or male—to God. See Almut Witt, "Anna Paulsen," 270–72, 277; Anna Paulsen, *Geschlecht und Person: das biblische Wort über die Frau* (Hamburg: Furche-Verlag, 1960), 69, 132, and passim.

135. We also can't say that Paulsen's achievement was greater than von Kirschbaum's. It was different, and one difference is that it is out there to measure, whereas von Kirschbaum's is blended into the work of someone else.

136. Busch, *Karl Barth*, 108; E. Busch, personal communication, 19 July 1994. Barth's family lived in Bern from 1889 onward, and Anna remained there till 1918, when she left to keep house for her son Heinrich, near Basel. Her activity might be a concrete link to the feminists Barth dislikes so much, but it seems far more likely that the groups she worked with fell within a religious orbit, sharing the dominant conservative ethos of the German *Frauenbewegung*.

this address in her own work.[137] Barth's sister Gertrud began a law career, though she ended her studies to marry.[138]

Barth taught a small number of female students at all of the universities at which he worked even in the twenties and thirties; he got along well with a considerable number of them and retained friendships with them through the course of their interesting and independent professional careers.[139] He described one of his students as "lively Gretel Herrmann with the bobbed hair" (bobbed hair means feminist, in the 1920s).[140] At Bonn and Basel, his loyal students (and lasting friends of von Kirschbaum) included Lili Simon and Erika Küppers.[141]

One might also note Barth's relationship with "the women of Bergli." The retreat was a gathering place that brought together, in conversation and planning for the struggles of the Confessing Church with Nazism, married couples and single women who were students or acquaintances of Barth and von Kirschbaum, such as Gertrud Staewen (the friend and close colleague in the church struggles who later became a social work teacher and social worker in the Berlin-Tegel prison).[142] Photographs of group gatherings at Bergli document this lively, egalitarian society.[143]

These women did not directly and continuously help the progress of the Church Dogmatics. However, to encourage a promising student to continue her or his studies is normal and expected behavior in the academic world now and earlier; to encourage and facilitate the way for a student who is going against social convention is, for most teachers both now and in the past century, an obligation. Barth failed here, presumably because he was not willing to lose von Kirschbaum's help or to return to his state of loneliness. We will return to this subject in our discussion of male-female encounter in the thought of Barth and von Kirschbaum. Immediately, we can only see that he was not willing to compromise or to try to devise alternatives and present them (without prejudice) to von Kirschbaum. In his intimate friendship and collaboration with Eduard

137. E. Busch (on Anna), personal communication, 19 July 1994. On Fritz: von Kirschbaum's quotation in "Role of Women in Proclamation," 112–13.

138. Busch, Karl Barth, 108.

139. Busch reports (Karl Barth, 181) that his students in Münster included Elisabeth Schulz and Anna Maria Rohwedder, who later became teachers and with whom he stayed on visits to Hamburg.

140. Ibid., 181. On feminism and short hair: Mary Louise Roberts, "Samson and Delilah Revisited: The Politics of Women's Fashions in 1920s France," American Historical Review 98 (1993): 657–83.

141. Busch, Karl Barth, 203; and Köbler, In the Shadow, 46, 49.

142. See Barth on Staewen in KB-ET Briefwechsel, 6 October 1929, 678, 680.

143. Photographs in Busch, Karl Barth, esp. 294.

Thurneysen—a collaboration that could be acknowledged with publication under joint authorship—Thurneysen was able to have his own personal life and his own job and responsibilities. He was certainly not expected to provide secretarial services or to be Barth's administrative assistant, as von Kirschbaum was. These two functions could have been bought: Barth—with some admittedly difficult adjustment to his late-night work habits—could have hired someone for them, supplemented with hardy student assistants.

We know that von Kirschbaum rejected one alternative to her life of work with Barth: marriage to Heinrich Scholz, the philosopher whom Barth respected when both were students of Harnack in Berlin in 1906 and whose friendship he valued from 1929 onward.[144] Von Kirschbaum was "assigned" to attend his lectures and then spend an hour in discussion with him, the content of which was to be relayed to Barth. When Scholz asked her to marry him, she said no without apparent regret.

Perhaps she would not have wanted to marry him under any circumstances; perhaps she expected to marry Barth. Did Barth think marriage to someone else—or to himself, for that matter—would fatally interrupt her intellectual life?[145] Besides the examples of his students, he might have considered the relationship of Karl Jaspers, his colleague in Basel from 1948 onward, and Hannah Arendt. Jaspers and Arendt had separate family, professional, and intellectual lives; their complex, interdependent, and rich relationship survived the war and separation by the Atlantic Ocean when Arendt emigrated to New York.[146] Hannah Arendt is not merely known as "someone in Karl Jaspers' life."

144. For this and the following on Scholz, see Busch, *Karl Barth*, 197, 206–7; Köbler, *In the Shadow*, 41–42.

145. It seems relevant to observe that von Kirschbaum would not have been overly burdened with domestic work in a marriage to Barth. H. Prolingheuer notes (in Köbler, *In the Shadow*, 132) that Nelly Barth "naturally had qualified personnel to take care of the housework and to care for the children."

146. For common social ground among Barth, Arendt, and Jaspers, see *Hannah Arendt/ Karl Jaspers: Correspondence 1926–1969*, ed. Lotte Kohler and Hans Saner, trans. R. and R. Kimber (New York: Harcourt Brace Jovanovich, 1992), in which Jaspers and Arendt make incidental references to Barth from time to time. For example, Arendt writes to Jaspers about an "American protégé" of hers who is studying with Karl Barth and will soon take some classes with Jaspers (17 January 1958); other examples on 168, 311; see also the references—usually impatient—to Heinrich Barth, Jaspers's fellow University philosopher— e.g., p. 92). The need Jaspers felt for contact with Arendt's mind evokes—and may surpass— Barth on von Kirschbaum. Writing to Arendt of his fleeting satisfaction with the overflowing audiences at his lectures, he says: "But then I think about Hannah Arendt and that there are a few 'Noahs' in the world, and I feel that what is more important to me than all this success I could easily dispense with is if you are of one mind with me" (20 July 1947).

Charlotte von Kirschbaum has a real but very limited independent existence as author of *Die wirkliche Frau*. Highly individualized and valued by Barth's friends and students, she is a stand-out flower in Barth's garden. Flowers don't move. With a shift in perspective, however, this charming deaconess-type, who chose whom she would serve, is an atypical New Woman in Weimar Germany. Her life was unconventional to an extreme. Eberhard Busch rightly stresses her bravery in following her choice despite the social condemnation it provoked.[147] And her life was open and cosmopolitan, sometimes more than one would wish for. With Barth she was involved in important and dangerous committee work for the church's struggle with Nazism. Some of the well-known anecdotes about Barth concern conversations in such places as Basel cafés, and she is part of them.

At the same time that she was tied to and controlled by one man, von Kirschbaum followed a path that was more intellectually satisfying and challenging than that of the Weimar New Woman. She had an apparently conservative doctrine of male-female relations that rationalized her situation, yet in her partnership with Barth, she was the one who insisted on dialogue with the Women's Movement. The movement was part of her consciousness, as a theological foil and as a social challenge that I think she proudly, if quietly, met. She was not a feminist by any but German standards. By any measure, however, she *was* a New Woman.

3. Feminist Approaches

I think it would be a mistake, nevertheless, merely to celebrate what von Kirschbaum achieved and to lift up the unconventionality of her life. We need also to recognize and regret what we do not have: an independent life and an autonomous, unconstrained body of work. Very little has been written about the Barth–von Kirschbaum relationship. One reason is that their correspondence has not been published. An edition of letters is in preliminary stages of preparation.[148] But it is unlikely that it will constitute a Rosetta stone for the complexities of their relationship. The intention in publishing it is largely to dispel the rumors that surround

147. Statement in Köbler, *In the Shadow*, 133.
148. Edited by Pfarrer R-J. Erler for the Barth *Gesamtausgabe* (with no access until publication). A publication year has not yet been designated.

the figures. The letters will shed further light on their work routines—
but we actually know a great deal about this subject from observations
and reports by their contemporaries, from students who worked with
them, and from von Kirschbaum's successor as assistant to Barth,
Eberhard Busch. The other and, I think, principal reason for the paucity
of commentary is that the relationship is an awkward subject for
Barthians and a charged subject for feminists. So it has not progressed
beyond the questions contained in the rumors.

Eberhard Busch, whose *Karl Barth: His Life from Letters and
Autobiographical Texts* is the major source for all Barth biographers, is
also the only Barth scholar to have confronted the relationship and
considered both its prime intellectual importance to Barth and the
enormous tensions and pain it provoked in the thirty-seven years of von
Kirschbaum's life in the Barth household.[149] Renate Köbler has published
the first freestanding work on von Kirschbaum, one that I have cited
often in this inquiry: *Schattenarbeit: Charlotte von Kirschbaum. Die
Theologin an der Seite Karl Barths*, translated by Keith Crim as *In the
Shadow of Karl Barth: Charlotte von Kirschbaum*. It consists of a short
biographical and interpretive portrait and tribute to her importance for
the work of Karl Barth, the texts of two lectures by von Kirschbaum, and
many observations by close friends and relatives who knew both of
them. The observations are invaluable, as is much of the biographical
information. Köbler recommends, but herself eschews, comparative
textual study to demonstrate von Kirschbaum's intellectual contribution
to *Church Dogmatics*.[150] Originally a research paper written under Hans
Prolingheuer at the University of Marburg, it is a valuable preliminary
study. The new Eerdmans translation of von Kirschbaum's lectures on
women contains another short survey, an introduction by Eleanor
Jackson.[151]

The biography and many of the comments by friends are sentimental. Von Kirschbaum is presented as happy and fulfilled in the life
she chose, and heroic or saintly in her devotion to Karl Barth. Several of
the observers are indignant that people have questioned the purity of the

149. Within the biography, see its many index entries for von Kirschbaum. Busch also
discusses von Kirschbaum in "Deciding Moments in the Life and Work of Karl Barth," 66,
and in "Theologie und Biographie," 333–34.
150. Köbler, *In the Shadow*, 148 (chap. 11 n. 9 and chap. 12 n. 3).
151. Jackson's introduction seems to make excessive claims for von Kirschbaum's role
in the writing of *CD* both with respect to the generation of ideas and the extent to which
she wrote "the" notes. In Parts 2 and 3 below I come to rather different conclusions,
though on the basis of an inquiry that was not Jackson's purpose to carry out.

Barth–von Kirschbaum relationship. They are indignant, not because the relationship was nonsexual, but because it must be viewed on a higher plane. One may agree with their rejection of puritanical judgment-alism but think the commentators have offered in its place something theologically unsound. Georges Casalis's wonderful letter of memories and reflections included in Köbler's book is typical of these. He suggests that in confronting the triangle of Karl, Nelly, and Lollo, we must accept it as something beyond our understanding but somehow good: that is, God-given in all its painful humanity. To think that divorce might have been a better idea is to miss this higher element. Marguerite Thurneysen (Eduard's wife) likewise speaks of accepting the enigmatic life of Karl Barth, his wife, and Charlotte von Kirschbaum.[152]

I fear there is some mythologizing in process here—the kind of romantic mythologizing that Barth sometimes warned against.[153] It should also be clear that I have reservations about von Kirschbaum's sense of fulfillment. I go back always to the absence of a life of her own and to Barth's selfishness—a selfishness that ignored the power that his mind and persona had to deprive von Kirschbaum of any choice. Or perhaps it is arrogance: the assumption that there could be no better choice than himself.

Köbler's work is an example of a biographical genre that seeks to redress the balance of attention for women who have collaborated with famous men. (Another is the literary historian Phyllis Rose's *Parallel Lives: Five Victorian Marriages*.) This is one possible feminist approach. Initially it was mine: I wanted to lift up von Kirschbaum's voice for others to hear. But whenever I wrote about her collaboration with Barth, I realized I was still paying more attention to Karl than to Charlotte. So I take another feminist view: we can't restore the balance because the life we would speak of was not lived.

Inge Stephan seems to have had an experience similar to mine. She includes a chapter on von Kirschbaum and Barth (one of eleven male-female pairs) in her *Das Schicksal der begabten Frau: Im Schatten berühmter Männer*. Intending to bring the women she studied out from the shadow of the great men with whom they labored, she found instead a pattern of exploitation and stifled creativity. It seems to me that she is right in attributing much of the problem to the myth of the creative genius: the great man, the one who is responsible for his *oeuvre*, though

---

152. Köbler, *In the Shadow*, 136–40 (Casalis); ibid., 132 (M. Thurneysen).
153. And which, we will later see, he did not always succeed in avoiding, on a subject of importance to us: the nature of women.

possibly inspired by a muse (or a perfect wife, secretary, or other provider of needs).[154] Likewise Linda Nochlin's question "Why have there been no great women artists?"[155] correctly sees, I think, that raising female heroes who are "just as good" as male heroes is a betrayal of the women who *might* have been as great, but were not. Such an approach also elides the more informative and helpful question: How was this allowed to happen? Or why did it happen this way?

We can and will study the limited number of texts we have from von Kirschbaum; we will also consider their paucity. I will try to find her voice within the *Church Dogmatics* and, in combination with *Die wirkliche Frau*, infer the directions and sound of what might have been. (I will also be interested in what might have been for a liberated Karl Barth.) But the subject of Charlotte von Kirschbaum must remain only a major part of the life and work of Karl Barth.

For this reason Wolfgang Schildmann's psychological study of Karl Barth is interesting indirectly as well as directly. How does he deal with von Kirschbaum in this analysis of Barth's reported dreams in reference to the key relationships in his life? By eliminating her. Her name appears only once, in an early reference that manages to delete her gender. The context is a discussion of the waning of Barth's closeness to Thurneysen. Thurneysen first became dispensable as theological colleague, "while the slackening of their pastoral relationship became evident with the entrance of Ch. von Kirschbaum into Barth's life."[156] Schildmann told Eberhard Busch that he did not have sufficient material to include her in his "Psychogramm." But von Kirschbaum's unacknowledged omission fits and reinforces all too well a pattern of evasion and repression I seemed to encounter in some of my research inquiries.[157] Part of any realistic response to the subject of Barth and von Kirschbaum must be anger.

In the last part of *Church Dogmatics* that Barth wrote and published, volume IV, part 4, "The Christian Life (Fragment)," he commented again

154. See Stephan's "Einleitung" and chapter on von Kirschbaum, 177–92, esp. 178. Stephan also recognizes the condescension in the (strategic) expressions of gratitude by these great men. She includes discussion of Illich's concept of "shadow-work," which Köbler drew on before her, as marginalization.
155. Nochlin, "Why Have There Been No Great Women Artists?" [1971], reprinted in her *"Women, Art, and Power" and Other Essays* (New York: Harper & Row, 1988), 145–78.
156. Schildmann, *Was sind das für Zeichen?* 26.
157. For example, I would be given information but told I must not attribute it; or I would be given information but told the informer could not remember the source from which he (always, he) got it. Notably, these men were not social conservatives.

on von Kirschbaum's role in his life and the life of the *Church Dogmatics*. *CD* would not be completed, in part because age and infirmity had slowed him down, in part because (he writes) "my faithful assistant Charlotte von Kirschbaum, who had been indispensable from 1930 onwards, suffered an even more serious illness than mine (definitively from the end of 1965 and beginning of 1966), so that she was out of action in relation to the *Church Dogmatics*, in whose rise and progress she had played so great a part."

In the pages that follow I shall try to discover what made Charlotte von Kirschbaum so indispensable an assistant to Karl Barth. Her role in their work together consists of both substantive contribution and specific function: I could as well use the terms *product* and *process*. Part 2 will look at the evolution of their collaboration to its mature form, forged in the late 1920s and the 1930s and continuing through their life together. I will consider her role in the compilation of the notes in *CD* and her role as first reader or first critical audience for Barth's arguments. (Barth's students were the first to hear the Dogmatics in their preliminary lecture form.) I will consider contributions not so easily categorized as process or product alone. Part 3 will be a more detailed examination of the collaboration on what I have been calling anthropology of gender. It is in many ways an example writ large for all their work together; it is also a special case. This is the subject that reflects upon their personal relationship, and it involves, more directly than other doctrines, cultural and historical contextualization.

As my study progressed, an unanticipated question arose and became increasingly intriguing: Why does it suddenly become, in *CD* III/1, so important and central to Barth to assert male-female differences or duality? And for von Kirschbaum to do the same? Here, besides historical and cultural perspectives, I have drawn upon theological concepts of relationality and alterity in my own milieu, the roots of which—this makes them more interesting—are in the 1920s. So we end, in part, with recollection of where we began.

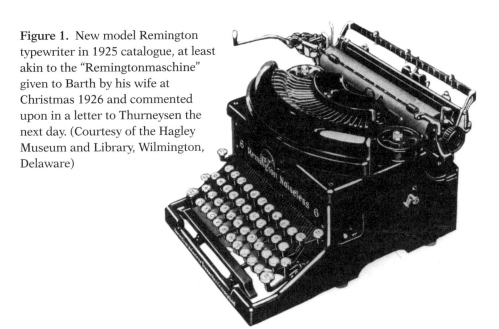

Figure 1. New model Remington typewriter in 1925 catalogue, at least akin to the "Remingtonmaschine" given to Barth by his wife at Christmas 1926 and commented upon in a letter to Thurneysen the next day. (Courtesy of the Hagley Museum and Library, Wilmington, Delaware)

Figure 2. Verband evangelischer Theologinnen Deutschlands at a conference in Marburg in the early 1920s. (Courtesy of AKET, the Archiv des Konvents Evangelischer Theologinnen in der Bundesrepublik Deutschland, Bovenden, Germany)

Figure 3. Charlotte von Kirschbaum in 1931. (Courtesy of the Karl Barth-Archiv, Basel)

Figures 4a and 4b. Two views of von Kirschbaum and Barth in the study at Bergli, 1929. (Courtesy of the Karl Barth-Archiv, Basel)

Figure 7. The Barth family, including von Kirschbaum. *Left to right:* Grete Karwehl (family friend), Peter Barth (brother), Markus (son), von Kirschbaum, Hans-Jacob (son), Karl Barth, Franziska (daughter), Christoph and Matthias (sons), Nelly Barth. (Courtesy of the Karl Barth-Archiv, Basel)

Figure 5. LEFT, ABOVE Von Kirschbaum and Barth working together in 1930. (Courtesy of the Karl Barth-Archiv, Basel)

Figure 6. LEFT, BELOW Von Kirschbaum mediating a discussion between Barth and Heinrich Scholz, c. 1930. (Courtesy of the Karl Barth-Archiv, Basel)

Figure 8. Von Kirschbaum, Barth, and Franz Hildebrandt (friend of Bonhoeffer) in a discussion in the garden at Bergli, September 1937. (Courtesy of the Karl Barth-Archiv, Basel)

Figure 9. Von Kirschbaum in Basel in 1943. (Courtesy of the Karl Barth-Archiv, Basel)

Figure 10. Von Kirschbaum on the steps outside the Barth home in the Pilgerstrasse, Basel, 1948. (Courtesy of the Karl Barth-Archiv, Basel)

Figure 11. Von Kirschbaum at Le Croisie, April 1950. (Courtesy of the Karl Barth-Archiv, Basel)

Figure 12. Von Kirschbaum, Helmut Gollwitzer, Barth, and Hermann Diem in Brione, March 1962.

Figure 13. Barth's study at Bruderholzallee 26 (now the Karl Barth-Archiv) with a view of the adjoining study of von Kirschbaum.

PART 2

Work

> Kurt leant his elbows on the table and looked at Anna
> busying herself with the dishes. He was too tired to speak
> but it gave him pleasure to sit there and watch her. She
> handled everything so deftly and quickly.
>
> —from the proletarian novel by Klaus Neukrantz,
> Barricades in Berlin (Barrikaden am Wedding:
> Der Roman einer Strasse aus den Berliner Maitagen), 1929

Kurt's view of Anna will seem very funny or very sad to most feminists, but Klaus Neukrantz did not intend it to be either. From Left to Right on the political and social spectrum, women were expected to take care of the menial tasks of life for "their men" so that the men could be free for "important" work. This cultural assumption is one context of the Barth–von Kirschbaum collaboration; so is the urgency of the political landscape in Germany in the 1930s and 1940s.

1. In the Light of Thurneysen

The correspondence between Barth and Eduard Thurneysen chronicles the beginnings of the Barth–von Kirschbaum collaboration. But it has additional use for our subject, for the collaboration of Barth and von

Kirschbaum can helpfully be approached through the lens of the Barth-Thurneysen relationship. To several observers (Markus Barth, Köbler, Busch, Schildmann, and this writer) Charlotte von Kirschbaum seems clearly to have replaced Thurneysen as dialogue partner and, in some sense, alter ego. The lens opens up areas and facets of the collaboration that might otherwise stay unnoticed—just as it serves to define aspects unique to each relationship.

Both relationships were grounded in an unusual degree of rapport that was noticed and widely commented upon. Barth self-consciously said of his early visits and walks with Thurneysen that the two became so engrossed in their conversation that villagers might have taken them for "two strange wanderers between two worlds." He recorded a wonderful anecdote current among friends in which he and Thurneysen were said to have "spent a whole afternoon sitting opposite each other and smoking. After an hour *I* said, 'Perhaps,' and after another hour of silence Thurneysen said, 'Or perhaps not!' That was said to be our conversation and the essence of our system."[1] In a similar way though in a different tone, the at-oneness of Barth and von Kirschbaum has been remarked. Gertrud Staewen said their congeniality as they worked in their study annex at the Bergli was "unforgettable and unrepeatable." At the end of their work on Barth's book on Anselm, they presented to Staewen "an unforgettable picture . . . in their oneness of intellectual communion."[2]

A distinctive part of the rapport in both collaborations is particularly important for us. A remark made by von Kirschbaum at Union Theological Seminary during Barth's visit to the United States in 1962 offers justification for the parallel as well as insight into its substance. Asked to describe how she and Barth worked together, she responded that it was really not possible to tell where the thoughts of one ended and the other began.[3] Consciously or unconsciously, she was paraphrasing a much earlier remark by Barth. In the Preface to the second edition of *The Epistle to the Romans* (1921), Barth said of Thurneysen's responses to his drafts of the new edition of the work:

Some of [his] additions penetrated deeper than my original comment, others were explanatory and added greater precision of expression. I have adopted these additions for the most part

1. Busch, *Karl Barth*, 73, 118.
2. Quoted in Köbler, *In the Shadow*, 36.
3. Christopher Morse, personal conversation, January 1992.

without alteration, and they remain a silent testimony to his self-effacement. So close has been our co-operation that I doubt whether even the specialist could detect where the one leaves off and the other begins.[4]

When Barth and Thurneysen published two volumes of sermons under joint authorship in 1917 and 1924, they did not indicate which of the sermons each one had written. Wolfgang Schildmann uses the technical term *fusion* for this relational phenomenon. It can include mutual idealization and a sense of necessary complementarity. Thurneysen felt energized by contact with Barth's thinking and writings. He felt that he owed his own achievements to the stimulus of Barth's work. In turn, Barth—who was uncomfortable in the pastorate and knew his congregation was dissatisfied with their pastor, at the same time that he wanted desperately to bind preaching and theology together in a new way—felt that Thurneysen was the ideal pastor. He was the one who truly loved and lived with his whole flock.[5] In Part 3 of this study we will see a different kind of complementarity (or perceived complementarity) in the Barth–von Kirschbaum collaboration, namely, one of gender. Barth's tendency toward relational fusion was another ingredient, I think, in his unreasonable decision to bring von Kirschbaum into his household.

When Barth left the pastorate and began to teach at Göttingen, his relationship with Thurneysen shifted almost entirely to written dialogue.[6] The more Barth wrote and published in his early years in teaching, the more he came to rely on Thurneysen as his "first reader"—that crucial role that is both critic and grand executioner. Even when von Kirschbaum became de facto first reader, Thurneysen was not displaced. He continued to be Barth's most important reader, the one whose opinion and validation were essential, through the end of the 1920s. What finally displaced him in this role was the waning of Barth's need for the kind of imprimatur he provided. Barth was sufficiently confident in his professorial role to dispense with it. Some of his confidence was

4. Barth, *The Epistle to the Romans*, trans. Edwyn C. Hoskyns (London: Oxford University Press, 1933 [1968]), 15.

5. Schildmann, *Was sind das für Zeichen?* 21–22.

6. Telephones were not yet used with modern frequency. The average prevalence for German cities in 1921 is about seven per one hundred people; cost was a retarding factor. See statistics by city in *World Almanac and Encyclopedia*. By the late 1920s, however, Barth seems to be using one regularly—for example, he refers to telephone discussions with H. Scholz in *KB-ET Briefwechsel*, 26 January 1930.

based on a function that he and von Kirschbaum developed as part of her work for him: the continuing construction of a library, a kind of hypertext, of long excerpts from the full history of Christian thought.

The dialogical need that Thurneysen had long filled continued, however, and it is here that von Kirschbaum did begin to replace Thurneysen. Logistics (some culturally constructed) favored her assumption of this role, and it is optimally a role for one unchanging partner to fill. We will see that she filled it in her own way; however, in several essential ways it was the same role. Barth's intensely dialogical personality required someone to function as sounding board and, most characteristically, someone with whom to think things through. This explains the situation von Kirschbaum described at UTS as well as Barth's remark about Thurneysen in the 1921 edition of *Epistle to the Romans*. As we proceed through the items in von Kirschbaum's daily agenda, it is essential to remember that she had to be available at any time for dialogue with Barth. Eberhard Busch's experience was the same. Barth needed to talk with—that is "with" as distinct from "to"—a *Gegenüber*, a counterpart, in order to become clear on a question.[7]

Such a dialogue partner could easily become an alter ego. Thurneysen was exactly this. In the Safenwil-Leutwil years, the two went to many conferences and visited many other pastors, theologians, and religious and social thinkers (largely friends of Thurneysen); and these contacts were of real importance for Barth's thought. But the two had to share these meetings even if both could not attend. The Barth-Thurneysen correspondence, even when Barth had moved to Göttingen, demonstrates Barth's need to report everything and to experience everything with Thurneysen, almost as if it did not happen or had not happened unless it was shared. The alter ego is a validator of the self and an ally in the project of life. As Barth said in a retrospective contribution to a Festschrift for Thurneysen in 1958, it must be understood that "we were at war with the world during those years."

The alter ego relationship (sometimes called twinship) is typically formed at a difficult transitional stage in self-development. Thurneysen accompanied Barth through the making of revolutionary theology and through the reorientation of Barth's life from parish to university.[8]

7. E. Busch, personal communication, 16 December 1993.

8. Busch, *Karl Barth*, 74. The concept of alter ego is most closely associated with Kohut; Schildmann (*Was sind das für Zeichen?* 22–24) draws on him too. See Howard S. Baker and Margaret N. Baker, "Heinz Kohut's Self Psychology: An Overview," *American Journal of Psychiatry* 144 (January 1987): 1–9; and see esp. F. von Broembsen, "The

Mutual need fulfillment, though with different intensity, is part of the alter ego or twinship relationship. Von Kirschbaum was largely isolated and had lost her affirming parent. The possibility that Barth functioned as a father figure for her is obvious but should not be exaggerated. In early twentieth-century Europe, their age difference of thirteen years is in the normal range for conjugal, not intergenerational, relationships. The psychological need Barth filled was, more probably, the affirmation of her intellectual and spiritual gifts that her father had provided. Barth had multiple needs in 1925: most of all, the final loss of Rösy Münger, and also the beginning of separation from Thurneysen that the very strength of their relationship made inevitable. Barth offers an extreme example of the alter ego phenomenon, and it would have been reinforced by his dialogical needs.

The second of the Thurneysen functions that von Kirschbaum assumed was that of *Seelsorger* or pastoral advisor. Schildmann considers this the most important of Thurneysen's roles.[9] His analysis of Barth's dreams is based in large part on the accounts of them in Barth's letters to Thurneysen. Some of the published letters were edited by Thurneysen to eliminate material that concerned their intimate lives (*Intimsphäre*); they are still replete with Barth's anxieties, annoyances, dilemmas.[10] Perhaps the most direct evidence of Barth's need for his theological collaborator or assistant to be *Seelsorger* too is in the accounts by Eberhard Busch of his own work with Barth as von Kirschbaum's successor. Barth did not draw a line—one could say he resolutely did not draw a line—between the personal and the professional. Busch said he worked his assistants hard and expected them to share his relaxation or recovery as thoroughly—they were comrades.[11]

In many an incident in recollections and in his journals, Busch presents a Barth of almost childlike vulnerability and trust. Barth presents Busch with dreams to interpret; he tells him he does not want to think about death though it looms before him. Thurneysen and Busch were pastors. Von Kirschbaum was a nurse-sister; and Barth includes, in letters to friends and family, various bits of health advice she gives him.[12] This caretaker role continued even through the onset of her illness in

---

Twinship: A Paradigm Towards Separation and Integration," *American Journal of Psychoanalysis* 48 (1988): 355–65.

9. Schildmann, *Was sind das für Zeichen?* 3ff.

10. Thurneysen, Vorwort, *KB-ET Briefwechsel*, vi.

11. E. Busch, personal communication, 16 December 1993.

12. See *KB-ET Briefwechsel*, 18 August 1928; Busch, *Karl Barth*, 436, 462.

1962. During his U.S. tour, Barth wrote to his son-in-law that "Lollo watches like a lynx that I am not overtaxed or do not overtax myself."[13] She concerned herself not only with his physical health. In July 1962 Barth wrote to Gollwitzer of his lack of appetite, "bordering on *acedia*," to write still another volume of dogmatics when all around him theological dullness prevailed. But he continues: "Lollo cannot stand this kind of thinking. She will be angry when she reads this, call me ungrateful, and try to stop me from sending the letter if possible."[14] Markus Barth thought von Kirschbaum understood Barth better than anyone else did. Lili Simon said von Kirschbaum advised him in small and large matters alike.[15] We know well—and shall see further—that she counseled him in time of political danger and that he listened to her.

The chronicle of von Kirschbaum's evolving role in Barth's life begins in August 1925, when Thurneysen tells Barth he spent some time with her and Georg Merz at the Bergli. She reappears in the letters in late 1926 when Barth is laboring to rewrite the dogmatics lectures he had delivered at Göttingen (only the Prolegomena would be published, under the title *Christliche Dogmatik im Entwurf*). He proposes to send some of the revised text to Lollo, who in turn would relay it to Eduard, in the hope that he would apply the same attention he had given the revision of *Epistle to the Romans* and tell Barth whether or not publication—to the eyes of hungry critics—is advisable. Barth will do whatever Thurneysen considers right—though as the publication decision becomes more complicated, he also seeks Lollo's opinion. She is starting to feel at home in the cross-currents of theology. In February of 1927 Barth told Thurneysen that she had returned another section of the Dogmatics and advised him to go ahead with the project, despite Althaus and Gogarten and a few others, because nothing like it was available.[16]

Von Kirschbaum is also becoming a useful intermediary. In April 1927 Barth tells Thurneysen to ask Lollo to explain Merz's dissatisfactions: relations with Merz were becoming burdensome for Barth.[17] Perhaps most important, by August 1927 a rhythm and sense of normalcy in working together have been established. On August 21 Barth wrote to

13. *Karl Barth: Letters 1961–1968*, ed. Jürgen Fangmeier and Hinrich Stoevesandt, trans. G. W. Bromiley (Grand Rapids, Mich.: Wm. B. Eerdmans, 1981), 43.

14. Ibid., 61–62.

15. Köbler, *In the Shadow*, 42f. and 145 nn. 11 and 12.

16. *KB-ET Briefwechsel*, 28 February 1927. Gogarten was an early ally who very soon became an abrasive critic; Althaus started as an opponent and soon became a respected colleague. They both knew Barth's work well, and Barth paid attention to them.

17. Ibid., 13 April 1927.

Thurneysen from Nöschenrode (in the Harz mountains) where he and his family were spending the summer: "Lollo and I have our hands full with the Dogmatics, so [all] our days are passed in the same tranquil tempo—interrupted by pleasant late walks, evening visits to the inn, and so on."[18]

The naturalness and necessary-ness of being together in work— difficult work, and work construed in the widest sense—is evident in a late December 1927 letter: "Together with Lollo I have delved into Heiner's [this refers to Karl's brother Heinrich] *Philosophie der prak-tischen Vernunft.*" Karl has always respected Heiner for the height and depth of his vision, and he takes special joy in the closeness of Heiner's and "unserer Problematik." "Unser" seems to refer to Thurneysen and now, implicitly, to von Kirschbaum too. Reading Heinrich Barth with von Kirschbaum is sharing an experience of a difficult and multileveled nature, for Heinrich, along with Anna Barth, strongly and openly dis-approved of Karl's relationship with von Kirschbaum.[19]

In the same letter, Barth refers to Thurneysen's observations on Heinrich's attitude toward Karl. Concurrent with Barth's reports about Lollo's activities, he still sends drafts of his work to Thurneysen for critical commentary. Barth *and* von Kirschbaum (who sends greetings to Thurneysen, as he does to her) seem to be trying to include Thurneysen in their relationship. One inevitably thinks of Thurneysen's and Gerty Pestalozzi's insistent acts of embracing both Lollo and Nelly in their letters. Barth tells Thurneysen that his voice, amid the voices of Gogarten, Bultmann, and Brunner, is the only one he cares to listen to.[20] However, Barth seems to be both isolated from the dialectical group and tired of it. Not only is he secure enough to write without affirmation from Thur-neysen, but his audience is differently defined than it was for *Epistle to the Romans*, and Thurneysen is not exactly a colleague anymore. "Their" war is over.

Before we proceed to von Kirschbaum's unique job and unique version of the intangible Thurneysen roles, we need to use the Thurney-sen lens one more time: for insight into what could be called the limits of the collaboration. We need to take a closer look at the way Barth described—as distinct from the way he evaluated—his colleague's con-tributions to "their" project.

18. Ibid., 21 August 1927.
19. Ibid., 30 December 1927; E. Busch, personal communication, 19 July 1994. (See above, page 7).
20. Busch, *Karl Barth*, 196–98.

The gratitude Barth expressed to Thurneysen in the 1921 preface to the commentary on Romans refers to editorial revisions and real theological contributions. It omits something that, in later years, loomed larger in Barth's memory and in other sources on his working method. If Barth and Thurneysen sometimes communed in virtual silence, they also batted ideas around at highest speed, and some of these hit the ground and never rose again, while others are with us still. There is a random, scattershot quality to the discussions Barth evokes. Barth characterized and valued Thurneysen as "a volatile man" whose thinking on details and whose opinions were not predictable.[21] Barth admired his openness and benefited from its eclectic nature. In the Safenwil years Thurneysen once suggested that they study Hegel, but "nothing came of that." It was the same Thurneysen who contributed the *Stichwort* or catchphrase "vertical from above" and, as momentously, the phrase "wholly other," when one day in 1916 he whispered to Barth that what they needed "for preaching and instruction and pastoral care is a 'wholly other' theological foundation." But if the concept of "wholly other" informed all of Barth's writing of *Epistle to the Romans*, Thurneysen had meant it in quite general (*allgemein gehaltene*) terms.[22]

Eberhard Busch, Barth's last secretary and assistant, described a function that seems closely related to Barth's earliest collaboration: the providing of keywords as stimulus, upon request in Busch's case. Barth was reviewing his unpublished manuscripts and working on material for *CD* IV/4 on baptism. When Busch expressed interest in Barth's thinking about baptism, Barth gave him a manuscript to read.

> Then he said, "It's been eight years since I wrote this and I think there are some points where the text should be changed. Now read it once more and tell me where." So I made some marks, but he said, "It is not enough. There is more to change. Write me some key-words to change." Then he made additions to the text and it was an amusing scene. When he dictated the text and was finished he said, "And now you are satisfied?" This was not only far better than what was given me, it was a whole other piece. But he liked to acknowledge my help. I think this was the form in which he thought. I don't know if I can generalize about this or

21. Ibid., 74.
22. Ibid., 97; Karl Barth, "Nachwort," in *Schleiermacher-Auswahl. Mit einem Nachwort von Karl Barth*, ed. Heinz Bolli (Munich: Siebenstern Taschenbuch, 1968), 294.

not. But it was my experience, and also while he was writing his *Dogmatics*, that Karl Barth needed others to give him key-words. I've spoken with other students who had the same experience.[23]

The stimulus Barth received from his congenial and talented assistants was more than a trigger: like his daily newspaper reading, it could traceably steer the writing that followed upon it. Busch was able to find in those writings responses to problems and personal concerns that he and others had brought to Barth, though they had not elicited an immediate response. But it remained Barth who carved out the theology.[24]

2. Von Kirschbaum's Days

Tasks, Routines, Habits

Von Kirschbaum became Barth's full-time assistant in the fall of 1929 (following the long sabbatical stay at Bergli), moving into the Barth household on October 14. On November 16, 1929, Barth, who was appointed dean of the faculty beginning in fall 1929 ("with long office hours and much minutia and representations of all kinds"), who was working on a radical revision of his lecture series on nineteenth-century Protestant theology and teaching a new seminar on the scriptural bases of the doctrine of justification, and who was watching the irreversible disintegration of the dialectical group, wrote to Thurneysen:

> Lollo is completely indispensable in these efforts. From early till late, she is concerned with the business of the Dean's Office, with production of the extracts that lie behind my lectures and form the ground for my later elaboration, and also with her own reading and subsequent reports thereof. I ask myself how I ever got along without her.[25]

---

23. Busch, "Memories of Karl Barth," 12.
24. Busch (ibid., 12) suggests it was not old age itself that prevented Barth from finishing *CD*; it was the loss of extended contact with students—combined with the loss of von Kirschbaum, we can safely add.
25. *KB-ET Briefwechsel*, 16 November 1929.

The new parts of von Kirschbaum's work with Barth—the secretarial and administrative tasks and the development of the card file that functioned as a reference library of church tradition—have emerged.

Von Kirschbaum's work with Barth was a combination of research, taking dictation (for books, articles, lectures, and speeches), editing texts that Barth wrote in manuscript form, and typing. Photographs taken at the Bergli are good sources for this subject. The two sat across from each other at a table next to a large window in the garret of the annex that Ruedi Pestalozzi built for Barth's work and work materials. Lollo had a typewriter—the pre-electric kind. Dialogue was interwoven with dictation. They passed pages back and forth and waited for each other's comments[26] (see figs. 4a and 4b). In Münster and Bonn, and in Basel from 1935 onward, they had separate, adjoining studies. Barth's large and ever-growing library was dispersed in both rooms.[27] Von Kirschbaum's study was part of her living quarters. Barth tended to work late into the night. Von Kirschbaum needed more sleep than he. Barth said he found it difficult to have to wake her to dictate a lecture that had to be typed for the next morning.[28] But Barth's greater endurance seems to be only relative. In one description von Kirschbaum is said to have worked "in the Barth style," which meant going from "early morning until often late in the evening, interrupted only by a short pause at noon with black coffee and a game of cards for diversion."[29] Omitted from this description are the daily family meals with their own tension and challenge, and the lunches in which Barth sometimes included students. Dietrich Ritschl, one of Barth's early students in Basel, summarized the Barth–von Kirschbaum collaboration:

> [Barth's] collaboration with Lollo in producing the text for the lectures, revising them in the light of spontaneous comments during the lecture, thereby completing the on-going text of the *Church Dogmatics*, a team-work following a disciplined time schedule—that was a truly phenomenal and noticeable experience.[30]

Barth estimated that for his four fifty-minute lectures each week, he needed thirty to forty hours of preparation, and in each of the four days

26. Köbler, *In the Shadow*, 36.
27. Busch, *Karl Barth*, 408–9.
28. E. Busch, personal communication, 16 December 1993.
29. Köbler, *In the Shadow*, 41 (includes description by Gollwitzer).
30. Ritschl, "How to Be Most Grateful to Karl Barth Without Remaining a Barthian," in McKim, *How Karl Barth Changed My Mind*, 87.

he had to produce at least eight publisher-ready pages of the Dogmatics.[31] As part of this process, von Kirschbaum attended all the lectures.[32]

Barth's seminar topics changed as his interests and curiosity dictated, adding to her workload. For the Dogmatics, von Kirschbaum assembled the primary and secondary texts that Barth would address and comment on. The texts were drawn from the file of excerpts she was working on as early as 1927, or from excerpts that she added as they were needed— Barth himself began the file in 1922 in that difficult first year at Göttingen.[33] In order to read patristic, medieval, and Reformation sources, she learned Latin. In the late 1920s, she worked under a tutor three times a week along with Barth's daughter Franziska.[34] In her own writing, she includes sources in French, Dutch, and English: she needed fluency in modern languages to keep track of modern scholarship, which Barth engages throughout the Dogmatics. It should be noted that Barth employed student research assistants too: his home was always a multi-shift factory of sorts. The duties of the student assistants (who included Herzog, Busch, and Hinrich Stoevesandt) overlapped with several of von Kirschbaum's. Besides adding to the great card file, they, like her, proofread and indexed individual volumes of the Dogmatics: Barth thanks five different students in prefaces to the volumes. A different kind of index, refined and expanded by von Kirschbaum, is noteworthy. She maintained a card index with entries for important sources under an extensive array of *Stichworten*. This subject index to the whole file was heavily used in the preparation for the lectures.[35]

Barth relied on von Kirschbaum to read very widely in current scholarship (both books and journals) and to report to him on her

31. Busch, *Karl Barth*, 373.

32. Köbler, *In the Shadow*, 41. Neill Hamilton reported that Barth's lectures were part of the sociocultural life of Basel; he described a front row of women whom the students called "the fur coats." John Hesselink remembers that Nelly Barth came to the lectures: she and von Kirschbaum arrived separately. (Both reports in personal conversations.)

33. *KB-ET Briefwechsel*, 22 January 1922. I use here the English translation by James D. Smart, *Revolutionary Theology in the Making*: "What do I do? I study. Chiefly the Reformation and everything connected with it. A voluminous card-index is coming into being in which everything of importance finds its place." Again, on 26 March 1922, Barth is temporarily "occupied with the scholastics whose essential ideas on all essential points, at least of *dogmatics*, I have now gathered together on some hundred cards as the *one* part of the foundation which I need urgently for the course on Calvin. The *other* part is Luther and Zwingli, with whom for the time being I must make myself acquainted in the same way, leaving a proper study of the sources for a later and better time."

34. *KB-ET Briefwechsel*, 29 April 1929, 16 November 1929, 26 January 1930.

35. E. Busch, personal communication, 16 December 1993.

readings. "Keeping up with the field" had two immediate purposes: to enable Barth to make efficient use of his own reading time and to protect him, so to speak, from surprise attacks. Von Kirschbaum's local surveillance duties included direct observation. In a December 1928 letter, Barth reports to Thurneysen that she went to a two-hour lecture by the German Jesuit theologian Erich Przywara and told Barth that he was the only opponent he had to fear and that he was a formidable one. At the Bergli half a year later, Lollo was making extracts from Przywara's book on Kierkegaard.

At the same time she and Barth were reading extensively in Augustine and Luther and she was excerpting from them, with "unearthly diligence," a store of "important notes about things hidden in the four volumes of [Luther's] sermons."[36] Behind all of the effort to have a library of Christian thought at his fingertips may be some of the panic Barth felt when he began his university career without the formal training that his colleagues had. In 1922 he had written to Thurneysen of his consciousness of his "thorn in the flesh," his "dreadful theological ignorance" that was sharpened by his "quite miserable memory that constantly retains only *quite* decisive things." "Oh," he said, "If only someone would give me time, time, time, to do everything *properly*, to read everything at *my own tempo*, to take it apart and put it together again."[37]

Von Kirschbaum needed significant preparation of her own to be what Barth wanted. This included gaining facility in philosophy: she was reading Kant and Plato in January of 1930. She did well enough for Barth to depend on her in the substitutionary (and somewhat absurd) relationship he devised for her with Heinrich Scholz, wherein she reported to Barth about Scholz's lectures and pursued with Scholz the issues that he and Barth debated by phone, letter, and in evening discussion. Sometimes she sat between the two of them as a mediator of sorts[38] (see fig. 6). Barth is famous for his commitment to reading a newspaper every day; he used von Kirschbaum's preliminary screening here, too.[39]

Von Kirschbaum was also Barth's organizer or, as he sometimes said, his business manager.[40] She kept his calendar, scheduling meetings and

36. *KB-ET Briefwechsel*, 21 December 1928, 29 April 1929. (This is the letter describing the idyllic spring at Bergli quoted in Part 1.) Pryzwara was soon to become a friend and welcome colleague for Barth (Busch, *Karl Barth*, 182–83).

37. *KB-ET Briefwechsel*, 20 March 1922. I use here the English translation in *Revolutionary Theology in the Making*, 20 March 1922.

38. *KB-ET Briefwechsel*, 29 December 1929, 26 January 1930.

39. Köbler, *In the Shadow*, 42.

40. Ibid., 70.

appointments in coordination with academic work and writing commitments. The appointments were for friends and visitors from afar—from universities and churches—and for public events: speeches, lectures, or simply attendance. She made sure Barth kept to the schedule and had the materials he needed. The semester of Barth's deanship at Münster required an unusual amount of unpredictable logistics work, though Barth's increasing fame and unchanging controversiality assured challenges beyond that semester. (He served as dean of the theology faculty at the University of Basel in 1938 and 1944. He did not relish administrative work, which suggests more delegating to von Kirschbaum.)[41] As the political scene developed in Germany, so did the confrontations leading to his return to Switzerland in the atmosphere of urgency, exigency, and pressure that Herzog felt so keenly when he was Barth's student assistant.

John Godsey has described Barth's wholehearted involvement in teaching. In a typical week in Basel, in addition to the four lectures in systematic theology, he conducted "a two-to-three-hour systematics seminar (in this setting Barth was at his best!), held a *Sozietät* [a form of discussion group] for a select group of German-speaking students and a Colloquium for either English-speaking or French-speaking students [they met on alternating weeks]."[42] At Göttingen and Bonn he held open evenings at his home for questions, and he held them at least in the early years in Basel. From the Bonn years onward, his student audience got larger and larger.[43] That von Kirschbaum was the orchestrator of his highly complex and tight schedule meant further erosion of her quiet time, further formal performance. She answered the telephone for Barth. She prepared tea for visitors to his study.[44] As Barth became more and more renowned, people sent books and manuscripts to him; and it was often his secretary, not he, who had to read them and respond appropriately. Von Kirschbaum also took on work connected with special occasions. She and Ernst Wolf co-edited a major Festschrift for Barth's seventieth birthday. It included seventy-eight contributors, and she compiled for it a bibliography of Barth's published writings from 1906 to 1955: 406 items, followed by a list of books and important shorter works

41. *KB-ET Briefwechsel,* 16 November 1929; Busch, *Karl Barth*, 285, 323.
42. John Godsey, "Portrait of Barth," in Karl Barth, *How I Changed My Mind* (Richmond, Va.: John Knox Press, 1966), 12.
43. Busch, *Karl Barth*, 129, 202, 266.
44. Werner Koch, in Köbler, *In the Shadow*, 131–32.

translated into twelve languages.[45] It is not only the sheer volume of her work that is astonishing but also the simultaneous claims, the conflicting demands for her time and attention.

Von Kirschbaum managed Barth's correspondence: sorting it, writing answers on the basis of instructions from him—and sometimes, when he chose, with no suggestions from him at all—and archiving copies of all documents. Eberhard Busch has described this role as he inherited it from her. Barth gave him free rein to answer some letters and often just signed them as presented to him. Conversely, Barth occasionally dictated complete letters and, for reasons personal or political, requested that Busch rather than himself be the signator.[46] Much of the correspondence fell between these extremes. It included incessant requests for lectures and speeches and participation in panels, discussion groups, and radio interviews; requests for pastoral and theological advice; and letters of all sorts from former students and from Barth's great flock of friends. Lollo also needed and found time for her own correspondence with friends in Germany (Erika Küppers, Lili Simon, Gertrud Staewen, Helmut Gollwitzer), most of whom she had met through Barth, and attempts, largely unsuccessful, to maintain relations with her family.[47]

Much of von Kirschbaum's administrative and organizational work was invisible: it became visible only when it was not perfectly or completely done. This began to happen during the U.S. visit when her memory began to fail and she forgot appointments, deadlines, and the location of papers that Barth needed. She also suffered increasingly from insomnia.[48] Until the beginning of the 1960s, however, she did perform, seamlessly and transparently. Much of the administrative work was protective in character: she took care of (or absorbed!) the distractions and material needs that threatened the free progress of Barth's career and writing—or as she may have seen it, as Ritschl and others did see it—the free progress of his creativity.[49]

Conversely, she protected students from the effects of Barth's single-mindedness. Hans Prolingheuer said that, with "gentleness and a smile"

45. Busch, *Karl Barth*, 416–17. The Festschrift was *Antwort. Karl Barth zum siebzigsten Geburtstag am 10. Mai 1956* (Zollikon-Zurich: Evangelischer Verlag, 1956). Its contributors include a good bit of the history of twentieth-century theology. Three women (besides von Kirschbaum) contributed to it; two, Lili Simon and Gertrud Staewen, were old friends.
46. Busch, personal communication, 16 December 1993.
47. Köbler, *In the Shadow*, 39.
48. Ibid., 70.
49. Ritschl, "How to Be Most Grateful," 87; Köbler, *In the Shadow*, 75.

and good intuition and finesse, "she knew how to put things right and thus to mediate matters that people would not so easily have taken directly from him." He also says that he, "like almost all students in those days [during World War II] was in love with her."[50] John Godsey dedicated his compilation of *Karl Barth's Table Talk* to "Fräulein Charlotte von Kirschbaum: the devoted helper of Professor Barth and his students." Less formally (and with a smile) Godsey remarked of Barth and von Kirschbaum that "he would have been impossible without her."[51] Busch, like Markus Barth, describes her as a kind of student-mother.[52] She sometimes tutored Barth's students in the intricacies of *CD*. She was considered to be a more correct and purer Barthian than Barth.[53] She occasionally loaned money to students and recommended useful books. They brought personal problems to her, and she listened and counseled.[54]

Von Kirschbaum's organizational skills were essential for the increasing number of academic and public events throughout Europe at which Barth spoke—in Hungary, Italy, Estonia, the Scandinavian countries, the Netherlands, France, England. (The United States was the only non-European country he visited.) In photograph after photograph, von Kirschbaum is at his side as they stand with other principal guests of an occasion. Sometimes Barth decided on trips that were largely recreational or restorative—for example, in the winter of 1948–49 he and von Kirschbaum went to Einsiedeln with a friend of von Balthasar. Barth and von Kirschbaum went to a Catholic mass, and they listened to Mozart recordings for almost twenty-four hours.[55] This excursion follows a pattern in two earlier trips in May and June of 1929. Barth and von Kirschbaum accompanied Ruedi Pestalozzi on a business trip to Dornach and then took a longer one with Ruedi and Gerty to Rome. They were reading guidebooks for the Italian trip, Barth wrote to Thurneysen, and "we're excited about it and hope to learn something of lasting value there." Emphatically, the tour was "purely for pleasure, travelling for travelling's sake, a deliberate and complete break from the purposeful pattern of the rest of our lives."[56] Closer to home, Barth and von Kirschbaum often

50. Prolingheuer, "Epilogue" in Köbler, *In the Shadow*, 138.
51. J. Godsey, personal conversation, October 1995.
52. E. Busch, personal communication, 16 December 1993.
53. Georges Casalis in Köbler, *In the Shadow*, 138; Gollwitzer, ibid., 47.
54. Ibid., 46, and E. Busch, personal communication, 16 December 1993.
55. Busch, *Karl Barth*, 362.
56. *KB-ET Briefwechsel*, 30 May 1929. They spent much time looking at St. Peter's with awe and criticism (Busch, *Karl Barth*, 186–87).

took advantage of lecture trips in Germany to take long walks and mountain hikes. In Basel many theological conversations with one or several of Barth's colleagues were peripatetic. We have photographs of Barth and von Kirschbaum strolling with their theologian friends, often close friends over decades, visibly intent on listening to one another (see fig. 12, for example). Von Kirschbaum and Barth were comrades everywhere. Barth expected his assistants to work beside him and relax beside him. All the more for von Kirschbaum, whose coming into Barth's life had meant an end to his loneliness.

Political Activity, Independent Study

For his refusal to declare unconditional loyalty to Hitler, Barth was suspended from teaching at Bonn in November 1934 and finally removed from the faculty in June 1935. It was von Kirschbaum who broke the news to the students in his cancelled lecture class and who made the arrangements for the return of the Barth family (with her) to Switzerland. In Basel, she continued to manage the extensive and now risky correspondence Barth maintained with resistance groups in Germany and in exile in Switzerland. Barth's resistance activities—manifold and with deep involvement—included committee work to aid exiled teachers and students, finding temporary housing for Jews and sending appeals to church officials in safer countries to provide permanent homes for them, and advising and trying to strengthen the Confessing Church, the church that had found him too radical and that seemed to him compromising to the peril of its survival.[57] Von Kirschbaum (who never gave up her German citizenship) worked with him and sometimes in his stead. Opinion among resistance workers was often divided on strategies. Dietrich Bonhoeffer seemed to Barth to be proceeding unrealistically. Bonhoeffer wanted to visit his revered senior colleague on one of his trips to Switzerland but needed assurance that Barth did not mistrust him so much that he was persona non grata. Von Kirschbaum wrote to him, successfully conveying both Barth's genuine eagerness to receive Bonhoeffer and his uneasiness about the younger man's political activities. (He and Barth had had several meetings in 1941; Barth told Bonhoeffer that he was sure the Allies would not agree to the German borders that Bonhoeffer's plan was intended to secure.) Yes, she told Dietrich, there were many things being said about him in Switzerland.

---

57. Busch, *Karl Barth*, 271–72. See ibid., chap. 6 passim, esp. 286–315.

Some of their friends wondered about his frequent, rather mysterious visits to the country. But when the Swiss border police (*Fremdenpolizei*) asked Karl whether he supported Bonhoeffer's visit, he did not hesitate to say yes. To be entirely open, she must also report that Barth finds something discomforting—*unheimlich*—in all attempts to rescue Germany by "national" undertakings. But that is no reason to delay his visit for even a moment.[58]

Photographs of group discussions and meetings with individual friends or colleagues in the late 1930s place von Kirschbaum beside Barth in the face of danger. The pervasive, existential at-oneness of Barth and von Kirschbaum had many uses in this time of danger and in the years immediately after the war that were so crucial for Germany's rehabilitation. The emergency years, starting with the rise of Nazism to power, also produced unprecedented needs that either enabled, required, or encouraged women to do work and assume roles ordinarily performed by men.

Von Kirschbaum twice entered public space as an individual separate from Barth though for a cause characteristic of Barth. The first occasion in mid-1933 has the character of emergency recruitment by him. Barth, on the spiral that was leading to Barmen and expulsion from Germany, felt increasingly isolated vis-à-vis the new regime. He opposed both the German Christians and the "Young Reformers," the alternative church group that was trying to accommodate Reformation ideals and present realities. In June 1933 he became the voice of opposition within the evangelical church through an uncompromising and electrifying state-ment in the first issue of *Theologische Existenz heute.* (Von Kirschbaum was among those who persuaded him to revise the even more strident first draft of the statement lest he risk being jailed.)[59] Elections were under way for the governing boards of the churches from lists compiled by the German Christians and the Young Reformers. Barth stated that "for the sake of the freedom of the Gospel one cannot vote for [either of] these two lists." His alarm was heard, and a third list was hastily com-piled for a new party called "For the Freedom of the Gospel." It won enough votes to qualify for minority representation in the Bonn parish, and Barth was one of those elected. So was another candidate on the

58. CvK to D. Bonhoeffer, 17 May 1942, in Dietrich Bonhoeffer, *Schweizer Korre-spondenz 1941–42. Im Gespräch mit Karl Barth*, ed. Eberhard Bethge, *Theologische Existenz heute*, Nr. 214 (Munich: Chr. Kaiser Verlag, 1982); Busch, *Karl Barth*, 315.
59. John Hesselink on von Kirschbaum's role, personal conversation, October 1991.

new list: von Kirschbaum.⁶⁰ It should be remembered that this was also a time of personal crisis. Karl and Lollo hoped to marry; Nelly Barth rejected Karl's request for a divorce; the Confessing Church disapproved of the Barth–von Kirschbaum relationship so much that it would shun Barth in the following year.

Von Kirschbaum's next public venture was on a larger scale and had a more independent character. In 1943 a heterogeneous group of German exiles in Switzerland, centered in Zürich, formed the Movement for a Free Germany (*Bewegung "Freies Deutschland"*). A branch was established in Basel in 1944. Its purpose was to work for the defeat of the Nazi government and the establishment of a viable and independent Germany after the defeat. As a member of the Movement for a Free Germany, von Kirschbaum took a leadership role, and Barth a supportive background role. The Movement was modeled after the Committee for a Free Germany formed in Moscow by German exiles and prisoners of war. Both the original committee and, to a lesser extent, the Movement included socialists and communists; however, the Swiss Movement was deliberately nonpartisan and strove to include, at all levels, middle-class as well as working-class members. Similarly, it chose to include representation of German Protestantism in its leadership council. Nevertheless, both the Moscow group and the Movement for a Free Germany were regarded with suspicion in Switzerland. A candidate for the church position on the council was chosen, but he withdrew because his church supervisors considered the Movement's work illegal. Von Kirschbaum averted a crisis by offering to serve on the council (called "Provisional Leadership" in the absence of Swiss state approval) as representative of the Confessing Church. The Movement was legalized by the time of its second national conference in May 1945, and von Kirschbaum, with the former Prussian Secretary of State Wilhelm Abegg and the actor and writer (and communist) Wolfgang Langhoff, was chosen to chair the leadership council.⁶¹

Six of the original ten provisional leaders were communists, and all but von Kirschbaum were men. Von Kirschbaum is identified in committee records as the close co-worker (*Mitarbeiter*) of Karl Barth. Barth said von Kirschbaum got along very well with "the red and reddish people" in the Movement. His words suggest she got along better than he

60. Busch, *Karl Barth*, 224–28; Köbler, *In the Shadow*, 47.
61. Köbler, *In the Shadow*, 54–57; Busch, *Karl Barth*, 324–25; Karl Hans Bergmann, *Die Bewegung "Freies Deutschland" in der Schweiz 1943–1945* (Munich: Carl Hansen Verlag, 1974), chaps. 1, 5, and 12.

did. He said the group provided him his first acquaintance "with notable communists and—less pleasantly—with communist methods."[62] But he supported "Free Germany," and his home became "almost like a branch office of this movement."

Through von Kirschbaum, moreover, his approach to the problem of German rehabilitation received further articulation. As early as July 1944, Barth asserted that it was now time to be both concerned and critical about the Germans, as is consonant with the church of the one who came to save sinners. And Barth meant critical in detail, not abstractly.[63] Von Kirschbaum's "Address for the Movement 'Free Germany'" matches very well his commitment to acknowledging the sins of the past so that there might be a genuine new beginning. In the address (delivered in St. Gallen, Geneva, and Montreaux in 1945), she points to the Lutheran two-realms doctrine behind the Confessing Church's ultimate passivity. She quotes at length a South German pastor who wrote about the German present and future after reading "the recent pamphlets by Professor K. Barth." The German people must be given factual material about the actual deeds of the Nazi state, and the church must play an important role in this education. The pastor and von Kirschbaum both point out that communist party members are acting in trustworthy unity with noncommunists to attain the goal of a free Germany, one in which people once again are "responsible for their own lives."[64] Barth had asserted his long-standing advocacy of openness to cooperation with communists before the Swiss–Soviet Union Society in March 1945.[65] In one way, von Kirschbaum was more than Barth's pupil and not exactly an alter ego, and she spoke more strongly for the difference. She could tell her audience what "we German men and women" must do, and declare (and shed light on her own self-image) that "we Germans living abroad [must] take the initiative ourselves in coming to the aid of our fellow country-men."[66] Barth spoke self-consciously in a Swiss voice, "eine Schweizer Stimme" (the title of a collection of political statements of 1938–45 that he published in 1945—a title containing some irony, for he had expressed much contempt for Swiss evasiveness during the war).[67]

---

62. Busch, *Karl Barth*, 324.
63. Ibid., 322–23.
64. Von Kirschbaum, "Address . . ." in Köbler, *In the Shadow*, 81–92.
65. Busch, *Karl Barth*, 322.
66. Von Kirschbaum, "Address . . . ," 84, 90.
67. Busch, *Karl Barth*, 326.

As an authority in the evangelical church, Barth could and did work to bring representatives of the Protestant exiles into the Movement (and generally found them less Christian than the self-proclaimed atheists, who seemed to him much more genuinely concerned with a morally sound German reconstruction). The Movement was proud to have Barth's support: he was a well-known cultural figure, and his remarks at meetings were received enthusiastically and sometimes had soothing and unifying effects. They particularly welcomed his openness (so rare in the church) to cooperation with socialists.[68] Barth clearly seems pleased with von Kirschbaum's leadership activity in Free Germany.[69] The activity was short-lived, however, for the committee dissolved itself in December 1945, seven months after the defeat of Germany and the end of the war in Europe.[70] The two postwar summer semesters that Barth and von Kirschbaum spent at the University in Bonn probably indicate a conviction that the work of the Movement was just as urgently needed now as it had been earlier.[71]

I think also that von Kirschbaum's work in the Movement for a Free Germany lent important impetus to her decision to speak out widely about women from an evangelical standpoint. On this subject, working independently, following her own passion, her standpoint was analogous and complementary to Barth's and certainly informed by that of Barth the political thinker. The solution she saw to the opposition between radical feminism and Catholic (and not only Catholic) traditionalism was lodged in the church, not because the church contained the rules but because it is the absolute criterion for any rules.

As part of her response to the Nazi regime, von Kirschbaum—like Barth and sometimes with him—tried to assist in the placing of German refugees in "safe" Swiss situations. In 1936 she wrote to Henriette Visser't Hooft Boddaert in Geneva about finding work for a certain Fraulein Löchner. Visser't Hooft Boddaert forwarded her letter to an Englishman working for the Christian Student *Weltbund* in Geneva, who in turn asked for clarification of Fraulein Löchner's reasons for seeking work in French-speaking Switzerland: von Kirschbaum had not stated

68. Bergmann, *Die Bewegung "Freies Deutschland,"* 84–86.
69. Busch, *Karl Barth,* 324–25.
70. The decision to disband was made by a two-thirds majority. Most of the exiles were eager to return to Germany and work there toward renewal; most of those who stayed in Switzerland regarded themselves as a colony of Germans living abroad and considered their work for Germany completed when the Nazi state was overthrown.
71. Bergmann, *Die Bewegung "Freies Deutschland,"* 165–70.

outright that she was a non-Aryan but had used words that suggested the matter was urgent. We do not know the disposition of this case, but it is very clear that both von Kirschbaum and Visser't Hooft Boddaert really wanted to help women like Fraulein Löchner and would exert whatever efforts they could.

It is also clear from the correspondence of Visser't Hooft Boddaert and von Kirschbaum (beginning in 1935, the year of Barth's expulsion from Germany and the move to Switzerland) that von Kirschbaum is involved with the women's movement to a much greater extent than we have hitherto realized. The letters—including their allusions to occasional conversations—reveal that von Kirschbaum was engaged in her own research on women in Scripture and in church history and theology and that she regarded this study as her own project, as "my work," separate though concurrent with her work for Barth. The letters shed light on her complex thought on the subject of women; and the discussion, congeniality, and sharp debate they contain allow us to measure von Kirschbaum's thinking—its mix of progressive and conservative suppositions—with that of someone very different: a Dutchwoman educated at a Quaker school in England and living in international church circles in Geneva. They also bring us closer to establishing—insofar as this can be done—the relative contributions of Barth and von Kirschbaum to some of the ideas they share.

Perhaps because of their social difference, Visser't Hooft Boddaert and von Kirschbaum address each other formally and use the "Sie" form. But Visser't Hooft Boddaert is the one who looks up to von Kirschbaum as the senior colleague in biblical theology and church history, the one from whom she solicits critical opinions of her own writings, and the one whose work she eagerly wants to see or hear about.[72] Barth's writings served as a common idiom for them: each weaves phrases from Barth into her letters; Visser't Hooft Boddaert asks von Kirschbaum to review her English-language summary of a chapter in *CD* II, which she originally did in Dutch for a young women's association; von Kirschbaum sends her an essay by Barth.[73]

We are also looking at still another piece of von Kirschbaum's ordinary activity. Visser't Hooft Boddaert—who, it should be remembered, criticized Barth for patriarchal thinking in 1934[74]—is certainly one who

72. See Part 1 above, pages 15–16.
73. E.g., HVH to vK, 16 March 1935, using the flute concerto/dead dog examples from *CD* I/1, or HVH to vK, 18 September 1947.
74. Part 1 above, page 21, note 84.

can use Barth against Barth, and she may have hoped her ongoing conversation with von Kirschbaum might influence Barth's thinking about women. But primarily she is hungry to talk to a woman like von Kirschbaum. For despite their intellectual differences, the two are united by the unshakable, passionate intention of defining and defending the nature of women against both religious conservatives (their concern is with Protestants) and contemporary feminists or "liberationists" who deny and threaten the realization of differences between male and female.[75] The two share exasperation as well as palpable disgust with the status quo and its options—those of both the non-Christian woman and the so-called Christian woman.

Von Kirschbaum's principal criticism of the work Visser't Hooft Boddaert sends her is that it undervalues the christological dimension of the pronouncements about women in Genesis and the New Testament epistles. Von Kirschbaum thinks Visser't Hooft Boddaert may be over-reacting against the upholders of the domestic Christian female ideal. Sounding a theme that will recur in *Die wirkliche Frau*, she writes that "all our strivings for freedom suffer because we frantically stare at the *man* instead of looking toward *the* man who alone can make us free."[76] Von Kirschbaum thinks that Visser't Hooft Boddaert attends too much to the earthly man, however much harm he has caused.

She is right about Visser't Hooft Boddaert's focus. In 1952 Visser't Hooft Boddaert has been reading Simone de Beauvoir's *Le deuxième sexe*. Like von Kirschbaum, she misses a Christian (or any other religious) framework; she too thinks that Beauvoir is driving out the devil with Beelzebub. But what she'd really like to do is write a book on "Le premier sexe." To talk of the woman question may be a male deflection from the real problem.[77] To focus exclusively on the differences between male and female and the value of the differences is not helpful; it may even lessen our awareness of the time when there will be no before and after, no A and B—she is echoing a recent formulation of Barth in *CD* III/4 as well as Galatians 3:28.[78]

Visser't Hooft Boddaert does not disagree with von Kirschbaum about the christological context of all scriptural pronouncements but does disagree on the sufficiency of any promise, including the great promise, for everyday life: "While it's good to listen to that music of the

75. E.g., HVH to vK, 22 October 1942.
76. vK to HVH, 20 November 1941.
77. HVH to vK, [day not legible] January 1952.
78. On the A-B formulation, see Part 3, page 141.

future, we human beings do not work well with promises," we need guidelines for living. In fact, she doubts that the women of the Old Testament, from whom von Kirschbaum draws her conclusions on living in hope, actually did so.[79] Her principal response to von Kirschbaum's criticism and, in the later letters, to *Die wirkliche Frau* is to point to the toxic effects that indiscriminate application of the one-sided Pauline doctrine has had throughout church history and the history of Christian thought. Unhindered by the lack of clarity and consistency in Scripture on the subject of women, von Kirschbaum too quickly seeks to establish a firm middle position for the Christian woman, one that too easily becomes rigid insofar as it is based on the scriptural superordination and subordination of male and female.

Visser't Hooft Boddaert is right about von Kirschbaum's orientation. Von Kirschbaum described her work as centering basically around 1 Corinthians 11, which best lays out the issues in the scriptural ordering of men and women.[80] Visser't Hooft Boddaert thinks that it would be naive to try to assert that order even in a world set right; she responds to von Kirschbaum's remarks on the New Testament transvaluation of values with wariness of any *Ordnung*.[81]

From any feminist viewpoint, Visser't Hooft Boddaert is more radical than von Kirschbaum. Her critical eye falls on scripture as it does on history. Men in the Bible have more rights than women; women are the subject of more prohibitions than men.[82] Visser't Hooft Boddaert's criticism of Barth was that he did not see the connection between the subordination of women and the ascendency of the Nazi state.[83] However, Von

---

79. HVH to vK, undated response to vK letter of 20 November 1941; HVH to vK, 7 May 1943.

80. vK to HVH, 20 November 1941.

81. HVH to vK, 5 March 1952, 24 November 1950, and 5 March 1952.

82. HVH to vK, 22 November 1942.

83. In an important but until recently little-read essay of 1934, "Eve, Where Art Thou?" *Student World* (publication of the World's Student Christian Federation, Geneva) 114: 208–20, Visser't Hooft Boddaert continued to argue that the failed relationship of male and female, from its resolution in Genesis through the course of history, is at the base of all human problems. Man has become the dictator of woman's soul and spirit (208) and has also suppressed the feminine element in his subconscious: the emancipation of men is as urgently necessary as that of women (212). She mocks the so-called Divine Orders of Creation in human institutions and uncovers the unconscious guilt women have brought upon themselves in trying to conform to them. (Besides the feminist studies noted in Part 1, Jürgen Moltmann has valued her work: see his chapter on her in *Gotteslehrerinnen*, ed. Luise Schottroff and Johannes Thiele [Stuttgart: Kreuz Verlag, 1989], 169–79.)

Kirschbaum is theologically more sophisticated and potentially richer as a resource for feminism—and for Karl Barth's theological anthropology—than Visser't Hooft Boddaert infers. In a letter of 20 November 1941, von Kirschbaum reproved Visser't Hooft Boddaert for neglecting the specificity of Genesis 2:18ff. on the creation of woman as the helper of man. She then proceeded to an analysis of the image of God. In the Genesis 2:18 account, it is the man who is *first* created as the image. Genesis 2:18, consistent with Genesis 1:27, makes it clear that the woman too is created in the image, though it was accomplished in a different manner. Furthermore, the woman is essential for the *realization* of the image in the man: she does this by seeing and responding to the image in him. And he sees in her the helper God intended her to be. Of course, it is true that historically the male has imposed his own self-serving construction of the image with its far-reaching implications for male-female life. Only Christ, the one true image, can make us free from all self-constructed images. Meanwhile, we have only hints of this reality, which we must apply to our lives ever again.[84] Visser't Hooft Boddaert concluded that von Kirschbaum denied the presence of the image in women; it is the presence of the hierarchy of superordination and subordination in von Kirschbaum that prevented Visser't Hooft Boddaert from seeing more.[85]

The discussion of the image is part of a response to Visser't Hooft Boddaert's request for criticism of an essay she apparently had sent to Basel for both Von Kirschbaum and Barth. Von Kirschbaum tells Visser't Hooft Boddaert that she is writing in Barth's stead (he was at that time very hard-pressed due to the preparation of the second part of his "Doctrine of God"—*CD* II/2). However, because Visser't Hooft Boddaert's subject has occupied her for some time in relation to her own work, she has read the essay with great interest and she hopes "this provisional echo from our corner will not be unwelcome."[86]

Von Kirschbaum's Christology and Old Testament exegesis have benefited directly from Barth's work on the doctrine of election in *CD* II/1 (1940). I think the new doctrine of the image of God that centers on the male-female relationship in *CD* III (from III/1 in 1945 through III/4 in 1951) has benefited directly from von Kirschbaum's work on the nature and possibilities in the male/female relationship *within* the

84. vK to HVH, 20 November 1941.
85. HVH, undated response to vK, 20 November 1941.
86. vK to HVH, 20 November 1941.

scriptural ordering. She does not yet equate the image and the male/female relationship, but she has begun to plumb the implications of scriptural teachings on man and woman in both Testaments for a christologically understood Christian life well before Barth. In a letter of 1942 she does not define the image as encounter, as will later happen in *CD* and *Wirkliche Frau* both, yet she describes male/female encounter in terms that place a Barthian frame around it. The typologies offered by psychologists and the images of men and women offered by mythologists (she has been writing to Visser't Hooft Boddaert about Jung and Bachofen) presuppose, first, a world of cruel loneliness (*grauenvoller Einsamkeit*). Second, in contrast to the "harmless" typologies of male and female offered by these psychologists and scholars of mythology, the "encounter of man and woman of which Gen 2:18f speaks" is something entirely different that we can't take care of (*bereinigen*) with such harmlessness. "It is a miracle, and every genuine account of man and woman (and implied here, of human and human) is a miracle. Here other categories than those of psychology apply."[87] Certainly the roots of *Die wirkliche Frau* lie as much in her own long-standing project, which included textual study, the history of exegesis and of theological anthropology, reading outside theology, and discussion with other women, as they do in her work for *CD* and Barth's mentoring.

The *Church Dogmatics* Notes

Volume I/part 2 of *Church Dogmatics* came out in 1939, II/1 in 1940, II/2 in 1942, III/1 in 1945, III/2 in 1948, III/3 in 1950, and III/4 in 1951. Barth was sixty-five in 1951, but that did not mean retirement. His work schedule, which was also von Kirschbaum's and which now included involvement in ecumenical affairs and major controversies with Bultmann and Niebuhr, was unrelenting for the next decade. Old age and the fear of not completing the Dogmatics before he died made him push even harder in this effort. He formally retired in March 1962 and then went on the great U.S. tour where thousands heard his lectures and he visited the places and historic sites he was curious about.

Von Kirschbaum would be sixty-three soon after they returned to Switzerland. It is during the U.S. visit that her distraction and exhaustion, the first signs of her illness, became apparent. It will be recalled that von Kirschbaum connected her waning mental powers to the

87. vK to HVH, 18 December 1942.

continual overwork of her years with Barth.[88] Though medically unsound, her statement that she had consumed and worn herself out in this work is a *cri de coeur* and a plaint. Barth had in effect exploited her remarkable ability to handle the demands of her job. This is both a rare and familiar situation in women's history. It must also be said that the very scope and weight of von Kirschbaum's job set limits on her actual authorial contribution to the notes in the Dogmatics.

Think of yourself as two people, or of a day that has forty-eight hours. As you sit down, on schedule, to take the next step in your major work, which is also your lecture preparation, you have on your desk detailed notes and relevant extracts from all the texts you will address in this step, references to kindred sources, and notes on the historiography of the subject and on current discussion of it. You also know you've done a thorough job and have overlooked nothing that could help clinch your argument or function as a trap for you. You know too that you can't overlook any of the note-cards: they have been screened for redundancy.

Barth, of course, achieved this state of preparedness by way of von Kirschbaum, who had some help from successive student research assistants. In addition, in the course of his work he availed himself of his sounding board and dialogue partner, always ready in the study next door. Von Kirschbaum, able to serve these functions because of her intellectual communion with Barth, because she was even more Barthian than Barth, *knew*, nevertheless, that *CD* was Barth's work, and she was frequently in great suspense to see how it would turn out.[89]

One student assistant described von Kirschbaum's research and the current reading she did for Barth as a mix of assignments and self-assignments.[90] This parallels, but is distinct from, the pattern that several assistants describe in which Barth delegated work areas, gave preliminary instructions, and then trusted the assistants to carry out the work responsibly.[91] Von Kirschbaum, as well as Barth, selected works to be excerpted for the card file, and, of great importance, she could supplement the excerpted materials that Barth requested through the *Stichwort* index that she created. She assembled and arranged such materials for Barth's work.

Did she write any of the notes, analogous to the way Busch handled some of Barth's correspondence? Assembling and arranging materials

88. Above, Part 1, page 10.
89. E. Busch, personal communication, 16 December 1993. Recall her remark on the breathtaking experience of watching the growth of *CD*.
90. F. Herzog, personal conversation, November 1992.
91. Köbler, *In the Shadow*, 60, based on information from Busch.

for a historical excursus or an exegesis can be very close to the final product. It is possible that she went a step further—it would be a seamless move—and sketched out some of the notes. I think such sketching is likely. Further than this indefinite possibility we cannot—and need not!—go. On the basis of their own assistantships to Barth and their observations of von Kirschbaum at work, Busch and Stoevesandt firmly consider the rumor of von Kirschbaum's authorship of the notes to be untrue.[92] But Busch also thinks we can assume she occasionally made supplementary inserts and that they fared the same way his own did in *CD* IV/4. Here is a further description of his IV/4 role:

[Barth] gave me the manuscript so that I could bring him proposals for corrections and additions. He accepted [*übernahm*] all of my proposals, made the additions partly himself (and I provided him in all these cases with the necessary literature), partly left it to me to write the actual inserts. (It was mostly but not always for one of the small-print passages.) He did not look at my inserts until they were in page-proofs [*Druckfahnen*], when he would first correct this and that.[93]

The experience he describes here in detail is the same that he discussed in "Memories of Karl Barth" to demonstrate the way Barth needed the contributions of others but turned those contributions into something truly his own. So it is that Busch can point to surviving handwritten manuscripts of parts of early *CD*, including small-print sections, in Barth's hand.[94]

So it is also that a reader can read published small-print sections of *CD* and published writings of von Kirschbaum and recognize immediately that the former were authored by Barth and the latter by someone else. Some of the richest exegetical and historical notes appear in *CD* II/2, chapter 7, "The Election of God." They do not merely supplement, but they form the foundation and scaffolding for Barth's argument on the irrevocability of election. When the Word became flesh,

[t]his coming was to the detriment of Israel. Face to face with its Messiah, the Son of David who was also the Son of God, Israel

92. H. Stoevesandt, personal communication, 11 May 1994; E. Busch, personal communication, 16 December 1993.
93. E. Busch, personal communication, 16 December 1993.
94. Ibid.

knew no better than to give Him up to the Gentiles to be put to
death on the cross. In so doing they confirmed the rightness of
God's dealings with them from the very first, when He cut them
off and destroyed them. And yet because the righteousness of God
stands fast like the mountains against the unrighteousness of
man, this coming was also to the benefit of Israel, and of the
Gentiles, and of the world.[95]

Insistently, the divine mercy toward the Jews is a present reality, and
it is "impossible for Christian anti-semitism (he that has ears to hear, let
him hear)" to relegate this mercy "into the realm of eschatology."[96] We
meet here Barth's dialectical mind as much as we hear Barth the citizen
of the church in the world. Again in the notes, we know we are encoun-
tering Barth's voice and mind when he criticizes Reformation theology,
Luther and Calvin alike, for failing to assert sufficiently that we are
"noetically to hold by Christ and Christ alone because ontically there is
no election, and no electing God, outside Him."[97] We will see in Part 3
that von Kirschbaum's exegeses use historical criticism quite differently
than Barth's. The notes in CD do not change after von Kirschbaum has
left the scene. Her role in their preparation was necessary and ample,
but it could be filled by someone else. Karl Barth is the author of the CD
notes. And the mystery of Barth's need for von Kirschbaum's full-time
presence is not yet resolved. Not so unexpectedly, the resolution lies in
the realm of process rather than product. But not entirely.

3. Influencing Barth

Barth formally described his theological development several times,
most famously in the Christian Century's "How I Changed My Mind"
series and in the 1956 essay "The Humanity of God."[98] The broad out-
lines are the same: his break with Liberal Protestantism dominates
through the 1920s; he later comes to recognize and correct its one-

95. CD II/2:57. See also ibid., 303.
96. CD II/2:305.
97. CD II/2:63.
98. See also, though from restricted perspectives, the "Nachwort" in Schleiermacher-
Auswahl and (with regard to eschatology) an autobiographical excursus in CD II/1:631–38.

sidedness and negativity (necessary though they once were), becoming christocentric in theology and more open and receptive in relations with other theologians.

In the *Christian Century* articles, the christocentric direction characterizes the decade 1928–38, and the gentling or new mildness characterizes the 1938–48 decade. He makes it clear—perhaps a little too much so— that he has not actually changed his mind; he has been occupied with the deepening and application of his theology. "Application" refers to his opposition and relations with the Nazi regime and to the church struggle. The "deepening" consists first of eliminating from his theology "the last remnants of a philosophical, i.e., anthropological . . . foundation and exposition of Christian doctrine" (which, in the preface to *CD* I/1, he further identified as existentialism) and second of learning that Christian doctrine, if it is really Christian and if it is to support the church in the world, must be "exclusively and conclusively" the doctrine of Jesus Christ as the living Word of God spoken to humankind. He wonders how it happened that he did not see this much sooner—but we human creatures are slow to learn the most important things. "My new task was to take all that has been said before and to think it through once more and freshly *and to articulate it anew as a theology of the grace of God in Jesus Christ.*" This is what he means by his "christological concentration."[99]

We know through the pioneering work of Bruce McCormack that Barth is collapsing into one movement (a shift in 1928) a longer, more complex development beginning in a conception of revelation—the *analogia fidei*—apparent in the *Göttingen Dogmatics* of 1924.[100] There Barth considered God's act of revelation, which (ever again) establishes a correspondence between God's self-knowledge and, through faith, human knowledge of God. I am focusing on the related, subsequent stage in which Barth seems to be thinking through and articulating a new theological orientation. In the retrospective sketches, Barth attributes his recognition of his new task to an increasing sense of difference and distance from Gogarten, Merz, and Brunner—which was clarified in relation to German politics—and to his work on Anselm; entering into

---

99. Barth, *How I Changed My Mind*, 42–43. Emphasis added.
100. Bruce L. McCormack, *Karl Barth's Critically Realistic Dialectical Theology: Its Genesis and Development, 1909–1936* (Oxford and New York: Oxford University Press, 1995). McCormack (pp. 1–14 and passim) acknowledges his own debt to the work of Ingrid Spieckermann and Michael Beintker, which challenged the widely accepted view of Barth's theology as dialectical from *Epistle to the Romans* to c. 1930 and then, emerging in great contrast in his book on Anselm, analogical.

genuine dialogue with church tradition (especially Calvin) was also important. He attributes his diminished contentiousness to the awareness and acceptance of mortality as he neared and passed the age of sixty. To his surprise and that of people who knew him, he became "definitely milder." He could empathize with his opponents and no longer felt compelled to attack others or defend himself, at least not as zealously and unfailingly. Moreover, it seems to him that "in this new character . . . I have accomplished more than in the belligerency of my early years."

Not only did he have a different persona, but "to say 'yes' came to seem more important than to say 'no' (though that is important too). Theologically, the message of God's grace came to seem more urgent than the message of God's law, wrath, accusation, and judgment."[101] In the same way, in "Humanity of God" he regretted having posited the "wholly other" in isolation and abstractly, more like the God of the philosophers than the living God of Israel. Only after the revolution initiated in *Epistle to the Romans* did Barth sufficiently grasp that the majesty and freedom of God includes his *togetherness* with us his creatures. We know nothing by ourselves. In God's togetherness with us as Jesus Christ the Word, we can and do *really* know him. It was both a tactical and a theological mistake to have missed this thoroughly christological perspective.[102]

We have reason to be concerned with Barth's development in 1928–38. In a letter to Thurneysen from the Bergli in May 1929, Barth joked about a historical account in a travel guide that had annoyed him insofar as it reminded him of both Brunner and Schleiermacher. But such annoyance doesn't correspond "to the irenic character of our most recent phase."[103] This is considerably earlier than the *Christian Century* account would allow. It is not incompatible with the 1934 debate with Brunner: Barth said he always retained the right to put up a good fight "when that is absolutely called for."[104] Moreover, other observers, some of whom we have encountered in this study, have pointed to a gentling in Barth and an openness in his theology, a diminishing of his aggressiveness and one-sidedness; and they have said that Charlotte von Kirschbaum brought this about. I think the ways and the extent to which von

101. Barth, *How I Changed My Mind*, 50–51.
102. Barth, "Humanity of God," in (essay collection) *The Humanity of God*, trans. John N. Thomas (Richmond, Va.: John Knox Press, 1960), 45–46.
103. *KB-ET Briefwechsel*, 30 May 1929.
104. Barth, *How I Changed My Mind*, 51.

Kirschbaum changed Barth's mind have barely been realized. Only Eberhard Busch, in the course of two articles written to suggest the close relationship between Barth's personal history and his theology, has approached them.[105]

In 1967 Busch found and discussed with Barth a sheaf of unpublished letters that included one to von Kirschbaum on 28 February 1926. It is in February 1926 that Barth and von Kirschbaum were alone in Münster and confessed and discussed their mutual love. In the letter, Barth wrote the following:

> What I have said [hitherto as a theologian] has had for many, not with injustice, a very harsh sound; I have been taken to task by many (including the beautiful and loved . . .) for my judgments. . . . I suppose it's true that I have spoken too sharply, with too much certainty. . . . A noticeable result of our experience [of meeting] will be that my summer lecture course will surely be much more merciful than otherwise would be the case.[106]

Busch sees here another major incident in Barth's life that led him "to say the same thing differently," the difference having decisive import for his thinking.[107] It crystallized and influenced the course of a shift already in the making, a shift also influenced by Barth's encounter with Catholics at Münster in 1925–29 and, in the early 1930s when Nazism becomes entrenched, his thorough jettisoning of natural theology. Though enveloped in sharp polemic, the exclusion of natural theology is a clearing of space for the thoroughgoing christocentrism that is emerging.

We should not miss Barth's reference to the fact that others had made the same criticism of his theology that von Kirschbaum has made. Examples of this run through the early interchanges of Barth with Brunner,

105. Busch, "Theologie und Biographie," 325–39, and "Deciding Moments in the Life and Work of Karl Barth," 51–67. In the same year they tell the same intriguing story, one in a scholarly journal in German theology and the other in a Canadian journal directed to a larger, English-speaking audience.

106. Busch, "Theologie und Biographie," 334: "Was ich [bisher als Theologe] gesagt habe, hat für Viele nicht mit Unrecht einen sehr harten Klang gehabt; ich habe Vielen Vieles (und zwar Schönes und Liebes . . .) genommen mit meinen Hinweis . . . auf das Gericht . . . Ich denke wohl, dass ich vielfach zu scharf, zu sicher geredet habe . . . Eine merkwürdige Folge unseres Erlebnisses wird die sein, dass mein Kolleg im Sommer . . . sicher sehr viel . . . barmherziger . . . ausfallen wird, als dies sonst der Fall gewesen wäre!"

107. The other incidents: acquiescing in his parents' insistence that he not marry Rösy Münger, and, very late in life, his relationship with the Roman Catholic nurse caring for his health. Busch, "Theologie und Biographie," 333; "Deciding Moments," 66.

Gogarten, Tillich, and Bultmann. In contexts of respect and gratitude, they variously regret Barth's theological one-sidedness; he responds by withdrawing further from them or pushing them further away.[108]

Bonhoeffer may offer the best example of one who told Barth that his work was too rigid, too categorical. He thought that Barth, in the focus of his "act" theology upon the individual at the crossroads before God, upon the individual called into *Krisis*, missed the continuity of "being" available in the community of revelation, the church. He thought that Barth's actualism, apart from that community, made justification a purely objective matter and devalued the significance of sanctification.[109] These criticisms anticipate Bonhoeffer's later charge of revelational positivism. Bonhoeffer remarked on the great difference between Barth the person, always eager to listen keenly to another's arguments or concerns, and Barth the formal theologian. What Barth heard in specific relation to his own theology did not creatively inform his subsequent work.[110]

That von Kirschbaum succeeded as a critic where others failed is in part the ironic consequence of sexual politics in the early twentieth century. Barth could afford to listen to her. She was not a threat. She was noncompetitive. She soon proved her loyalty—more irony—by becoming totally dependent on him. It is probably safe to assume that colleagues of Barth used her, or tried to use her, to get messages through to him—and that she enjoyed the responsibility and trust that this role presupposed.

The letter of 28 February to Charlotte is one of two communications between the two that Busch found. The other was a poem he came upon while straightening out von Kirschbaum's desk. Barth wrote the poem to her in the same year, 1926, which was also the year after Rösy Münger's death. In it, he wrote of going through life alone, *ganz allein*, certain that that was how it must always be for him. And then he met von Kirschbaum

108. See the collected writings in James M. Robinson, ed., *The Beginnings of Dialectical Theology* (Richmond, Va.: John Knox Press, 1968)—for example, Bultmann's review of the second edition of *Römerbrief* (100–120) and Barth's response to Bultmann in the preface to the third edition (126ff.) and in comment to Thurneysen (24), and see the interchange with Tillich (133ff.); see also, of course, the climax of Barth's interchanges with Brunner in *Nein!* (ET: *Natural Theology, Comprising "Nature and Grace" by Prof. Dr. Emil Brunner and the Reply "No!" by Dr. Karl Barth* [London: Geoffrey Bles/Centenary Press, 1946]).

109. In *Act and Being*, quoted in R. Umidi, "Imaging God Together: The Image of God as 'Sociality' in the Thought and Life of Dietrich Bonhoeffer," Ph.D. diss., Drew University, 1993, 222–23.

110. Busch, *Karl Barth*, 215. See ibid., 381, for Barth's reaction to Bonhoeffer's post-humously published characterization of his work as revelational positivism: Barth said he just couldn't make sense of the criticism and saw nothing in *CD* that it could apply to.

and found at once a human being and a woman who understood him.[111]
The poem and a short discussion that ensued with Barth led Busch to
two conclusions about the change signaled in the 28 February letter.
First, the surprising realization that he was no longer lonely was an
occurrence that opened up space for the full knowledge of God's mercy
or graciousness (*Barmherzigkeit*). In Barth's view, loneliness, the essence
of all human misery, was the inescapable concomitant of nineteenth-
century theology (grounded as it was in subjectivity and individualism).
Second, the mercy that Barth the theology professor now resolved upon
would be applied immediately to that hitherto-rejected theology.[112]

The gentling that Barth retrospectively attached to the 1938–48 decade
in fact coexisted with the increasingly christocentric character of his
theology in the preceding decade. One could say that von Kirschbaum
both crystallized and shaped the changing of Barth's mind by changing
his perspective on and for his life. Now he was *able* to see christologically.
She also provided him a different "horizontal" life, alongside the always-
dominant "vertical from above" and distinct from the social concern that
was a consequence of his theology. She represented constantly, unfailingly, God's graciousness to his lost creature.

Several of Barth's writings in the late 1920s and early 1930s form a
sequence of markers of the shift in his thought. In the fall and winter of
1926–27, in the same letters in which he portrays von Kirschbaum's
developing role as his assistant, he described his labors, day and night,
to revise the *Göttingen Dogmatics*. He regarded the revision as a recon-
ceiving and likened it to the revision of *Epistle to the Romans*.[113] The
differences may seem less thoroughgoing to later readers; they may
seem more progressive than contrastive, yet they still are perceptible. In
both the *Göttingen Dogmatics* (1924) and the new *Christliche Dogmatik*
(1927), Barth eschewed the preliminary subject matter of "modern"
dogmatics—the "general presuppositions" of the Christian faith—as
impossible and unnecessary. Indeed, their presence, it seems to him,
indicates insecurity.[114] Rather, Christian dogmatics and Christian proclamation alike will proceed from God's Word. This can and will occur
because God has permitted and commanded it to occur.[115] McCormack

111. E. Busch, personal communication, 16 December 1993.
112. Ibid.
113. *KB-ET Briefwechsel*, 8 November 1926. He told Thurneysen that "here, too,
almost no stone is being left unturned." See also ibid., 14 October 1926.
114. *Göttingen Dogmatics*, 18–19; *Christliche Dogmatik*, 27.
115. *Göttingen Dogmatics*, 51ff.; *Christliche Dogmatik*, 27–28, 109ff.

has pointed to Barth's heightened appreciation in *Christliche Dogmatik* of Anselm as guide to a theological method of "ac-knowledgment" (An-Erkenntnis) rather than knowledge.[116]

Fides quaerens intellectum (1931), the book on Anselm that Barth later held up as the signal of his complete rejection of natural theology—and that he and von Kirschbaum worked on so intensively—is the concentrated exploration of Anselm's congenial methodology, in itself and as manifested in his proof of the existence of God. That Barth is still experimenting with different approaches to a theology of God the sole giver of life and light is suggested by his lecture of 1929 on the Holy Spirit and the Christian life. The Spirit is "God the Lord in the fullness of Deity, in the total sovereignty and condescension, in the complete hiddenness and revealedness of God." It is by the action of the Spirit that Christ the Crucified and Risen One is present for the believer; it is in our being grasped by the Spirit that we participate in the occurrence of revelation.[117] At the start of this lecture, Barth rejects any understanding of the image of God as a given in the human being, as a human property. There is neither innate awareness nor innate orientation to God. The discontinuity between God and his creature can only be changed by the Creator in his relation to the creature.[118]

Christocentrism in liberal theology—as in Wilhelm Herrmann—was intimately tied to the ethical impulse, to some form of *imitatio Christi*. Contact with the inner life of Jesus was available; it was direct, certain, and decisive for the course of the individual's life.[119] Barth said he remained grateful for Herrmann's christocentric impulse.[120] Barth came—in the phase we are describing—to combine christocentrism with the rejection of all human capacity. Busch sees the lecture "Das erste Gebot als theologische Axiom" (The First Commandment as Theological Axiom), delivered on 12 March 1933, in Copenhagen, shortly after the burning of the Reichstag on 27 February, as the first product of a radical new christocentrism in Barth.[121] His resolution of the problem presented in

116. McCormack, *Karl Barth's Dialectical Theology*, 424–25. (To be sure, McCormack makes this observation in the context of his argument for continuity.) On Anselm, see Barth, *Christliche Dogmatik*, 131–36.

117. Karl Barth, *The Holy Ghost and the Christian Life*, trans. R. Birch Hoyle (London: F. Muller, 1938), 10, 18–20.

118. Ibid., 14–16.

119. Claude Welch, *Protestant Thought in the Nineteenth Century*, vol. 2: *1870–1914* (New Haven: Yale University Press, 1985), 44–54 and passim.

120. Busch, *Karl Barth*, 45.

121. Busch, "Theologie und Biographie," 333.

Epistle to the Romans, that we are called upon to speak of God but just this we cannot do, is clarified in a new perspective. If we refuse commitment to all authorities but the God of the Old and New Testaments, excluding absolutely the claims of all human creations and capacities (the political reference is obvious), then, and only then, can God find us and grace us with his presence.

Two new themes pervade this lecture, and they are themes of linkage and continuity. First (and in contrast to general scientific axioms), Barth insists that we see revelation as a historical event and specifically as interpersonal address in I-Thou form. References to the address of God's *Ich* to the human *Du* resound through this lecture. Second, the God who spoke to Israel and who speaks to us is, as Calvin said, the *Deus ecclesiae*. For in all his speech to us, God is speaking of his relationship to us his elect, to us the people he has called. In Calvin's words, *subest locutioni relatio*.[122] Barth is specific in his christological encompassing of all the Commandments: "That the Word became flesh, that God spoke humanly to humankind [*menschlich zum Menschen*], and thus in the human mode of being and in time, that is already the sense of the Book of Exodus."[123] The God who claims us in the First Commandment is the covenantal God, and the human response is an obedience that is gratitude. The First Commandment "cannot be separated from this soteriological or, we say with the same concreteness, from this christological connection."[124] And, if the God who speaks to us is the *Deus ecclesiae*, this becomes the God of whom we can speak. The Word is proclaimed in the *church*. This is the focus Barth needed for the Dogmatics begun in 1931–32. It is a horizontal focus, a shift that is both necessary and possible to him in these years of political challenge and personal change.

That it is also a connective perspective is particularly clear in the treatment of modern Protestant theology in "Erster Gebot." On the one hand, Barth exasperatedly points out that the theological voices dominant since the eighteenth century have persisted in finding other sources of religious knowledge to place alongside revelation, such as reason, religious consciousness, *kultur*-ethos, the history of religion, human *Existenz*, or the orders of creation.[125] This is very familiar to readers of Barth. On the

122. From *Institutes* II.viii.14: "For underlying this expression is a mutual correspondence contained in the promise: 'I will be their God and they will be my people'" (I:380).
123. Karl Barth, "Das erste Gebot als theologische Axiom," Lecture in Copenhagen and Aarhus, March 1933, in *Theologische Fragen und Antworten*, Gesammelte Vorträge 3, p. 130.
124. Ibid., 133.
125. Ibid., 137.

other hand, Barth gives these theologians of the "Revelation *and*" mindset a hearing more open than usual. He asks whether they have truly subordinated the second element that they pair with revelation, to make it only incidental. He thinks the Reformers correctly discounted the contributions of natural theology even though they included it in their theology. Later theologians have not done the same. Barth has opened a possibility, in a questioning format similar to the final set of questions he posed about Schleiermacher in his *Nachwort*. He names his past and present adversaries and finds them all unable to hold to the absolute primacy of God's Word even though they say they do. At least he has heard them say this.[126]

In the years around 1930, Barth is paying a lot of attention to his lecture course on modern Protestantism. In November of 1929, in the last semester at Münster and the time that von Kirschbaum became his full-time assistant and joined his household, he is preparing new material on Kant, Herder, Novalis, Hegel, and Schleiermacher. In the first version of the course, he had begun with Schleiermacher. He thinks the new design should result in a new picture (*ein neues Gesicht*) of him.[127] Teaching a summer seminar and a discussion group on Schleiermacher in 1931, he tells Thurneysen he is trying very hard (though with little success) to get his students to look at Schleiermacher positively, even if only for his historical significance.[128] Then in 1932–33 Barth gives the new version of the nineteenth-century Protestant theology course at Bonn. It is the most direct marker of the shift we are tracking, if not the most complete. In published form it often surprises students familiar only with Barth's treatment of Schleiermacher in the *Church Dogmatics*, and it surprised his own audience.

Barth pointed out, when asked whether he had withdrawn his previous harsh criticism of nineteenth-century thought, that one can afford to be milder with figures who are dead; criticism would do them no good. Furthermore, biblical exegetes and dogmatic theologians alike must prove themselves by the extent to which they grasp the historical reality of their predecessors and by becoming more impartial in doing so: "We need openness toward particular figures with their individual characteristics and interest in them; . . . a little grace in expressing even the most

126. Ibid., 138–39, 141. His concluding remarks are reminiscent of passages in the final parts of *Epistle to the Romans*. No one is absolutely right; many of our debates are *"gute notwendige Streit,"* and they *all* are covered in God's mercy.

127. *KB-ET Briefwechsel*, 16 November 1929.

128. Busch, *Karl Barth*, 214.

profound criticism; and finally (even in the worst cases) a certain tranquil delight that they were as they were."[129] The theological reason for such attention is that "the Church means that the eternal revelation entered not only into time but also into the sequence and the changes of time."[130] On the one hand, we are obliged to search out the particular view, in an age and in its individual exponents, of our common unity "of perplexity and disquiet" and "of richness and hope."[131] Barth did more than find positive compensations amid his predecessors' sins. He discussed fundamental concepts and positions in their work that placed him in their debt.[132] On the other hand, "care will always be taken that this openness is not too wide." Good historical study is further justified because it serves to clarify and deepen our differences with the theologians with whom we are preoccupied.[133]

In his biography of Barth, Karl Kupisch described von Kirschbaum's work in relation to the *Church Dogmatics* as watching over, "energetically, single-mindedly, and knowledgeably, and with a firm hand, tenacious zeal, and direction," the development of that enormous work.[134] She did have a sense of the whole, and could situate Barth's current thinking in the context of his own work as well as in the context of tradition and contemporary debate. When Gollwitzer said that in her work with Barth's students she was more Barthian than Barth himself, more radical and unconditional, he was also describing the grounds for Barth's trust in her.[135] Von Kirschbaum was able to steer Barth's theology, not toward compromise, but—to use a phrase of Renata Adler's—toward a radical middle. To do this, she convinced and persuaded him to reconsider his historical and systematic theology of negation. She also made human otherness part of his consciousness and vision. We now proceed to her role as Barth's counterpart, wherein gender moves to the foreground.

129. K. Barth, Foreword, *Protestant Theology in the Nineteenth Century: Its Background and History*, trans. B. Cozens and J. Bowden (London: SCM, 1972), 12.

130. Ibid., 29.

131. Ibid., 27.

132. For example, Kant's critical philosophy that by implication cleared an independent space for theology and insisted that it have methodological integrity; Hegel's important stress on God's aliveness and on truth as act, as event. See the chapters on each in Barth, *Protestant Theology in the Nineteenth Century*.

133. Ibid., 24, and chap. 1, "The Task of a History of Modern Protestant Theology," 15–29 passim.

134. Kupisch, *Karl Barth in Selbstzeugnissen und Bilddokumenten*, 104.

135. Quoted in Köbler, *In the Shadow*, 47.

PART 3 | # Dialogue

"You stole that from me."
—Von Kirschbaum to Barth, as he dictated
textual material on the *imago Dei*
(recounted by Barth to Eberhard Busch)

1. Further Questions

As Barth recalled it, Von Kirschbaum sighed and made this remark again and again.[1] Yet this study began with Barth's grateful remarks about von Kirschbaum in the midst of their collaboration, five years after the publication of *CD* III/1 (1945), in which the *imago* material first appeared and two years after its elaboration in III/2. We have also seen that Barth attributed his inability to complete *CD* in good part to the unexpected end of von Kirschbaum's collaboration with him.

These are general tributes. In III/4 (1951) Barth paid a different kind of respect to von Kirschbaum: he cited her as an authority on the subject matter of the text, the *imago Dei* as the I-Thou relationship between male and female. There are two such references. First he states, "cf. for what follows [works by Rasker, Leenhardt and Blanke, and Meyer] and along the lines we have been following, Charlotte von Kirschbaum, *Die wirkliche Frau* (1949)." Then, on the following page, he states, "cf. *CD*

---

1. E. Busch, personal communication, 16 December 1993. Barth told Busch that ". . . beim Diktat diese Lehre Ch.vK immer wieder aufgeseufzt habe: das und das habe er ihr ja gestohlen."

III/2, p. 309, cf. von Kirschbaum, op. cit., p. 42."² The passage in III/2 (1948) that Barth cites is, like that in von Kirschbaum's work, an exposition of the scriptural verse that is the subject of the III/4 discussion. In III/2 he also cites, as presupposition for all subsequent discussions of the male/female relationship, his foundational exegesis of Genesis 1:26f. and 2:18ff. in III/1 (1945), in which the doctrine of the *imago Dei* in its mature form first appears. Is he not also saying, in III/4, that his exegesis was not entirely derived from von Kirschbaum? Barth seems to be asserting independence of, as well as dependence on, von Kirschbaum at this intersection of their theological interests.

In turn, von Kirschbaum cites Barth's exegesis of Genesis 1:26 in *CD* III/1 at the beginning of her first lecture, she cites him on the significance of the Virgin Birth in *CD* I/2, and she quotes him on Christian servanthood.³ We have here something like a braid, and it is tempting to say that the strands cannot be sorted out, that we should just accept the results and benefit from its richness. That is an approximation of my final position. But von Kirschbaum's accusation and Barth's own uncertainty of its meaning ask for further attention. We also need to remember that von Kirschbaum had long been interested in the subject of women and the male/female relationship and considered it her own project, *her* work as distinct from work she did with Barth.

Several scenarios seem possible. One must first wonder about the extent of the co-opting. Barth told Eberhard Busch that he agreed with her comment but thought they were at one (*einverstandlich*) about borrowing from each other. Busch thinks von Kirschbaum was referring to her biblical exegeses and her commentary on the feminism of Simone de Beauvoir, not to theological ideas. It is also possible that she meant the latter as well. However, if von Kirschbaum contributed the new content of the *imago* (or part of it) in III/1, her version was grown in soil prepared and fertilized by Barth over a long time. Furthermore, the new material in the doctrine is not exclusive to Barth and von Kirschbaum. The foundational work of Buber on the I-Thou relationship and the work

2. *CD* III/4:172, 173 (*KD* III/4:192, 193). The references are in a long, small-print subsection of III/4, par. 54 (Freedom in Fellowship), sec. 1: Man and Woman. The subject of the subsection is male-female ordering in the New Testament epistles, primarily Paul in 1 Corinthians 11. (The reference for III/2 should be to *KD* III/2:372f., not 374, and to *CD* III/2:309–11.)

3. Von Kirschbaum: first chapter in *Wirkliche Frau* (henceforth *WF*), 7 (Shepherd: 56); chap. 4, p. 67 (Shepherd: 133); revised lecture, "The Role of Women in the Proclamation of the Word," in Köbler, *In the Shadow*, 96 (Shepherd: 176). (For the last point, which will be further discussed below, she cites Barth, *Theologische Studien* 22, p. 25).

of Brunner, Gogarten, Bonhoeffer, and Vischer—especially Bonhoeffer and Vischer—and indeed the whole movement of dialogical personalism in the 1920s and 1930s was Barth's and von Kirschbaum's theological environment. Barth cites the work of these figures in reference to the *imago* in III/1. But it is also the case that these resources were available to Barth long before he turned to them.[4] The doctrine of the *imago* in *CD* I does not draw on them.

Might someone, of whom the likeliest candidate is von Kirschbaum, have precipitated a new interest in these sources or convinced him of their importance? Or might Barth, as he thought about and around the subject, have encountered this material in his memory? Remembering might have been aided by the tradition of interest in women and their emancipation in the Barth family, from Karl's father and mother to his son Markus. Women's emancipation is not the same as theology—or church polity—but we can recall that Karl Barth briefly joined the discussion about the role of women in the Reformed churches in 1932. Finally, might the relationship of von Kirschbaum and Barth itself be the major source or precipitant of the doctrine for Barth? One cannot read their discussions of relationality without thinking of their relationship. Eberhard Busch thinks that Barth experienced with von Kirschbaum an I-Thou relationship in which each felt understood by the other and fully trusted the other. Frederick Herzog, another student who knew Barth and von Kirschbaum, has suggested that Barth might have seen their relationship as an I-Thou one in an attempt to understand it better.[5] And the mirroring possibility has many modes: it could have been quietly observed by Barth or occasionally discussed by the two, or it could have been "set up" as an experiment by Barth—there is an exploitative character to the latter. Although many of these questions must remain speculative, they may still be useful to raise.

We will also need to consider the evolution of Barth's thought on women per se in his anthropology, and part of this story is the status of the *Frauenfrage*, or woman question, in late nineteenth- and twentieth-century European theology and culture. I think Charlotte von Kirschbaum made a substantive contribution to Barth's anthropology and doctrine of the *imago*, helpfully evaluated by his remark in III/4 about *both* III/2 and her work in *WF*. Her correspondence with Visser't Hooft Boddaert is also

---

4. Brunner is a special case. See below, pages 116–17, where the context of their disagreement on the *imago* is discussed.

5. E. Busch, personal communication, 19 July 1994; F. Herzog, personal conversation, November 1992.

helpful because it enables us to trace, not the origin of common ideas, but the relative origin of *interest* in them. The latter may be more helpful for a study such as this. At the least, I think von Kirschbaum is responsible for seeing to it that the subject got full-scale attention in *CD* III.

I am most interested, however, in what each of the two makes of the doctrine of the *imago Dei*, because it has very different aspects and emphases in each. I think we can track some of the exchange of ideas through textual comparison, and we certainly can track their independent appropriations of their common material. Two people in an unusual relationship are discussing the theology of relationship and differentiation within relationship. In our own discussion we will be concerned with dialogue and listening, with authoritarianism and hierarchy, and with alterity.

2. Barth's First Anthropology of Gender

Women were theologically important to Barth at two loci: the doctrines of the Virgin Birth and the image of God. Exposition of *natus ex virgine* occurs in the *Göttingen Dogmatics* (or what we presently have of it in volume one of either the German or the English translation), in *Christliche Dogmatik*, and in *Church Dogmatics* I/2 and (briefly) IV/1. Barth's doctrine of the *imago Dei* was completely revised after its appearance in I/1: the new version, which construes the *imago* as male/female relationship, first appears in *CD* III/1 and is expanded in III/2 and III/4. Von Kirschbaum's work gives greater stress to the doctrine of the *imago* but gives significant attention to Marian theology. Together the two doctrines define the framework within which Barth and von Kirschbaum exchange ideas as well as pursue ideas independently in directions of special interest to each. The separate tracks or appropriations of each seem, in some instances, to comment on and correct or revise the work of the other. Because the doctrines that constitute the framework themselves undergo change, we must first survey their development.

Cultural Équipage

The doctrine of the Virgin Birth was rejected by Barth's theologically conservative father, a rejection that probably disqualified him for academic promotion twice in his career.[6] A generation later when Karl Barth affirmed the doctrine, he was going against the grain of many major Protestant theologians (including Emil Brunner, whom he frequently reproaches for denying the doctrine) as well as against his father. He was also speaking on a culturally charged subject. It will be recalled that women's emancipation—the *Frauenfrage*—was infused with new energy by the exigencies of World War I that brought women into new socioeconomic situations, including the male sphere within the church, and by the simple fact of the massive loss of male life in the war. Yet the professions remained overwhelmingly closed to women, and factory and office work did not provide a new identity to many middle-class women, who continued to identify with and defend the domestic life of which they were unexpectedly bereft.[7] In response to the loss of lives in the war (and its larger context of the decline in birthrate in Europe) and in reaction to inroads into the traditional gender spheres, the political right in Germany reasserted separate spheres for men and women, allotting to women the domestic sphere (later summarized in the Nazi slogan, "Kinder, Küche, Kirche") and protecting it from the male spheres of work, war, and state.[8]

The political right was able to exploit a century-long fascination with the identity of "the feminine." The century of Marian devotion in the Roman Catholic Church, marked by promulgation of the dogma of the Immaculate Conception in 1854 and the dogma of the Assumption in 1950, exalted motherhood through the Virgin Mary.[9] The Catholic Church in France was a close, valuable ally of antirevolutionary political movements in the nineteenth century. Protestant churches also reflected what has been called a feminization of religion, albeit with different results for U.S. and European churches—and especially different for German Protestantism.[10] We have encountered the socially and politically

6. Busch, *Karl Barth*, 10.

7. Sheila Briggs, "Images of Women and Jews in Nineteenth- and Twentieth-Century German Theology," in *Immaculate and Powerful*, ed. Atkinson, Buchanan, and Miles (Boston: Beacon Press, 1985), 243; Smith, *Changing Lives*, 423.

8. See essays in Friedlander, *Women in Culture and Politics*, especially Claudia Koonz, "Some Political Implications of Separatism: German Women Between Democracy and Nazism, 1928–1934," 268–85. The decline in birthrate was largely the result of more effective birth control technology and heightened expectations for individual lives (Smith, *Changing Lives*, 346–47, 411).

9. Barbara Corrado Pope, "Immaculate and Powerful: The Marian Revival in the Nineteenth Century," in *Immaculate and Powerful*, 173–200. Barth reminds us of the logical intermediate step of papal infallibility in 1870 (*CD* I/2:146).

10. Ann Douglas, *The Feminization of American Culture* (New York: Doubleday/Anchor, 1988 [1st ed. 1977]) is a very frequent reference point in the discussion of the subject (e.g., Corrado Pope, "Immaculate and Powerful," 193).

conservative ethos of women in the German church. C. G. Jung thought the declaration of the dogma of the Assumption of Mary was part of a wider assertion of what he called the feminine principle.[11]

Behind these varied phenomena, and part of nineteenth- and twentieth-century German Protestant theology, was the pervasive assumption and theme in Romanticism,[12] especially German Romanticism, of the natural affinity of women for religion. And despite the truly new roles of women, first in the salon and then in religious revivals and the deaconess movement, their common message of inner moral reform had the effect of creating a separate-but-equal role for women in culture: that of moral education or formation.[13] Religious laywomen increasingly turned to works of charity and sometimes reform in the institutions of health, religious education, rehabilitation of prostitutes, temperance, and poverty relief.[14] Schleiermacher, among other Romanticists, came to speak increasingly of the complementarity of the sexes.[15]

However equal in value each was said to be to the other, women were locked into a social construct that defined them and their activities contrapuntally in relation to men.[16] The male belonged to the public world; he was the builder and critical thinker. The woman's sphere was private life, and the ideal of women was motherhood. To the woman were attributed feeling and spontaneity, intuition, nurturing, and forgiveness. Attuned to both nature and the supernatural, she fulfilled her true nature when she raised children and oriented them to the higher life of God and church. With this upbringing men would be prepared for the further work of shaping the moral communities that constituted

11. Quoted by Corrado Pope, "Immaculate and Powerful," 199 n. 36, from Jung's *Answer to Job*.

12. I use the term *Romanticism* to refer to ideas and sensibilities in Europe c. 1800 through the 1830s with lasting effect into the next century. Occasionally I will use its adjective form. Barth uses the term in the pejorative senses of sentimental, subjective, or unrealistic: e.g., on attempts to reconstruct the early church (*CD* IV/2:686 [*KD* IV/2:776]); on Schleiermacher's, Schubart's, and Bovet's "apotheosis of Eros" (*CD* III/4:126–28 [*KD* III/4:139–41]).

13. Smith, *Changing Lives*, 122–31. See also *RGG* on the salon roles of Varnhagen and Karoline Schlegel, and Schleiermacher's *Catechism of Reason for Noble Women* (s.v. Frau, sec. 5); see also Olive Banks, *Faces of Feminism: A Study of Feminism as a Social Movement* (New York: St. Martin's Press, 1981), 71–72.

14. Smith, *Changing Lives*, 129.

15. Briggs, "Images of Women and Jews," 228–29. An alternative to the Schleiermacherian view had a short-lived existence: that of Friedrich Schlegel, in whose concept of Romantic love the free woman was united with an equally unconventional man (Frevert, *Women in German History*, 58–59).

16. Smith, *Changing Lives*, 130–31.

civilization, and they could continue to find almost sacred respite in the domestic sphere. It was men who daily confronted the tensions between individualism and universality, between religious faith and modern culture (articulated in Schleiermacher's *Weihnachtsfeier*, to which Barth refers in his discussion of the Virgin Birth); and these tensions were the wellspring of progress.[17] Women, in their one-sidedness and insulation from the male spheres, were pure and (in a favored nineteenth-century term) angelic. Bound to the sphere of children, they were also, inevitably, childlike. With more accuracy than he intended, one of Schleiermacher's characters in *Weihnachtsfeier* approvingly quotes "the old proverb, 'We women go right on being children while you men must first be turned about to become so again.'"[18]

Richard Rothe, whose work Barth knew very well, perpetuated this view; so did Barth's teacher Wilhelm Herrmann.[19] The compelling simplicity of the gospel message in Liberal Protestantism, freed from its extraneous trappings, meshed well with nineteenth-century female spirituality. In Herrmann's ethics, the sexual stereotypes were strengthened by the late nineteenth- and early twentieth-century conceptual framework of the orders of creation: marriage and the family, civilization and the state.[20] In the 1930s "civilization" would be largely replaced by *Volk*. In the second edition of his *Ethics* in 1920 (the first was 1911), Reinhold Seeberg introduced the notion of male and female natures and echoed another, more time-specific theme when he correlated women's emancipation with contempt for culture and morality.[21]

Seeberg is drawing on, and speaking to, another image of women in the minds of his audience: the dangerous woman—in this case, the transgressor. This image too has its roots in Romanticism.[22] The Romantic restoration of the treasures of darkness and the infinite gave new life to the perennial notion in world myth, art, and literature of woman as mystery. In the Romantic decades, and increasingly in the post-Romantic

17. Briggs, "Images of Women and Jews," 254.
18. Friedrich Schleiermacher, *Christmas Eve: Dialogue on the Incarnation*, trans. Terrence N. Tice (Richmond, Va.: John Knox Press, 1967), 54.
19. The first of many *CD* references to the works (as well as the personality of Rothe, whom Barth seems to find congenial despite their differences) are in I/1 (266, 281) and I/2 (372).
20. Briggs, "Images of Women and Jews," 226–42.
21. Ibid., 248–53.
22. Peter Gay, *The Bourgeois Experience: Victoria to Freud*, Vol. I, *Education of the Senses* (New York: Oxford University Press, 1984), 188–213 and passim.

period or "bourgeois century," the image of the angel in the house coexisted with its opposite: the *femme fatale*. Contradictory and incomprehensible, sinister and treacherous, the *femme fatale* became strikingly common in literature and the arts.[23]

The early twentieth-century depth psychology that was part of Barth's environment—literally, in the case of the distinguished Basel citizen C. G. Jung—was nurtured by Romantic literature and reflected the two-sided image of the female. Especially in the work of Jung, psychology incorporated this image along with the age-old notion of the complementarity of male and female.[24] Barth was sufficiently familiar with the ideas of the depth psychologists to reject the one-sidedness of Freud's sexual determinism and cite Jung and Adler in support of his rejection.[25] Wolfgang Schildmann has recounted Barth's interested but wary relations with the psychoanalyst Ewald Jung, a cousin of Carl Gustav, who lived in Anna Barth's house as a boarder for six years after the death of Barth's father in 1912. Barth found some of their discussions intriguing: in a letter to Thurneysen in 1915 he told his friend of the "splendid father complex" that Ewald Jung had "unearthed" for him. But in general he felt that Ewald Jung misunderstood him both as theologian and as pastor.[26]

As we have noted, Barth regarded psychoanalysis as a narcissistic deflection from a theological anthropology defined by the Word of God; he correspondingly preferred to lodge psychological health in an outward move to the Christian community.[27] In fact, Barth was ambivalent about psychology. Usually dismissive, he was occasionally fascinated with it. His striking esteem for C. G. Jung even in disagreement (as in his criticism of Jung's *Answer to Job*) is not surprising.[28] In fact, some central

---

23. Ibid., and a source Gay values: the classic study by Mario Praz, *The Romantic Agony*, trans. Angus Davidson (New York: Meridian Books, 2nd ed., 1956), esp. chap. 4, "La Belle Dame Sans Merci," 187–286.

24. See Henri Ellenberger, *The Discovery of the Unconscious: The History and Evolution of Dynamic Psychiatry* (New York: Basic Books, 1970), esp. 292–94. Catherine Keller discusses the originally Aristotelian association of male with soul and female with body, along with the active/passive dichotomy and the notion of woman as the deviant one, and stresses that the problem is not the notion of complementarity but "the culture of sexist complementarity" (*From a Broken Web: Separation, Sexism, and Self* [Boston: Beacon Press, 1986], 10, 49–50).

25. *CD* III/4:136 (*KD* III/4:150).

26. Schildmann, *Was sind das für Zeichen?* 8–9.

27. Ibid., chap. 1, "Karl Barth und die Tiefenpsychologie," esp. 11–12.

28. *CD* IV/3:384. The family of C. G. Jung (1875–1961) had close ties to both church and university in Basel. See Ellenberger, *Discovery of the Unconscious*, 660–63.

ideas of Jung may have found greater resonance than Barth's remarks on psychology reveal. Though careful to say that the figures of Eros and Logos are merely conceptual aids, Jung spoke often of the paternal Logos and the maternal Eros in describing the structure of the unconscious. He called upon them "to describe the fact that woman's consciousness is charac- terized more by the connective quality of Eros than by the discrimination and cognition associated with Logos."[29] Although such stereotyping diminishes both male and female, its latent content is less even-handed. *Magna mater*, the mother archetype in Jung and Romanticism and their mythic sources, includes monster—remember the *Todesmutter* of Barth's dream—as well as *mater spiritualis*. Catherine Keller zeroes in on Jung's analysis of the roots of consciousness in matricide and recognizes this consciousness as specific to Western culture. Jung presupposes that consciousness can only occur through the discrimination of opposites: "This is the paternal principle, the Logos, which eternally struggles to extricate itself from the primal warmth and primal darkness of the maternal womb; in a word, from unconsciousness. Unconsciousness is the primal sin, evil itself, for the Logos. Therefore, its first creative act of liberation is matricide."[30] In actual life the archetype is projected onto an individual's mother, and varying parts of it are reinforced by the "real" mother: the combined impression is the individual's lasting mother/woman image. A dream such as Barth's would demonstrate this process.[31]

Archetypes have their own history. The two sets of female images, the holy and the deadly or demonic, are a recurring dyad in history and have, in their nineteenth-century prominence, elicited several explana- tions. Certainly the dyad comprises that which the self defined by the post-Cartesian male does not comprise.[32] Historians of the Victorian era have traditionally seen its fascination with the female figurings of evil as compensatory to its unrealistically high moral standards; psychohistorians

29. "In men, Eros, the function of relationship, is usually less developed than Logos. In women . . . Eros is an expression of their true nature, while their Logos is often only a regrettable accident" (C. G. Jung, "Aion," in *Psyche and Symbol: A Selection from the Writings of C. G. Jung*, trans. Cary Baynes and F. C. R. Hall, ed. Violet S. de Laszlo, 1-60 [New York: Doubleday, 1958], 13).

30. From "Psychological Aspects of the Mother Archetype," quoted and discussed by Keller, *From a Broken Web*, 62, 12, and chap. 3 passim.

31. Keller, *From a Broken Web*, 106ff.; Ellenberger, *Discovery of the Unconscious*, 705. On Barth's recurrent dream and Schildmann's analysis of it, see Part 1 above (page 18).

32. My understanding of the phenomenon has been informed by Alice A. Jardine's *Gynesis: Configurations of Woman and Modernity* (Ithaca, N.Y.: Cornell University Press, 1985).

have added the dimension of fear in men poised to conquer the world by virtue of their various kinds of superiority. In Peter Gay's picture, the image of the dangerous woman was both an Oedipal projection *and* a reasonably accurate warning system about the effects of expanding and restructuring the economic sphere into male thinkers, doers, and controllers and female drones or drudges.[33] The prospect (and in the women's movement, the reality) of offensive women elicited defensive men (Gay's phraseology); they projected their fears and at the same time explained to each other (in the texts we still read) why it was urgently, vitally necessary to keep women under control.

Gay has described the many manifestations of "the pervasive sense of manhood in danger" in Victorian Europe and America in popular literature and belles lettres, in newspapers, and in sermons. Medical texts met the fiction of the dangerous woman with the reassuring counterfiction of women's (i.e., wives!) lack of any sexual appetite.[34] The nineteenth-century list of *femmes fatales* prominently includes Salome, Judith, Delilah, and characters in Dostoevsky.[35] The woman who seduces, humiliates, and destroys is the subject of Zola's *Nana* in 1880; and some forty-five years later the type, along with female transgressors in politics, across sexual boundaries, and in role reversals, is familiar in Weimar cinema.[36] *The Blue Angel* (1930)—the script for which Heinrich Mann wrote an early version and Carl Zuckmayer (Barth's friend in old age) a major part of the final version—could serve as a cultural icon.[37] The New Woman, the subject of endless "savage or nervous" jokes as well as virulent hate literature, represented or re-presented to men what they unconsciously or vaguely feared: "women's eternal power over man."[38]

---

33. Gay, *Bourgeois Experience*, chap. 2, "Offensive Women and Defensive Men," passim.

34. Ibid., 193, 197; see also Banks, *Faces of Feminism*, 71. Banks points out that the idea that women, if they experienced sexual desire at all, had to be aroused, in contrast to the sexual spontaneity of men, supported the nineteenth-century view of the higher moral nature of women.

35. Gay, *Bourgeois Experience*, 201.

36. Smith, *Changing Lives*, 445.

37. It is the story of an infatuated English teacher, who gives up his career and, after public humiliation, his life, when he allows himself to be seduced by the cabaret singer, Lola (played by Marlene Dietrich). See John Baxter, *The Cinema of Josef von Sternberg*, International Film Guide Series (London: A. Zwemmer, 1971), 64–75. We note also that Barth the movie-goer most admired films with "the immortal Marlene Dietrich . . . (I don't know where she will have a mention in the *Dogmatics*—perhaps in eschatology, because she is such a borderline case?)" (quoted in Busch, *Karl Barth*, 312).

38. Gay, *Bourgeois Experience*, 435.

Freud testified to his ultimate incomprehension of the female unconscious, of female sexuality "veiled in unpenetrable obscurity."[39] The many
nineteenth- and early twentieth-century images of confrontations with
the sphinx also capture the fascination of male intellectuals with the
mystery of women.[40] Thomas Mann, whose novels were part of Barth's
cultural capital,[41] often presented women as distillations of multiple
Romantic themes: Gerda (in *Buddenbrooks*) is the Woman of artistic
temperament and soul: she is "unique, puzzling, ravishing."[42] In *The
Magic Mountain* (1924), Claudia Chaucat is Woman as foreign and
exotic—and likened by the rationalist Settembrini to Lilith.[43]

We will see that Barth shared this fascination. It is held separate, or
segregated, from his intense annoyance, his snarling derision toward
those transgressive, "sexless" females who clamor for the rights that will
enable them to be just like men—that is, to confuse the boundaries that
place women where men need them to be. Such rights would contradict
their very nature. (Others, including C. G. Jung, more calmly opposed
feminism as unnatural and therefore self-destructive.)[44] I have suggested

39. Ibid., 167.
40. On the sphinx in art and literature: Ibid., 204–6.
41. See Barth's letter to Thurneysen on a visit to Lübeck, which Barth calls "die Stadt
der Buddenbrooks" (*KB-ET Briefwechsel*, 20 December 1923).
42. When Thomas Buddenbrook tries to tell his sister about the complex woman he
has fallen in love with and intends to marry, he says that "she can't be measured by
ordinary standards." As the sister and brother talk evening falls, and the chapter ends
with this image:
    The door to the hallway opened, and a tall, erect figure stood before them,
    surrounded by twilight and dressed in a pleated, flowing robe of snow-white
    piqué. Heavy chestnut hair framed the white face, and bluish shadows brooded in
    the corner of the brown, close-set eyes.
    It was Gerda, the mother of future Buddenbrooks. (Thomas Mann, *Budden-
    brooks* [original German ed., 1900], trans. John E. Woods [New York: Alfred A.
    Knopf, 1993], 266).
43. When the infatuated Hans Castorp confronted Claudia and addressed her, in a
language foreign to both of them, as *Tu*,
    "She stood there . . . and looked him up and down, with a smile that betrayed
    no trace of pity, nor any concern for the ravages written on his brow. The [female]
    sex knows no such compassion, no mercy for the pangs that passion brings; in
    that element the woman is far more at home than the man, to whom, by his very
    nature, it is foreign. Nor does she ever encounter him in it save with mocking and
    malignant joy" (Thomas Mann, *The Magic Mountain* [original German ed., 1924],
    trans. H. T. Lowe-Porter [New York: Alfred A. Knopf/Vintage, 1969], 332).
44. Keller, *From a Broken Web*, 260 n. 37, comments on Jung's often overlooked
antifeminism. He argued, in "Women in Europe" (in "Civilization in Transition") that "by
taking up a masculine profession, studying and working like a man, woman is doing
something not wholly in accord with, if not directly injurious to, her feminine nature."

that the qualities that annoyed Barth so much in his mother and wife—
their domineering behavior, their harshness—are part of his perception
of feminism. Early feminism is like a blip in a corner of Barth's radar
screen. He is worried and annoyed that feminists want to suppress
male/female differences, which to him are positive distinctiveness. He
also goes out of his way to make the point that a female ideology of
womanhood is as bad as a male ideology of manhood.[45] His distorted (and
contradictory) perception of feminism is intertwined with his romantic
view of women to the detriment or blocking of his attention.

We will see that von Kirschbaum largely concurs with him on feminism but does not share the romantic view of women. She is very familiar
with Jung's work, and she is skeptical both about its usefulness for the
Christian life and about its truth value: "Maybe each human unconsciously
dreams this primordial dream of humankind [*Urmenschheitstraum*] and
this really shows in our dreams. It is very interesting to know that (though
I do not believe it)."[46] Notorious as Barth's—and von Kirschbaum's—
hierarchicalism is, the residual stereotyped vision of male and female
may be the more insidious problem.

Thinking Through the Virgin Birth

The doctrine of the Virgin Birth has for Barth the character of a favorite
theme or *Lieblingsidee*—much as it had for Luther in his expositions of
the Magnificat, of grace come to us in our very lowliness, which Barth,
and later von Kirschbaum, quote at some length. Three elements or
themes of constant importance to Barth are present when he speaks of
the Virgin Birth: mystery, the necessary link with the Holy Spirit, and the
idea that everything is from God.

But there is more to the doctrine for Barth. He insists that it is not
the absence of either sexuality or sexual concupiscence that the Virgin
signifies and that the theologian must inquire into, but the absence of
the male, the creature that signifies human action and generativity. Barth
is hereby rejecting negativity on human sexuality, and this is a resound-
ingly healthy core that runs through his anthropology and doctrine of

45. *CD* I/2:193 (*KD* I/2:211).
46. Von Kirschbaum to H. Visser't Hooft, 18 December 1942. Similarly, von
Kirschbaum considers the work of such scholars of myth as Bachofen necessary for the
understanding of the Bible but not of general applicability for life: "The image of the
woman, which one perceives here, is certainly also interesting, but in the end it is an
unreal image, a dream" (ibid).

the Christian life. As part of his explications of *natus ex Maria virgine*, it is parallel to the theme of Mary's importance in locating the miracle of revelation within human reality.[47]

Most important for Barth, the doctrine of the Virgin Birth occasions the development of the theme of revelation in hiddenness.[48] The very implausibility of the story serves a noetic function. The doctrine states that the revelation of God can only be accomplished in God's way, not in the way of human creatures, and it can only be understood in faith, not in human terms. In this sense, the doctrine is akin to that of the empty tomb.[49] In *CD* I/2 and again in IV/1, Barth affirms an idea he had once rejected (in a marginal note to *Christliche Dogmatik*): that acceptance of the doctrine of the Virgin Birth may even be a criterion of the genuineness and seriousness of Christian belief.[50] This view of the doctrine finally explains why an alternative, more plausible story, placing the birth of Jesus within the marriage of Mary and Joseph, would not be theologically preferable, even though it could be more serviceable for a Christian ethic of marriage.[51]

It is only when Barth develops the theme of the peculiar inappropriateness of the male and appropriateness of the female for the miracle of Christmas that problems arise. Here one finds inconsistencies and prejudices about gender, along with slippage from "signifies" to "is." The path taken by Barth's remarks on gender in relation to the doctrine is a move toward equalization of the worth or honor that male and female have as God's creatures, but he achieves this by redefining male and female natures in a way that undermines their equality.

From the *Göttingen Dogmatics* onward, the male is defined as the actor, the doer, the maker of human history—that whole, sometimes glittering, sometimes sorry and disastrous, sinful course of the world. This is patriarchal history with two theses. First, it is the male "who is preponderantly (though of course not exclusively) the historically acting and effecting being whose deeds stamp world history and the history of the arts and sciences and economic history which characterize individual

---

47. *CD* I/2:185 (*KD* I/2:202).

48. For example, *Die Christliche Dogmatik im Entwurf* (Zurich: Theologischer Verlag, 1982 [1927]), 368.

49. *CD* IV/1:207 (*KD* IV/1:226–27).

50. Ibid.; *Christliche Dogmatik*, 371 n. gg.

51. From *Göttingen Dogmatics: Instruction in the Christian Religion* [hereafter *GD*], trans. Geoffrey W. Bromiley, ed. Hannelotte Reiffen (Grand Rapids, Mich.: Wm. B. Eerdmans, 1991), I:163, onward; von Kirschbaum, *WF*, 67 (Shepherd: 133).

times and cultures. These are male deeds [*Männertaten*]."⁵² Second, the male is the carrier and provider of individual human identity—of "the human person" as distinct from "human nature."⁵³ It is the father who provides (to his son!) "name, class, status [*Recht*], place in history, character as this or that actual person or this individual."⁵⁴

Barth is aware of the vulnerability of his position from the start. His presentation of the theme of male privilege and preeminence in world history defensively asserts that "this is how it is . . . no matter how much it is open to criticism."⁵⁵ In *CD* I/2, apparently in response to such criticism, he retreats on the importance of inquiring into the absence of the male, Joseph, in the story and redefines the question as a *parergon* (a secondary, supplementary matter), presenting it in small print (though not in fewer words!), in contrast to "the excessive dominance" it had in *Christliche Dogmatik*. But the same story about male humanity and its twofold significance is told.⁵⁶

Barth may be attributing more to the male than responsibility for historical action, social location, and personal identity. The very fact of being the doer, the one who acts, confers upon the male the aura of a basic motif in Barth's theology.⁵⁷ It is also held, in the first two versions (*Göttingen* and *Christliche Dogmatik*), that the male commands history by virtue of being created in God's image. Emphatically, in both the early Dogmatics, it is *Adam* who is created in the image of God; through Adam sin came into the world, and the first Adam must be removed so that the second Adam can come to renew humankind.⁵⁸

52. *Christliche Dogmatik*, 371–72; *GD*, 163. Barth italicizes "Männer" in "Männertaten."
53. *GD*, 163.
54. *Christliche Dogmatik*, 371.
55. *GD*, 163.
56. *CD* I/2:192-93 (*KD* I/2:211 [published in 1938/9]). Note that Barth still refers to the *Christliche Dogmatik* as the first version of his dogmatics. Joseph's exclusion from the story means the exclusion of "willing, achieving, creative, sovereign man." And it is the human father who bequeaths to his son "everything that marks his existence as his own—his name above all, and with it his position, his rights, his character as such and such an individual, his place in history" (ibid). Again in *CD* IV/1:207 (*KD* IV/1:227), the exclusion of a human father is the exclusion of "the will and work of man."
57. E.g., George Hunsinger, *How to Read Karl Barth: The Shape of His Theology* (New York: Oxford University Press, 1991) on "the motif of actualism," 30–32, 67–75.
58. *Christliche Dogmatik*, 372; *GD*, 163. Barth is also criticizing the Eve/Mary typology of early Christianity. The criticism reappears in *CD* I/2:140–41 (*KD* I/2:154–55) and he includes Luther among those who mistakenly hold Eve to be the one who introduced transgression, basing his mistake on a narrow reading of 1 Tim. 2:13–14. (In this view Adam ate of the fruit too, but out of love for his wife rather than submission to temptation.) Barth, like most modern commentators, follows Rom. 5:12f. on Adam's

The Son of God, begotten of the Father in eternity, has no need of human personhood; what he must assume to fulfill his mission is human nature or creatureliness.[59] The Virgin is the sign that "the sinful life of sex" is excluded *insofar* as this involves generativity, "the work of the willing, achieving, creative, sovereign man." Mary too is "entangled in sin and guilt," but sin in the woman is derivative. The male is responsible for sin; the woman is the co-sinner (*Mitsünderin*).[60]

Woman as such represents a humanity that is not creative—Barth's account strangely resonates with the biology of earlier centuries about conception—but is "the bearer of human creatureliness."[61] "Not the one gifted with original genius [*nicht geniale*], not the creative one, not the one who has the capacity to stamp history," she is thus "*the* possibility of man [i.e., humankind] for the actuality of the Word of God."[62] She is a receiving vessel, an organ for God insofar—and only insofar—as God's miracle makes her this.[63]

As the nonmale, Mary is defined negatively, while the *woman* Mary is defined restrictively. She "is the bearer of the predicate of humanness [*Menschheit*], just as in male-created history she is also indispensable as the object to its subject, the form to its content, the sound to the word, the intuition to the concept—yet just for these reasons she is the substratum of the act of the male [*der Tat des Mannes*] in which humanness becomes actualized."[64] This tribute is the active/passive dichotomy, and it would have weighed into the conservative side of post–World War I debate. Further in this direction, Barth states in *Christliche Dogmatik* that Schleiermacher had some correct things to say about "the other relation of woman to reconciliation [*Versöhnung*] in his *Weihnachtsfeier*." Here Barth refers to the idea (spelled out in *CD* I/2) that the female was naturally or spontaneously religious and did not need to be converted as

---

transgression by which sin entered into the world, on the second Adam of which the first is the type or figure, and on the universality of sin.

59. *Christliche Dogmatik*, 371, and *CD* I/2:193 (*KD* I/2:211) on the need to preserve the mystery of enhypostasis.

60. *CD* I/2:192, also 191 (*KD* I/2:210). *GD*, 163, and in *Christliche Dogmatik*, 374.

61. *GD*, 164.

62. *Christliche Dogmatik*, 374 (Barth's italics).

63. Barth comments in the first two dogmatics that there is, of course, a connection from the Virgin Mary to the Roman Catholic ideal of celibacy. To him the connection is neither totally incorrect nor totally correct, for in Christianity in this world, the sexual sphere will inevitably exist under a shadow. *GD*, 164–65; *Christliche Dogmatik*, 374.

64. *Christliche Dogmatik*, 373; see also *GD*, 163, regarding the impersonal substratum of history.

did the male.[65] Eve and the daughters of Eve are somewhat cleaner and purer than Adam. The romanticization or sentimentalizing exaltation of women is complementary to patriarchal history.

In *CD* I/2 there are changes in content beyond shifting the status of "the Joseph question" to parergon. The male acquires his power and creativity—the full extent of which we have seen—not as a distinction (in the *imago*) but as a result of the Fall. The lordship over the woman, and "therefore" the male's significance "for world history," is the sign of this situation and is the post-Fall punishment for both.[66] Barth also makes an implicit—almost explicit—response to the feminist criticism that can be presupposed in German and Swiss culture in the late 1920s and 30s. The response focuses on world history in a tentative but considered way. Nodded at in the post–World War I *Göttingen Dogmatics* ("Economics, politics, art and science, with some exceptions and exceptional circumstances such as we find today, are male affairs")[67] and again in *Christliche Dogmatik*, the possibility of historical significance for women is confronted in *CD* I/2:

> God alone knows whether the history of humanity, nations and states, art, science, economics, has in fact been and is so predominantly the history of males, the story of all the deeds and works of males, as it appears . . . or whether . . . the hidden factor of female cooperation and participation has not in fact always turned the scale in a way of which chronicles, acts and monuments give us no information, because it involves an element which is deeply concealed both psychologically and sociologically . . . though no less potent for that reason. Be that as it may, if there had been a matriarchate instead of a patriarchate and if perhaps there actually still is a matriarchate, nevertheless it is— well, "significant" that the historical consciousness of all nations,

---

65. *Christliche Dogmatik*, 373; *CD* I/2:195 (*KD* I/2:213). In *Weihnachtsfeier*, the child Sophie saw Mary in her own mother, and her mother concurred: "Every mother is another Mary" who devoutly sees and nurtures "the stirrings of the higher spirit" in her child (Schleiermacher, *Christmas Eve*, 48). Calmly loving and honoring Christ (and the divine in their children), women are contrasted to men, who only contend about him. Men, drawn into the world and its "restless striving" and "passionate conflict," must be "converted" to the Christian life. It is here that "the old proverb" cited above is brought into the discussion: women always remain children while "men must first be turned about to become so again" (ibid., 55).

66. *CD* I/2:193–94 (*KD* I/2:212).

67. *GD*, 163.

states and civilizations begins with the patriarchate. . . . The Biblical witness assumes this view.[68]

Female humanity is also reevaluated contrapuntally—and the evaluation is as much closed to correction as the question of male dominion is opened. On the one hand, Barth regrets that he was not clearer that Mary's virginity was not the *condition* for the revelation of God in Jesus Christ but a reference or indicator. This is a familiar Barthian motif. "The *ex virgine* must always be understood as a *pointer* [*Hinweis*—italics his] to this penetration [of God into historical humanity] and new beginning, but not as the conditioning of it."[69] Barth firmly rejects the Mariology that "involves a relative rivalry with Christ." Such reverence for Mary herself, apart from Christology, is the equivalent of the Roman Catholic conception of the church. He condemns both and notes that the rejection of Marian devotion in modern Protestantism is tainted by the same human-centeredness.[70] Mary's virginity in the birth of the Lord "is the denial not of man in the presence of God but of any power, attribute or capacity in him for God." Man lost "the capacity for God" through disobedience. "Upon this human nature a mystery must be wrought."[71] Clearly the active/passive dichotomy reinforces, and is reinforced by, Barth's theology of overwhelming grace.

On the other hand, despite Barth's "clarification"—which is theologically necessary—that he is not attributing a special capacity to woman as such, he raises a question that uncharacteristically muddies the water. It is prefaced by the self-conscious and highly defensive statement that "our language here cannot be too careful." Many years later in *CD* III/4 in 1951, when Barth and his world were very different, we encounter the same wariness. As he proceeds to develop his doctrine of superordinance and subordinance in the male/female relationship, he writes: "Every word is dangerous and liable to misunderstanding when we try to characterize this order."[72] The question in I/2 is whether "in contrast to the significant inappropriateness of the male to be the father of Emmanuel something positive should be said about a corresponding appropriateness in the female to be his mother."[73] He has already raised this question passingly

68. *CD* I/2:193 (*KD* I/2:211–12).
69. *CD* I/2:189 (*KD* I/2:207).
70. Ibid., 139–46, esp. 140–41, 145–46 (*KD* I/2:153–60).
71. Ibid., 188–89 (*KD* I/2:206).
72. *CD* III/4:169 (*KD* III/4:189).
73. *CD* I/2:194 (*KD* I/2:213).

in the *Christliche Dogmatik*. The suggestion by Schleiermacher that was cited in *Christliche Dogmatik* is specifically rejected here: those remarks about the connection between women and religion "would have been better unsaid."[74] However, Barth now notes as relevant to his question "what Goethe may have meant by 'the eternal feminine,'" although it cannot be said in any important theological sense [Barth's safety-hatch] that [the feminine] draws us 'upwards.'"[75] He also suggests, with a warning not to be led down the road to Rome, that some Catholic Mariology may legitimately point to the honor conferred upon Mary, *as* the representative of human nature, in God's revelation: the female, then, "is as significant for human nature as such as the male is for human history."[76] To think "further along these lines," Barth introduces the idea, which will be developed further by von Kirschbaum, that the Virgin Birth is a countersign to that of the post-Fall attainment of dominion by the male—though he does so with some grumbling. The male exclusion from the birth of our Lord is a "limitation of male preeminence" which should satisfy any woman who demands "justification and rehabilitation in face of the significant preeminence of the male for world history"— which "it is better that she should not do."[77]

Barth seems intrigued with the question of gender in the story of the Virgin Birth. The idea of the Virgin Birth as countersign is not only in line with "some Roman Catholic theology." It is also a more developed version of his earlier presentation of the Virgin Birth as a "reversal [which] takes place in favor of the female."[78] Barth changes the symbolic contrast for Mary from the traditional typology of Eve/Mary to that of woman/man. He is interested in the structure and meaning of scripturally based male-female differentiation as part of theology. His understanding of the relationship of male and female as illuminated in the countersign proves very fruitful: it reappears in III/1, III/2, and III/4, transformed

74. Ibid., 195 (*KD* I/2:213). Note that Schleiermacher's "deep knowledge of man and woman," which "cannot be denied," will inform Barth's later discussion of the *imago Dei* in *CD* III/4:124 (*KD* III/4:137).

75. *CD* I/2:195 (*KD* I/2:213). At the end of *Faust*, the Holy Virgin/Mother/Goddess is pure and graciously forgiving: love is the dominant note, as "die Ewig-Weibliche zieht uns hinan." Friedrich Heiler, whose Mariology Barth criticizes in *CD* I/2:141, also referred approvingly to Goethe as one of the princes of poetry who understood and wrote of the Madonna ("The Madonna as Religious Symbol," in *The Mystic Vision: Papers from the Eranos Yearbooks*, trans. Ralph Manheim, Bollingen Series 30, vol. 6 [Princeton: Princeton University Press, 1968], 350).

76. *CD* I/2:195 (*KD* I/2:213).

77. *CD* I/2:194 (*KD* I/2:212).

78. *GD*, 163.

into the dynamic of inversion, a basic concept in his new doctrine of the *imago Dei*, in which superordination and subordination are relativized. The new *imago* doctrine in III/1 changes and undermines Barth's particular doctrines of man and woman; however, his prejudices about both male and female humanity remain and affect his exposition of the *imago*.

From the early 1930s onward, Barth seems more open to the recognition of women as equal in value to men and of greater value than church and culture have allowed. He is willing to advocate this recognition and he *wants* to benefit from this value. Further evidence of his openness is in the three-way debate in the *Reformierte Kirchenzeitung* in 1932, cited by von Kirschbaum for the light it sheds on "an inappropriate stubbornness" in Reformed circles on participation by women in church proclamation.[79] The exchange began when Gertrud Herrmann, who identified herself as a *Theologin*, wrote to the Swiss church newspaper in defense of a female pastor in the canton of Graubünden ("Frau Caprez") who lived apart from her husband in order to do her job. Herrmann argued that God can call particular women in particular situations to atypical paths, and we can neither censure the women who follow such calls nor close our minds to other possible callings in the future. In a *Nachwort*, the editor ("Pastor" D. Wilhelm Rolfhaus) took the position that Herrmann opposed: that the orders of creation with regard to women were universal and inviolable. Barth jumped in to defend Fräulein Herrmann. He did not champion the opening of the pastorate to women; he did expand on Herrmann's point about God's freedom and about the lack of total clarity in scripture—which was such, he notes, that it was once used to defend slavery in the U.S. southern states.[80] If we also remember that in the 1930s Barth became increasingly dependent on von Kirschbaum, there seems to be a disjunction between his life and work on one hand and his theological anthropology on the other.

79. In von Kirschbaum, "The Role of Women," 103 (Shepherd:183).

80. *Reformierte Kirchenzeitung*, 1932, nos. 25 ("Ungehorsam gegen Gottes Gebot?" by G. Herrmann and "Nachwort" by D. W. Rolfhaus); 28 ("Der Schrift gehorsam" by Karl Barth and response by Rolfhaus); 30 ("Noch einmal: Der Schrift gehorsam" by Barth and response by Rolfhaus). On Gertrud Herrmann, see Andrea Bieler, "Aspekte national-sozialistischer Frauenpolitik," in '*Darum wagt es, Schwestern*,' 253–54. In 1932 Herrmann also opposed the Nazi ideology as the replacement of the living God by a human self-projection. She said that Nazism, like the Marxist *Menschenbild*, obscured the reality of sin.

Enter von Kirschbaum

Charlotte von Kirschbaum disliked stereotypes about women, among which she included the "Marian woman," the "eternal feminine," "the religious one," or Mary as the cosmic force of selfless devotion (*Hingebungsgewalt des Kosmos*):[81] we can expect differences between her treatment of Mary and Barth's, although the differences exist in the context of deep agreement. Von Kirschbaum talks about the Virgin Mary extensively in two essays (the fourth and fifth in *WF*) and in a separate excursus in which her attention is devoted to criticizing Catholic Mariology. The essays are "Die 'Mutter der Lebendigen'" (The Mother of All Living), with an excursus on Mary in current mariological discussion, and "Kritische Ausblicke" (Critical Views), a review of Gertrud von Le Fort's *Die ewige Frau* (1934, Swiss ed. 1947) followed by a review of Simone de Beauvoir's *Le deuxième sexe*. The two form her dialogical situation. Le Fort's work is a principal Catholic source for Barth too. Because it is itself critical of excesses in the cult of Mary, Barth and von Kirschbaum can focus on the central issues.[82]

Like Barth, von Kirschbaum regards recognition of any positive human role in salvation, any mediatory or intercessionary role, as a denial of the exclusive purpose and accomplishment of Christ. To speak of the reception of grace, of a positive, effective quality in Mary's response to the annunciation, is similarly unchristological. But to von Kirschbaum it is also unrealistic and unfair to women to posit a connection between female nature and religiosity. Here she proceeds independently of Barth. She affirms his idea that the Virgin Birth is a countersign to the post-Fall dominion of the male. She highlights the honor Mary received through grace in bearing Jesus, which counterbalances the subordination of Eve to Adam after the Fall,[83] and she is (as we shall further see) very preoccu-

---

81. Von Kirschbaum, "The Role of Women," 117 (Shepherd:196); *WF*, 79, 83–84 (Shepherd:150, 156–57).

82. Von Kirschbaum: *WF*, 57–87 (Shepherd:121–60); Barth: *CD* I/2:145 (*KD* I/2:159). Note that each found personally relevant material in Le Fort. Barth points out that Le Fort converted to Catholicism after editing and publishing Troeltsch's *Glaubenslehre* after his death: Barth sees her course as parallel to his own rejection of Troeltsch's synthesis of "Bible, history, and inner experience" (*CD* IV/1:386–87 [*KD* IV/1:427]). Von Kirschbaum (*WF*, 80–87 [Shepherd:149–60]) appreciates Le Fort's recognition of the male need of the female for totality and of positive possibilities in the husband/wife relationship apart from child rearing and of relationships between a male and a female friend or *Arbeitsgehilfin* (though she thinks Le Fort undermines the possibilities by focusing on the two privileged female roles of virgin and mother).

83. *WF*, 67 (Shepherd:133).

pied with denying that scriptural precepts for female subordination to the male are either demeaning or inhibitory. But there are more than differences of emphasis between von Kirschbaum's writings on Mary on the one hand and Barth or her Catholic sources on the other. Unencumbered by notions of female passivity and orientation to higher reality, von Kirschbaum can counter Catholic *and* Protestant—Liberal Protestant and dialectical!—anthropologies of gender with another view of women.

A comparison of von Kirschbaum's explication of the Virgin Birth as countersign to the dominance of the male in human history with Barth's parallel text in I/2 offers a very clear example of the appropriation and rewriting that, I think, best describes their collaboration. Von Kirschbaum cites the Barth text.[84] Remember that she is composing her lecture some ten years, and a world war, after Barth wrote I/2. She begins with a reference to Mary's experience in pregnancy: "Mary was the first to experience—and did so in her own body—the incarnation of the Son of God."[85] Barth would not object to this, but he didn't say anything like it. Next von Kirschbaum uses Barth's exact words and phrases to rewrite one of his sentences in a woman's version: "World history may ascribe the historical deed to the male, but the history of Jesus Christ is not a history of men!"[86] Then she repeats, with no change, Barth's observation that the location of the conception of Jesus in the marriage of Mary and Joseph might have been more beneficial to a Christian ethic of marriage than the actual story: no alternative vision needed here.[87] Von Kirschbaum goes on to conclude, of the countersign, "Here woman is given primacy in a way that surpasses all other privileging."[88] Barth's gruff conclusion, it will be recalled, was that, if a woman demands rehabilitation in face of the significant preeminence of the male for world history—which she should not do—then she can find it here. Von Kirschbaum's use of Barth's work, at a post–World War II conference on women in Bièvres, demonstrates gratitude, adaptiveness, and ingenuity.

Georges Casalis expressed his gratitude to Charlotte von Kirschbaum for opening to him a feminist reading of scripture.[89] An essential part of

84. Ibid., 67 (Shepherd:133), referring to *CD* I/2:194–95.
85. "Maria darf als Erste die Fleischwerdung des Sohnes Gottes an ihrem eigenen Leib erfahren" (ibid., 66 [Shepherd:133]).
86. Ibid. ["Mag die Weltgeschichte dem Manne die geschichtliche Tat zuschreiben, die Geschichte Jesu Christi ist keine Männergeschichte!"]
87. Ibid.
88. Ibid. ["Hier wird die Frau in einer Weise vogeordnet, die jede andere Vorordnung überbietet."]
89. Statement in Köbler, *In the Shadow*, 139.

von Kirschbaum's adaptation of Barth is a different utilization of scripture and scriptural interpretation. The major contrast is that Barth's exegetical commentary is theological rather than historical-critical, whereas von Kirschbaum's engages equally with historical context and contemporary application. Barth's approach was well known since he published his commentary on Romans (see his prefaces to the first and second editions) and debated with Harnack.[90] Von Kirschbaum's different path is in unexpected contrast. Her approach may be based on lesser confidence as a theologian, and it probably reflects her role as maker of the card file. The proximity of Oscar Cullmann's classroom to Barth's and the collegial relationship of Barth and von Kirschbaum with Cullmann may have encouraged her independence: she uses Cullmann on the liturgy of the first Christians.[91] We must also remember that it is sometimes only in the outward, final result of his exegesis that Barth is "unhistorical."[92] But the contrast in von Kirschbaum's text also reflects disagreement and perhaps mild criticism.

Barth is ready enough to do exegesis on significant women in the Bible to illustrate non-gender-specific theological points— for example, his lengthy commentary on Abigail, wife of the fool Nabal, in *CD* IV/2:427ff. His treatment of women in Acts, which is a very important source for von Kirschbaum, is similarly focused. Barth censures the "egoistic partnership" of Ananias and Sapphira, contrasting it to the "positive example" of "inner fellowship and outward witness" of Aquila "and his possibly more noteworthy wife Priscilla."[93] Von Kirschbaum sees Priscilla as evidence of the considerable share women played in the mission of the early church, including participation in proclamation, however much modern church historians dispute or deny this role. For her view, she cites Zscharnack, *Der Dienst der Frau in den ersten Jahrhunderten der christlichen Kirche* (1902)—a source Barth does not use—and excitedly cites Harnack's opinion that Priscilla might even be the author of the epistle to the Hebrews. She goes on to discuss two

90. See their exchange in James M. Robinson, ed., *The Beginnings of Dialectical Theology*, 165–87.

91. Von Kirschbaum, *WF*, 51 (Shepherd:111–12).

92. Bruce McCormack makes this observation in "Historical Criticism and Dogmatic Interest in Karl Barth's Theological Exegesis of the New Testament," in *Biblical Hermeneutics in Historical Perspective: Studies in Honor of Karlfried Froehlich on His Sixtieth Birthday*, ed. Mark S. Burrows and Paul Rorem (Grand Rapids, Mich.: Wm. B. Eerdmans, 1991), 322–38.

93. *CD* III/4:225 (*KD* III/4:252).

other female co-workers with Paul in Philippi, Euodia and Syntyche, noting that Harnack includes their importance in proclamation.[94]

Von Kirschbaum sees in the women of Acts and the Epistles a concrete historical message. Fully aware from her study of Simone de Beauvoir that gender roles are historically constructed and historically varied, she is open to, and finds in scripture, a reality that is adaptable and relevant for women in her own time. Barth, by contrast, does not focus on the New Testament women *as* women, and he seems, moreover, to expect less than he might find. The examples he highlights serve as illustrations of general moral precepts rather than models for structuring communities. This is consistent with his rejection of attempts at historical reconstructions of the original church communities as in Brunner's concept of *ecclesia*.[95] Such reconstructions import their own programs, to the detriment of church law and the institutionalized church. They obscure and reject the only normative ideals we can (and should) take from scripture: the "brotherly" and "living community of the living Lord Jesus Christ."[96] For the latter point Barth cites E. Schweizer, in whom von Kirschbaum had found support for her close focus: for example, on the relation between church congregation and minister.[97]

The two also use Markus Barth's *Der Augenzeuge* very differently. Barth draws from it support for the absolute historicity, as well as the uniqueness, of revelation in Jesus Christ as recounted in scripture.[98] Von Kirschbaum's use of the work seems to be a very rare instance of overzealousness in highlighting the positive role of women in Christianity. She draws upon *Der Augenzeuge* to explain why women were not included among the apostles and in their mission after the resurrection. It is because the Twelve, and they alone, were given the specific office of witnessing to the wider world. So it was *not*, she tells us, because of an inherent weakness in women, nor was it to satisfy social convention.[99] After all, the New Testament makes it clear that neither rationale prevented women from being among Jesus' community and fulfilling their

---

94. Von Kirschbaum, *WF*, 39 (Shepherd:97). Her statement of Harnack's opinion: "Harnack even thought Priscilla might be the author of Hebrews!" Harnack was one of the very few male supporters of university education for women in his time (Moltmann-Wendel, "The Women's Movement in Germany," 123).

95. Barth detects a pietist background in the concept. *CD* IV/2:685–86 (*KD* IV/2:776–7).

96. *CD* IV/2:686 (*KD* IV/2:776).

97. Von Kirschbaum, "The Role of Women," 119 (Shepherd:197).

98. *CD* III/2:439f. (*KD* III/2:527f.).

99. *WF*, 24 [citing *Der Augenzeuge*, 254, and referring, in disagreement, to a recent Dutch study by Rasker] (Shepherd:78).

own roles in God's economy on Easter morning and, afterward, as representative of the *Gemeinde* that is the church.

Barth's reservations about the uses of early church history are consistent with his particularistic reading of scripture as the history of God's elect people that is revealed ultimately in Jesus Christ. Thus "when Scripture speaks of man it does not allow our attention or thoughts to lose themselves in any self-selected generalities. In the Bible we are not concerned with the abstract concept of man, or with the human race as a whole, or with the being and destiny of the individual man as such."[100] So we should not expect a conclusion or set of conclusions on the role of women in the church and church community, or the story of women as a distinct part of the history of God's people. There is an exception: in his exegesis of Genesis 1:27 and 2:18–24 in the III/1 presentation of the *imago*, Barth will pursue his interest in gender balance and the inversion of genders in God's economy that he first found in the sign of the Virgin Birth. We shall return to this below.

Von Kirschbaum typically works from successive stories of individual women in Old and New Testaments and sees emerging patterns. She begins her lecture on the "Mother of All Living" with an effort to find out from scripture what motherhood means. "The mother of all living" points us necessarily (i.e., traditionally) to the name of Eve and then to a reading of Genesis 3:16. The bearing of children in pain must be understood in the context of the whole Hebrew Bible: this childbearing is also serving as an instrument of God's grace.[101] Barth's exegesis of Genesis 3:16 focuses only on the dominion of husband over wife; he simply does not include the bearing of children in his line of attention.

Von Kirschbaum reminds her audience that a woman in ancient Israel could attain a worthy position only through bearing and giving a son to her husband. Following Wilhelm Vischer, she likens the history of Israel to a body that hopes and waits for a son.[102] Though God alone decides who will fulfill his promise, it is understandable that Old Testament women would do anything to preserve and advance the cause of their sons. The mothers of the living whom von Kirschbaum presents are those women who were first barren and only conceived after God heard their (or their husbands') prayers—Sarah, Rebecca, Rachel. They are also those women who schemed and deceived to protect their sons and thereby secure God's plan—for example, Rebecca. So it is no

100. *CD* II/2:55.
101. *WF*, 62 (Shepherd:127).
102. *WF*, 57–58, 60 (Shepherd:121–23, 125).

surprise that Matthew begins his gospel with a lengthy Old Testament genealogy of Jesus that, departing from the ancient convention of naming males only, includes four female ancestors (*Stammütter*).The four are not moral paragons, and they are not, in fact, Israelites. The distressing lives and deeds in the stories of Tamar, Rahab, Ruth, and "the wife of Uriah" (Bathsheba) and the fact that they are actually foreigners in Israel constitute a riddle, a mystery, until one realizes that their human inadequacy is the point. "The red thread [*rote Faden*] that connects them" is that they are chosen to be, as they could only be, work tools of God.[103] The incongruity of Sarah's motherhood also demonstrates this theme. Over and over again God fulfills his promise despite the unfaithfulness of his people.[104] Nothing in Israel is as one would expect.

Von Kirschbaum has painted a feminine vista of the strange new world that Barth found in the Bible. Barth's exegesis of the wisdom of Solomon in 1 Kings 3:16ff.—the story of disputed motherhood—declares "the red thread that runs through the whole history of Israel" to be the coexistence of two peoples—the hidden true (or elect) and the untrue, the one that looks outside itself to serve that which is God's and the one that looks only to itself.[105] Von Kirschbaum agrees in her own way. To her the enigma of which of the two women in the story of Solomon is the genuine mother "goes through the whole history of this people." The two harlots of the story demonstrate the difference between a true "motherhood of living hope" and an untrue motherhood of self-interest.[106] It is spiritual (*geistliche*) not biological motherhood that is decisive. Thus Isaiah—one can assume this has special meaning for von Kirschbaum— could praise the barren one whose children will people the desolate cities (Isa. 54:1ff.). The prophetic women of the Old Testament are examples of such spiritual mothers or mothers of living hope. Deborah, Zipporah, Abigail, and Huldah brought the power of God's word to Israel in its time of need.

Mary is the fifth *Stammütter* in Matthew's genealogy. Von Kirschbaum, like Barth, finds the miracle of Christianity reflected in Mary's acceptance of what she cannot understand, that it truly is God who has chosen her for his purpose. Von Kirschbaum quotes Luther at length here; she observes that Joseph, in accepting the child into his household,

103. Ibid., 59, 60–62 (Shepherd:124, 126–27).
104. Ibid., 59 (Shepherd:123).
105. *CD* II/1:434 (*KD* II/1:488–89).
106. *WF*, 62–63 (Shepherd:128).

gave Jesus the social conditions for his temporal life required by ancient law. She is also interested in Mary's postnativity and postcrucifixion life and its significance. Mary retreats to the background of the Gospel stories after fulfilling her service in salvation history—a background that is brought forward at the crucifixion (and we might note that Barth's comments about Grünewald's depiction do not include Mary). Mary's only future is with the apostles, with the disciples of the Lord—no more and no less. For Mary is another one of scripture's mothers of living hope. Immersed in human life, she happens to be the foremost representative of God's community from Israel (*Gemeinde aus Israel*).[107] As Mother of the apostles ("Woman, there is your son . . . Son, there is your mother"), she is the future of God's *Gemeinde*.

Women, all women, are potentially mothers of the living. Creativity—the defining attribute that Barth assigns to the male—is von Kirschbaum's subject. Von Kirschbaum is an early feminist in religion. She thinks in terms of the structures of the institutional church and shares Barth's hierarchicalism about male vis-à-vis female. But she does not define women or men restrictively by spheres. Thus the creativity of motherhood, depicted unambivalently and vibrantly, can be a dominant theme in von Kirschbaum's biblical exegeses and Marian theology. It contradicts the passiveness in post-Romantic Catholic and Protestant anthropologies of women alike.

In deifying Mary, von Kirschbaum argues, Catholic Mariology deprives us of the one we can trust, the one who makes it clear (quoting and paraphrasing Luther, as does Barth) that Christ might dwell in us as he did in her.[108] The Roman Catholic Mary is not the Mary of the Gospels, not Mary of Nazareth. The Queen of Heaven is the human dream of the possession of grace. Grace imprisoned in that perpetual image separates us from the possibility of any real encounter with grace.[109] Marian devotion also isolates believer from fellow-believer and believer from the world. Oriented toward a myth, it bypasses reality (*Wirklichkeit*).[110] This is Barth's understanding and teaching on the Christian life, freed from his notions about gender and its role in human history. We will later see that despite all of von Kirschbaum's disagreements with Simone de Beauvoir, she likes her historicity: the concreteness, the prioritizing of

107. Ibid., 8 (Shepherd:134).
108. Ibid., 70–71 (Shepherd:137–38).
109. Ibid., 84 (Shepherd:157).
110. Ibid., 87 (Shepherd:160).

existence or act over essence and abstraction.[111] We live in the thick of the real world—and it must be remembered that the community in which von Kirschbaum thinks one must immerse one's self in order to serve is the church and the world of Weimar Germany, Nazi and anti-Nazi Europe, and postwar Europe.

Von Kirschbaum's approach to Marian theology is typical of her work. One finds a similar laying of scriptural foundations for a theology of women's role in proclamation. She confronts in detail texts that she recognizes as obstacles—most notably the injunction to silence of women in the church in 1 Timothy 2:11. She draws on exegetes ranging from Calvin to her contemporaries, some well known and some not, in search of the specific context of the epistle. She concludes that the women of Ephesus to whom the epistle refers were rejecting the role of bearing children: it is their gross misunderstanding of the coming of Christ that had to be silenced.[112]

When von Kirschbaum looks at individual women in the New Testament, she finds that many perform, and define, the function of witness. The entourage (*Umgebung*) of Jesus includes married and unmarried women: neither chastity nor childbearing has special meaning. Some New Testament women illustrate types of encounter that Jesus had with his *Gemeinde*: he performs healings; he treats the community as his counterpart (*Gegenüber*). A very Barthian doctrine of the life of the church is read off here.

3. Toward a Theology of the Image of God and a Collaboration

In exegesis, Von Kirschbaum is drawing as much on the doctrine of the *imago Dei* that she and Barth have come to share as on her rejection of female stereotyping. In contrast to Marian devotion, male and female in a life of solidarity, of genuine encounter, *are* living in gratitude to God—such a life is worship.[113] Only such a man and woman are *actual* humanity—*wirkliche Mensch*, a phrase Barth uses prominently in *CD* III/2, and a phrase surely alluded to (along with "ewige Frau") in von

111. Ibid., 94–95 (Shepherd:169).
112. Ibid., 53–55 (Shepherd:115–17).
113. Ibid., 86 (Shepherd:158).

Kirschbaum's *Wirkliche Frau*.[114] Echoing Barth on sin, von Kirschbaum maintains that "a christologically-based anthropology cannot seriously consider an isolated human being. Relational existence in the world is God's command and God's gift to us."[115]

To Barth's and von Kirschbaum's joint and dual development of the doctrine of the *imago Dei* we now turn. Here the collaboration as one between equals seems to quicken. In the pattern that emerges, von Kirschbaum follows or appropriates Barth's exegeses of the principal Old Testament texts in Genesis and the Song of Songs. Apparently she did not read Hebrew: there is no evidence that she did, as there is for other languages.[116] But we must remember that it is during Barth's dictation of the *imago* material that von Kirschbaum said, "You stole that from me." In this light, his exegesis seems in considerable part to be the result of their discussions. Barth, in turn, follows or appropriates von Kirschbaum on the principal New Testament texts on women per se (e.g., 1 Cor. 11:3f. and Eph. 5:22f.). But it seems highly likely that the Old Testament exegesis is in her mind when, in regard to Ephesians 5:30, she echoes the decisive move of Barth's on Genesis 1:27—the significance of the shift to the plural "Let us."[117] As important as the verse in Ephesians is to Barth, he does not focus here on the grammatical change. The grammatical observation is the signature of a student of Barth working independently. My analysis of parallel text clusters below is intended to further describe the pattern of their collaboration. Where there seems only to be unison, I will quote from them alternately.

Before III/1, Barth's doctrine of the *imago* moves through several stages and reflects tentative, slowly emerging interest in the subject. In the first stage, from the *Göttingen Dogmatics* through *CD* I/1 and I/2, he treats it only as part of other issues, and it is largely conventional. In *Nein*, his response to Brunner's *Natur und Gnade*, he sharply rejects Brunner's distinction between formal and material image. But Barth's concern is with the doctrine of the knowledge of God that Brunner based on the "point of contact," the formal image that remains in humankind after the Fall. He corrects Brunner's theology and his reading of Calvin; he does not himself offer a "correct" doctrine of the image of

114. Ibid., 85 (Shepherd: 158); *CD* III/2:32 (*KD* III/2:36) and then as the title of par. 44, sec. 3.
115. *WF*, 85 (Shepherd:158).
116. Köbler, *In the Shadow*, 36, 41, on von Kirschbaum's study of Latin and English.
117. *WF*, 21: "Förmlich jubelnd macht der Text diese Aussage und geht dabei plötzlich in die Wir-Form über" (Shepherd:74). On Barth's grammatical analysis, see below, page 139.

God. His concern is to assert humanity's total dependence on the work of the divine: the *imago* is actualized by the Holy Spirit.[118] Within Barth's dogmatics are nuances and departures from tradition that will be important when he moves into his final version of the *imago*. In *CD* II the doctrine moves toward central importance, but all ingredients are not yet in place.

In the *Göttingen Dogmatics* and *Christliche Dogmatik* (as we have seen) Barth characterizes the *imago* in Adam as the creativity and activity by which the male has dominion in this world. Perverted in the Fall, the image must be restored by a second Adam.[119] This characterization is conventional in Barth's time and in his theological tradition. *Die Religion in Geschichte und Gegenwart* (*RGG*), a reliable source for early and mid–twentieth-century German Protestant thought explicitly and by example, discusses the *imago* tradition in the article "Anthropologie," where it is described as dominion over the world along with love for humankind.[120] The dominion of humankind over creation had also been accepted by Luther and Calvin as part of God's created order. Luther distinguishes between pre-Fall dominion, based on wisdom and harmony with all of creation, and the post-Fall dominion of fear and discord, which has only a shadow of the effectiveness that it had before the Fall.[121] The dominion of husband over wife is part of the post-Fall dispensation.

It is sometimes pointed out that there are two traditions in the history of the doctrine of the *imago Dei*: on the one hand, the substantialist or essentialist (and basically Greek) tradition; on the other hand, the relational and dynamic tradition, which looks to biblical, especially Old

118. Barth had stressed this point earlier in the important lecture of 1929, "The Holy Spirit and the Christian Life," which identified the image of God in humankind with the Holy Spirit as (and only as) it brings grace to us (*The Holy Ghost and the Christian Life*, esp. 15–18). Joan E. O'Donovan, in "Man in the Image of God: The Disagreement Between Barth and Brunner Reconsidered," *Scottish Journal of Theology* 39 (1986) makes the important suggestion (452–53) that Barth's rejection of Brunner's stress on human capacity—on *Wortmächtigkeit*—to respond to God's call has a contemporary dimension in 1934. Barth requires that the image of God be common to all humans including "newborn children and idiots." This is a rebuke to the emerging Nazi ideology of racial purification.

119. *GD*, 163, and *Christliche Dogmatik*, 372.

120. *RGG*, s.v. "Anthropologie," part 4 [col. 421]: "Nur im wirklichen Glauben an Gott ist der M. gottebenbildlich, seinem Gottähnlich in der Lieb zu den M.en und in der Herrschaft über die Welt."

121. Jane Dempsey Douglass, "The Image of God in Women as Seen by Luther and Calvin," in *Image of God and Gender Models*, ed. Kari E. Børreson (Oslo: Solum Verlag, 1991), 238.

Testament, narrative. *Relational* can refer to the human/divine relationship or to interhuman relationships.[122] Wolfhart Pannenberg situates the Reformers largely, if not entirely, in the relational tradition. For them the image of God consists in the actual relation to God, whereas for medieval Latin Scholasticism the image is a presupposition for this relation and is a formal structural property of human nature. Pannenberg compares the latter to the "remnant of the image" in Brunner's doctrine.[123]

Barth's first discussion of the *imago Dei* in *CD* (in I/1) is part of his presentation of the *analogia fidei*. Though he evokes Reformation—especially Reformed—doctrine, he does not exploit the relational tradition. First, the image of God is consonance with God's word or conformity with God's will or, in Barth's favored phrase, conformity to God. Second and *contra* Brunner, the image was decisively lost—"totally annihilated"[124]—in the Fall. Conformity can only be restored by God, through the atonement of the Son and through the Holy Spirit. Barth adapts a favored term of Calvin, *rectitude*: "man's possibility for the Word of God through faith."[125] More specifically, "to the image of God in man which was lost in Adam but restored in Christ there also belongs the fact that man can hear God's Word. . . . [it is] as a capacity of the incapable."[126] It is acceptable to call such hearing a "point of contact," and this is "what the theologians call 'the image of God in man.'" It should not be confused with Brunner's "point of contact" or with the Roman Catholic *analogia entis*. The point of contact of which Barth speaks is *not* proper to the human as part of one's humanity and personality.[127] Ultimately, this capacity or conformity exists only in God's eyes. Though it is darkness to us, "the possibility of the human" can become "the adequate divine possibility."[128] How is it manifested and how do we have access to it? Through the analogy of faith and in proclamation. "In faith and confession the Word of God becomes a human thought and a human word, certainly in infinite dissimilarity and inadequacy, yet not

122. See survey in R. Umidi, "Imaging God Together," chap. 1.
123. Wolfhart Pannenberg, *Anthropology in Theological Perspective*, trans. Matthew O'Connell (Philadelphia: Westminster Press, 1985), 50. With respect to both traditions, however, Garrett Green has observed that "virtually all" versions of the *imago* "from the Church Fathers to the Enlightenment assume the creation, fall, and restoration of the image to be something affecting the soul" (*Imagining God: Theology and the Religious Imagination* [San Francisco: Harper & Row, 1989], 98).
124. *CD* I/1: 238 (*KD* I/1:251).
125. Ibid., 238, 239 (*KD* I/1:251).
126. Ibid., 241 (*KD* I/1:254).
127. Ibid., 238–39 (*KD* I/1:251–52).
128. Ibid., 243 (*KD* I/1:256).

in total alienation from its real prototype, but a true copy for all its human and sinful perversion, an unveiling of it even as its veiling."[129] At the close of the discussion, Barth evokes the Luther who knew faith to be "a mighty, active, restless, busy thing, which alike reneweth a man, beareth him elsewhere, and leadeth him altogether into a new way and nature, such wise that 'tis impossible that the same should not do good works without intermission."[130] But the fruits of faith do not dominate Barth's discussion of the *imago*, for he is here concerned with "the vertical from above." His discussion "is meant only as recollection of the promise and as expectation of its future fulfillment."[131]

It is important to note, in contrast to the *Göttingen* and *Christliche Dogmatik*, that dominion is not part of the *CD* I/1 discussion of the image. This is consistent with *CD* I/2 in which (as we have seen) dominion in the world—not just the dominion of husband over wife—is attributed to the male as a post-Fall condition rather than "an original mark of distinction."[132] Also notably absent (in light of Barth's final doctrine) are male/female differences. These were sometimes important in the early church and of moderate interest in the sixteenth century—either to give higher status to the male or to contend that position by denying gender specificity for the image.[133]

In III/1 there is something truly new that is at the same time absolutely consistent with what precedes it: the *imago* as male/female I-Thou relationship. This follows upon another necessary foundational concept: that of the covenant or *Bund*.[134] In *CD* II, parts 1 (1940) and 2 (1942), the *imago Dei* is involved in the doctrine of Election, for it is the image of God in humankind upon which the election of humankind is based. The likeness of God in us means that we are created to bear witness to God's existence in our existence.[135] Barth does not elaborate on the content of

---

129. Ibid., 241 (*KD* I/1:254).
130. Ibid., 246 (*KD* I/1:259–60).
131. Ibid., 241–42 (*KD* I/1:254–55).
132. *CD* I/2: 194 (*KD* I/2:212).
133. Neither Luther nor Calvin was very interested in gender differences in the image, though they occasionally dealt with the subject and Calvin inclined toward inclusiveness. From this viewpoint, he questioned whether dominion was a *major* part of the *imago*. On the whole, in the traditional view that they too accepted, Eve was included in the image though she was assumed to be weaker: the male was "more fully made in God's image" (Douglass, "The Image of God in Women," esp. 307–8).
134. See Wolf Krötke, "Gott und Mensch als 'Partner.' Zur Bedeutung einer zentralen Kategorien in Karl Barths Kirchlicher Dogmatik," in *Theologie als Christologie: Zum Werk und Leben Karl Barths*, 106–20.
135. *CD* II/1:188 (*KD* II/1:211).

the image, but he does elaborate on its dynamic. The divine likeness that is in us, though not from us, is necessarily active. It will be manifested *as* we live rather than in discreet actions that we perform, and it will always take place in unity with others. "To hear and obey the command of God is always to be on the way to fellowship."[136]

I must underscore the abrupt and genuine newness of the male/female, I-Thou identity of the *imago*. It is not in the passages on the image of God in II/2. Nor is there a gap to be filled there. While Barth argues there that true relationship with God necessarily means true relationship with fellow humanity, his thinking on relationships in II/2 is different from that in the I-Thou concept. Moral fellowship among Christians is still construed as a convergence or finding of oneness amid diversity, not the mutual apprehending and embracing of otherness. God's will is one, and it is the command of his goodness. It is one "in spite of the diversity of its expression."[137] All the differences among humans—historical, national, social, and vocational—are the gifts of one grace. And God's will applies to *all*: Was not Paul's purpose to preserve inner unity as the root of the outward unity of the body of Christ?[138]

Despite a reference in *CD* II/1 to the creation of woman as man's helper "who can also be an opposite [*Gegenüber*] to him," Barth's thinking about women is fundamentally unchanged in *CD* II.[139] The story of the creation of this helper and opposite has two meanings. First it demonstrates that the man God created is not merely a sexual being. He was created to love and nourish and cherish the woman as the creature of his own flesh. In Ephesians 5:31, Paul related Genesis 2:18ff. to the great mystery that is Christ and the church. And thus—Barth's second point—the creation story in Genesis points "far and fundamentally beyond and above the man." Like nonbiblical stories, it is a cosmogony and anthropogony, but at the same time it is the promise of revelation and reconciliation. It is the characterization of the world as "good," as determined and adapted as the theater of revelation, which will be called Jesus Christ.[140] The one earlier *CD* exegesis on the creation of male and female, in I/2, comments only on the absence of superordination and subordination before the Fall.[141]

---

136. *CD* II/2:413, 717 (*KD* II/2:457, 801).
137. Ibid., 714 (*KD* II/2:798).
138. Ibid., 714–16 (*KD* II/2:798–800).
139. *CD* II/1:118 (*KD* II/1 [1940]:130).
140. Ibid.
141. *CD* I/2:193–94 (*KD* I/2:212).

Something extraneous seems to have happened to account for the important change in III/1. George Hunsinger has referred to the I-Thou concept, which Barth attributes to Confucius, Feuerbach, and Buber, as an assimilated concept rather than a derived doctrine: within the theology of the *imago* only the doctrine of co-humanity is derived (essentially) from Barth's own theology, namely from Jesus' self-giving in Barth's Christology.[142] As students of Barth's life know, he always learned from others.[143] III/1 is a perfect development but not a necessary one, not a "missing piece of the puzzle" or the solution to a problem. In addition to being new, the III/1 doctrine of the image of God requires some revision of previously presented material about order and difference in relationships. However, it is strikingly congruent with an earlier presence in Barth, one that many also recognize as a continuing subcurrent in all of *CD*: dialectical theology itself.

In summary, the *imago Dei* in humankind is, first, an I-Thou relationship: that of male and female in encounter, understood and modeled (from an infinite distance) after the way God loves—freely and with unshakable commitment. God's love has been revealed to us in the covenant of the Old Testament (and the I-Thou relationship of God and the individual believer that follows from the covenant) and in the trinitarian being that God chose for Godself and showed forth in Jesus Christ. The relationship in the *imago*, like that between the divine and the human in the scriptural model, is personal, occurring between two subjects rather than subject and object, and consisting of personal address and response. And it is between two who are radically "other"— to one another and for one another.

Like the covenant, marriage is the "indestructible connection and fellowship between two subjects which are indestructibly distinct."[144] The relationship consists of love or, rather, defines love. The I-Thou relationship of husband and wife is the human paradigm. Other human relationships can and should follow the paradigm for genuine encounter, though they do so with less potential for it. (Isolated existence, like sin, is a theological impossibility.) It is also the case, Barth states with wonderful clarity, that the *imago* was neither lost nor virtually lost in the Fall.[145] This, in contrast to his earlier conception of an image that was

---

142. Hunsinger, *How to Read Karl Barth*, 62–63.
143. This is a motif in the writings of Eberhard Busch on Barth.
144. *CD* III/2:320 (*KD* III/2:386).
145. *CD* III/2:324 (*KD* III/2:391). Gunnlauger A. Jónsson (*The Image of God: Genesis 1:26–28 in a Century of Old Testament Research* [Stockholm: Almqvist & Wiksell, 1988], 72)

"totally annihilated" when Adam, and with him Eve, brought sin into the world.

Second, this I-Thou relationship is an ordered one, and its order is hierarchical. To Barth and most of his contemporaries, order had to be hierarchical but did not necessarily entail an ascending and descending scale of value or loss of freedom: Barth spoke most often of coordination and mutuality. In this sense, the order of creation that prioritized male humanity over female could also be egalitarian. The effect of the Fall was to disturb the mutual relationship of male and female: the "definite order" established in creation was thrown into confusion, giving rise to the blind dominion of the male and to female resentment of dominion.[146]

In the *imago Dei*, through faith the woman is subordinate and obedient to the man but chooses to be so, just as the man is subordinate to Christ, and the Son of God is subordinate to God the Father. For the male/female I-Thou relationship of husband and wife, von Kirschbaum's preferred analogy is the relation of church community and Christ, its head. Thus she can point to the relation of Christ and community to help us to see marriage no longer in the sense of the old dispensation as a destroyed relationship, but rather in its original beauty.[147] Barth urges an understanding of the marriage relationship in light of the Trinity.[148]

Both Barth and Von Kirschbaum stress the nature of superordination and subordination as *relative*. Freedom in obedience is the core of the Reformation idea of Christian freedom. Barth's version or understanding of freedom in obedience is more fluid and, one can only say, more rationalized than the traditional doctrine. The fluidity comes from the concept of inversion, and this shifting of hierarchies within relationships is important. To say that the shifting is largely perceptual is to point to the analogy of faith, which is transformative. Yet there is a limit to the relative nature of superordination and subordination: the limit of the order of creation, *especially* as affected by the Fall. This order is parallel to the asymmetry of the I-Thou relationship between the human and the divine: the order is always from divine to human, from above or superior to below or inferior.

Third: If order is essential for Barth, dualism in the traditional sense of spirit versus flesh or soul versus body is not, and to oppose this

---

notes that Barth's revised position (that there is no radical loss of the *imago*) brings him into line with most Old Testament scholars.

146. *CD* III/1:310–11 (*KD* III/1:355–56) and again III/2:295–96 (*KD* III/2:356–57).
147. *WF*, 18 and parallel 86 (Shepherd: 70, 159).
148. *CD* IV/1:202 (*KD* IV/1:221–22).

dualism is a specific, pervasive intention of his thinking on relationality. We have seen that the rejection of dualism was a concern in his exposition of the doctrine of the Virgin Birth: Barth took pains to ensure that God never seemed to be excluding the realm of sexuality per se. Walter Lowe has elaborated on the full extent to which Barth opposed traditional dualism in his *Epistle to the Romans*.[149] Barth respected the same theme within Schleiermacher's discussions of marriage and did not hesitate to praise him for it: it was Schleiermacher's "most eager concern" to abolish "the dark shadow" of dualism implicit in Roman Catholic teaching on the higher perfection of celibacy.[150] Schleiermacher likewise insisted that a married couple that turned away from the world to be "all in all to each other" were impairing their full vocation of worldly existence.[151] Sexual intercourse is positive within the human unit of husband and wife in genuine I-Thou relationship.[152] Barth's most perfect expression of the human wholeness of the male/female relationship is in his insistence on seeing the eroticism of the Song of Songs as the second part and completion of the Old Testament statement on the man/woman relationship that was only begun in Genesis; though less extensively, von Kirschbaum makes the same point.[153]

Another essential element in the doctrine of the *imago* in von Kirschbaum and Barth is the separation and distinction of the marriage relationship from that of family: they are talking about the I-Thou relationship of wife and husband, apart from their roles as parents, apart from children. And beyond the sexual. What Barth intends (colorfully and with pastoral wisdom) is a three-part emancipation of the sphere of marriage: demythologizing, decentralizing, and de-demonization.[154] Demythologization will occur when all tendencies to divinization, as in Roman Catholic sacramentality and the unhealthy aspects of Schleiermacher's doctrine of marriage, are renounced.[155] De-demonization will occur when sex is viewed nondualistically.[156] And decentralizing will

149. Lowe, "Barth as Critic of Dualism: Re-reading the *Römerbrief*," *Scottish Journal of Theology* 41 (1988): 377–95, and *Theology and Difference: The Wound of Reason* (Bloomington: Indiana University Press, 1993), chap. 2.

150. *CD* III/4:124, 122 (*KD* III/4:137, 134).

151. *CD* III/4:225 (*KD* III/4:252).

152. *CD* III/2:306–7 (*KD* III/2:369–70).

153. *CD* III/1:313 (*KD* III/1:358), III/2:294 (*KD* III/2:355); von Kirschbaum, *WF*, 11–12 (Shepherd:61–62).

154. *CD* III/4:140 (*KD* III/4:155).

155. See *CD* III/4:122 (*KD* III/4:134) on Schleiermacher's merging of "the omnipotence of love, the divinity of man and the beauty of life."

156. *CD* III/4:134ff. (*KD* III/4:148ff.).

occur when it is understood that "the sphere of male and female is wider than that of marriage, embracing the whole complex of relations at the center of which marriage is possible."[157]

The husband/wife relationship regarded in this way has major implications for a Christian, especially Protestant, ethic of marriage, which, Barth and von Kirschbaum both argue, is urgently in need of the help and corrective it would supply. Barth develops this idea more extensively: ethics, he has maintained from the start of *CD*, is not an appendix or a detour or a separate chapter in systematic theology. It should be recalled that von Kirschbaum's objective in *Die wirkliche Frau* is always to define a Protestant doctrine of women, whereas Barth's concern with regard to the *imago* is a Protestant doctrine of marriage. Barth regrets that Luther focused on procreation in his teachings on marriage, which, though historically understandable, later hardened into the "order of creation" teachings on marriage as an obligation, intended to ensure another created order, the family. Barth recommends his threefold reform because "such an emancipation and decrease of tension are necessary in face of the haste with which refuge is often sought . . . in the haven of marriage and of the compulsion with which the telos or center is immediately envisaged and its particular problems are tackled and expounded."[158] The husband and wife relationship will be strengthened when it is understood as an interpersonal relationship apart from sex and apart from parenting, and this strengthening will lead to a healthy sexual relationship and healthy family.

The husband/wife relationship so strengthened will also be the foundation for other male/female relationships. This outcome is as important as the sequence of husband/wife to father/mother and is of obvious importance to von Kirschbaum and Barth. It is likely that Barth learned from von Kirschbaum to see and assert that marriage is less absolutely required in the New Testament than in the Old Testament regime: this is inherent in her discussion of Christian witness in the unmarried state.[159] In *CD* III/4 Barth also credits N. H. Søe for daring to break with Christian tradition by including the unmarried as well as married state.[160] As often, Barth—like von Kirschbaum—draws on multiple sources or resources.

157. *CD* III/4:140 (*KD* III/4:155).
158. Ibid., 141 (*KD* III/4:156).
159. *WF*, 16, 63 (Shepherd:67–68, 128–30); Barth, *CD* III/4:143 (*KD* III/4:158).
160. *CD* III/4:141 (*KD* III/4:156).

There is another theme that, though following from the idea that the *imago* remains and persists in post-Fall life, is stated so emphatically by Barth and von Kirschbaum that it constitutes a distinct element of the doctrine. It is that the *imago Dei* is hidden within "the mortal sickness" in human life and relationality. As such it is twice-removed from our apprehension of it. We are dependent on the grace of God to certify its persistence, and the analogue by which we know it—as revealed in scripture and in the loving trinitarian life of God—is infinitely different from its likeness in us. The mortal sickness of which both Barth and von Kirschbaum speak[161] comprises the discord and tension between husband and wife and between male and female in other relationships. It includes the distortions, temptations, and fears that mar the human. Sometimes Barth discusses the *imago Dei* in its historical reality as a human condition, further defined as the post-Fall human condition, and sometimes he gives a cultural explanation: human sexuality, and by extension all male/female relationality, has been condemned and defined and constituted vis-à-vis the early Christian ideal of celibacy and the negativity that exists even in the Epistles.[162] Most often the presentation of this element of the *imago* is, nevertheless, positive: the pattern the two follow is to say that even in this life, this sad, sick life, we know the *imago* exists to guide, sustain, and testify. Indeed it is in this vein that Barth placed an excursus on Mozart in his discussion of Nothingness (*das Nichtige*) in III/3 (and hung portraits of Calvin and Mozart facing each other in his study).[163] The activity of husband and wife in itself "is no doubt a denial of their divine image and likeness, and laden with all the mortal sickness which is a consequence of this denial, but this does not in any way alter the fact that this activity as such is the sign of the hope given to man; the sign of the Son of Man and of His community."[164] The rejection of divorce follows from this conviction.

These are the elements—with some necessary overlap—of the doctrine of the *imago Dei* in Barth and von Kirschbaum. Barth does not make formal use of the traditional distinction between *image* (which is lasting) and *likeness* (which was lost in the Fall), but a conception of analogy per se is integral to his theology. He stresses that "analogy, even as the analogy of relation, does not entail likeness but *the correspondence of the*

161. *CD* III/1:191 (*KD* III/1:214); *WF*, 22 (Shepherd:76).
162. Barth includes this idea in his expositions of *natus ex virgine* in *GD* 164–5 and *Christliche Dogmatik*, 374.
163. *CD* III/3:298. See figure 13.
164. *CD* III/1:191 (*KD* III/1:214).

unlike" (my italics: this is a recurrent phrase).[165] It is true (following Paul, for example in Col. 1:15) that in Jesus Christ "the image and the reality are not two different things but the reality is present in the image."[166] On this basis Barth distinguishes between the Old Testament understanding of *imago Dei* in humanity as always a hope and the New Testament understanding, in the light of the relationship between Jesus Christ and his community, as reality.[167] Most characteristically, he reminds his reader that "terms like image, original, copy, correspondence, analogy, parity, likeness, and similarity" are finally wrapped in mystery.[168]

I think there is considerable negation in both Barth's and von Kirschbaum's insistence that the superordination and subordination inherent in the order of creation is not demeaning, not a sign of lesser value to God. I find even more negation in von Kirschbaum.[169] There is certainly much compensation in both. But more than negation or compensation, the conception of the *imago Dei* in their work is complex, cautionary, and fruitful.

We need to look closely at the texts of each writer to find the extent and pattern of commonality and interchange and to lift up the particular emphases and unique elements within the commonality. Prior to this, however, we need to investigate the extent to which the doctrine as they understood it was present among their contemporaries or in other available resources. Barth's mutually fruitful dialogue with his contemporaries—as also, I think, von Kirschbaum's quieter participation in this dialogue—is especially important for this doctrine.

4. Dialogical Personalism

In 1922, in the aftermath of World War I, Barth published the second edition of his commentary on Romans, and one year later the Jewish philosopher and theologian Martin Buber published *Ich und Du*. The

165. "Entsprechung des Ungleichen": ibid., 196 (*KD* III/1:220).
166. Ibid., 205 (*KD* III/1:231).
167. Ibid.
168. *CD* III/2:319 (*KD* III/2:384).
169. *Negation* is the psychoanalytic term for statements that are ultimately self-directed in order to override internal doubts or counterarguments. Instances in von Kirschbaum occur in discussions of Paul's teachings on submission and silence—e.g., *WF*, 50f. (Shepherd:111f.). Cf. Barth, *CD* III/1:301 (*KD* III/1:345).

impact of the first event has been characterized (by Karl Adam) as a bomb falling into the playground of the theologians. And it was Barth himself who described the advent of Buber as one who arrived amid "the confused humanism" of the postwar time "like a guest from a long forgotten world."[170]

The result—largely—of the first book was the formation of the movement known as dialectical theology; that of the second, the movement known as dialogical personalism. The two movements in thought overlapped, and on that common ground a decisive critique of individualism, transcendental idealism and the philosophy of identity, and Liberal Protestantism was forged.[171] So too was forged a relational concept of the image of God. Of particular importance in the reception of the nexus of new ideas, and reinforced by them, were existentialism and an early twentieth-century Luther revival. The new philosophical anthropology of the 1920s, incorporating ideas on community in social thinkers like Weber and Löwith, was a helpful background, especially to theologians like Bonhoeffer.

Dialogical personalism is the view that individuals exist not in themselves, not as isolated entities, but are constituted by their relation to an other, the Thou. This "social constitution of individuals" (in Wolfhart Pannenberg's phrase) is the beginning and foundation of their existence in society. This concept is the polar opposite of the idealistic principle that the individual constructs his and her world. The I-Thou relationship between two human beings is distinguished from, and understood in contrast to, the I-it relationship, which objectifies (and dehumanizes) the other. Dialogical personalism rejects both the isolated subject and an abstract, supratemporal subject, which exists "in the form of individual subjects but which is asserted to be the basis of all experience."[172] The new conception was formulated in the Jewish theologian Franz Rosenzweig's *Stern der Erlösung* and the Roman Catholic theologian Ferdinand Ebner's *Das Wort und die geistigen Realitaten*, both

170. Barth on Buber in a source used by Dieter Becker, *Karl Barth und Martin Buber— Denker in dialogischer Nachbarschaft? Zur Bedeutung Martin Bubers für die Anthropologie Karl Barths* (Göttingen: Vandenhoeck & Ruprecht, 1986), 21. Becker draws extensively on an unpublished 25-page typescript by Barth in the Barth-Archiv. It is an excursus on Buber prepared in 1944 for a course titled "Des menschen Menschlichkeit." Written at the same time that Barth was preparing material for *CD* III, it directly engages Buber's *Ich und Du*. (Becker reports that Barth's copy of that book—also in the Archiv—does not reveal when he first read it.)

171. I am drawing here on Pannenberg, *Anthropology in Theological Perspective*, 179ff. for the impact of dialogical personalism.

172. Ibid., 180, 179.

of 1922. However, it was Buber (*Lehrbeauftragter* at the University at Frankfurt am Main, 1922–33, then to the University at Jerusalem) who articulated and developed it in the form that quickly spread.[173]

In his retrospective sketch, "The History of the Dialogical Principle," Buber unforgettably described his emergence from a self-imposed "spiritual ascesis" as he worked to finish writing *Ich und Du* in 1922, to find that, in an uncanny way, "in this our time, men of different kinds and traditions" were devoting themselves to the same "search for buried treasure." The time was the World War I period and the years immediately following that so insistently disclosed the human situation. Quickly spreading among theologians and philosophers, "a strange longing awaken[ed] for thinking to do justice to existence itself."[174] Buber is specific about the particular strengths and the successive, cumulative contributions of his co-laborers in this new field. Hermann Cohen—whom the young student Karl Barth may have heard in Marburg—renewed a much earlier idea (first recognizable in Jacobi), that it is "the discovery of the Thou that brings me to consciousness of my I," and augmented and transformed it with the dimension of correlation between two different relationships: the divine-human and the interhuman.[175] Franz Rosenzweig, "Cohen's astonishing disciple," took the next decisive step by conceiving of encounter as dialogical, as a *spoken* event, grounded in the biblical address of God to the human being, which originates life and the form of life.[176] Buber then characterizes his own contribution: to conceive of the dialogue between God and the human creature not as the mode of communication but as "the happening itself" and to turn his full attention to description of this dialogue.[177]

173. Pannenberg (p. 180) thinks Buber was the popularizer of Rosenzweig's and Ebner's idea. To Helmut Gollwitzer (in a lecture at a 1978 conference on Buber, published as "The Significance of Martin Buber for Protestant Theology" in *Martin Buber: A Centenary Volume*, ed. Haim Gordon and Jochanan Bloch [New York: KTAV, 1984], 385-402) Buber's *I and Thou* of 1923 is the basic text for the movement in Protestant theology called theological personalism.

174. Buber, "Afterword: The History of the Dialogical Principle," in *Between Man and Man* (New York: Macmillan, 1965 [first pub. 1947]), esp. 211-17. Note that Rosenzweig was as aware as Buber of the direction and ferment of thought in the late war and postwar years; he called it New Thinking (Maurice Friedman, *Martin Buber's Life and Work: The Early Years, 1876–1923* [New York: E. P. Dutton, 1981], 284–85).

175. Buber, "Afterword," 212.

176. Ebner is further important on the centrality of speech, though Buber considers him as one who—like Kierkegaard—is "in the last instance ananthropic" despite his love of the fellow-human (ibid., 213).

177. Ibid.

It seems certain that Barth's intensely dialogical personality would have rendered the new movement highly plausible. But his response was complicated by the fact that theologians he increasingly distrusted were identifying themselves with it. Brunner, Gogarten, and Karl Heim have been seen as the most direct "users" of Buber; Buber recognizes their contributions as well as those of Hans Ehrenberg and Eugen Rosenstock-Huessy.[178] Counterbalancing these representatives for Barth, Buber had some key publicists. Thurneysen met and engaged in theological conversation with Buber and was extremely enthusiastic about his work in letters to Barth—he thought Buber was really sympathetic with "our concern [*Anliegen*]."[179] Hans Urs von Balthasar recognized Buber's importance for Christian theology and indeed all Western thought.[180] Barth resisted personal contact with Buber—apparently the result of some miscues in an exchange of letters during the debate with Brunner and impatience with what he saw as rejection of the obvious: the Christian foundation of the Hebrew Bible.[181] We will see that some ten years later he could be very appreciative of Buber—and still critical. His most public statement on Buber in *CD* III/2 reflects his ambivalence perfectly and ungraciously: "The pagan Confucius, the atheist Feuerbach and the Jew Buber" are outsiders who have something to say to us about fellow-humanity.[182]

Bultmann was another who found much in common with the movement of personalism. Wilhelm Vischer and the young Bonhoeffer, both very interested in dialectical theology as well as dialogical personalism, published several of their parallel writings on the I-Thou relationship, the biblical divine-human relationship, and the image of God by the late 1920s and early 30s. Jónsson has used the phrase "circle of influence" to describe the way Vischer and Bonhoeffer, who were decisively influenced by the writings of Karl Barth, developed a doctrine of the *imago*, which Barth in turn absorbed into his own work, citing them and describing how he further developed their doctrines.[183]

178. Gollwitzer, "The Significance of Martin Buber," 389-92; Buber, "Afterword," 216-17.

179. See esp. *KB-ET Briefwechsel*, 7 December 1923.

180. Quoted in Michael Theunissen, *The Other: Studies in the Social Ontology of Husserl, Heidegger, Sartre, and Buber*, trans. Christopher Macann (Cambridge, Mass.: MIT Press, 1984), 353.

181. Gollwitzer, "The Significance of Martin Buber," 396; see also Michael Wyschograd, "A Jewish Perspective on Karl Barth," 156–61, on Barth's emotional response to Jews (and his regret about this response).

182. *CD* III/2:277–78 (*KD* III/2:333–35).

183. Jónsson, *The Image of God*, 67–68.

Gollwitzer has connected the Protestant reception of Buber's "person-oriented thinking" to Luther's theology, the theology that had as its center the "event of the Divine Word in its address to the human being," simultaneously revealing sin and grace: "Constitutive of man's existence is the situation of being face to face with the God who addresses him."[184] Of course the Reformed author of "The Strange New World Within the Bible" shared this sensibility. It permeates his early reading of the Hebrew Bible as word event, as decisive word event, and his insistence on the *Deus dixit* that meant *both* the reality of God *and* address to the covenant partner of God. It should be noted that as Barth's circle of dialectical theologians broke up in the late 1920s and early 30s and Barth became increasingly concerned about the political Lutheranism of Gogarten and others, Charlotte von Kirschbaum, schooled in Lutheranism by Georg Merz, remained with him and perhaps strengthened the core of affinities Barth always shared with Lutheran theology.

Lutheran theologians in the 1920s could draw on the vocabulary of existentialism to describe the overwhelming, shattering impact of encounter with God. So too could Barth, as *Epistle to the Romans* demonstrates. The conceptual vocabulary of *Krise*, paradox, and existentiality were really modish among German (and Swiss-German!) intellectuals and cultural avant-garde, as Peter Gay's portrait of Weimar culture makes clear.[185] The affinities of dialogical personalism with existentialism lie also in the immediacy of encounter and the boundless openness it requires.

Neuser reminds us that Barth's thought was stamped by the 1920s.[186] It is also true that as the '20s progressed and Barth distanced himself from his original theological group, he distanced himself from existentialism. In the preface to *CD* I/1 he distinguished the new dogmatics from the *Christliche Dogmatik* by its expurgation of everything "that

184. Gollwitzer, "The Significance of Martin Buber," 388.

185. Of the resonance that Heidegger's writings found, Gay observes that key terms in his philosophy—*Angst*, existence, nothingness, decision, and death—had already been made "thoroughly familiar even to those who had never read a line of Kierkegaard" by the Expressionist poets and playwrights (*Weimar Culture*, 82). Heidegger gave "philosophical seriousness . . . to the love affair with unreason and death that dominated so many Germans in this hard time" (ibid.). The affinities in Barth's work with important aspects of Expressionist art have been persuasively suggested by Stephen Webb in *Re-Figuring Theology: The Rhetoric of Karl Barth* (Albany: SUNY Press, 1991).

186. W. H. Neuser, *Karl Barth in Münster, 1925–30* (*Theologische Studien*, 130 [Zurich: Theologischer Verlag, 1985]).

might appear to find for theology a foundation, support, or justification in philosophical existentialism."[187]

Barth was not successful in this effort, however. He never entirely broke with Bultmann, and he remained sympathetic to, and interested in, the work of Jaspers, who became his very respected colleague in 1948: their lecture rooms were connected by a staircase, a Jacob's ladder that Barth enjoyed describing.[188] In a section in III/2 prior to his development of the doctrine of the *imago* as "the basic form of humanity," Barth discusses at length Jaspers's concept of frontier situations (*Grenzsituationen*), those paradoxical situations "of suffering and death, conflict and guilt," in which human existence is felt to be "unavoidable, inexplicable, and totally questionable." Just here, where we experience disruption (*Zerrissenheit*), we can also encounter the transcendent other that does not answer our questions but renders our questioning meaningful.[189] Barth is finally critical of the "closed circle" of existentialist thought, of its ignorance of true opposition—and relationship—between the human and the divine.[190] But he values Jaspers's recognition of "the mystery of transcendence" to which the frontier situation points. And he particularly welcomes in Jaspers (and other versions of contemporary existentialism) the recognition of "the historicity of man and his relatedness to another."[191] Facing the questioning of the other is a primal situation for Barth. Hans Urs von Balthasar linked Buber and Jaspers as the two great dialogicians of his time.[192] It may be the case that I-Thou philosophy came to "contain" existentialism for Barth.

Martin Buber's I-Thou idea challenged the great ideal of Western civilization and its philosophical tradition, the ideal of finding a higher unity amid divisive and superficial disunity, with another great ideal: that

---

187. *CD* I/1:xiii (*KD* I/1:viii).
188. Busch, *Karl Barth*, 351.
189. *CD* III/2:112–13 (*KD* III/2:132–33).
190. There are interesting parallels in Buber's appreciation and criticism of Jaspers. Buber thought he wrongly rejected as arbitrary the analogy between the I-Thou human relationship and the I-Thou relationship of God and humans, i.e., that which "is common to these two relationships otherwise so utterly uncommon" (Buber, "Afterword," 219–21).
191. *CD* III/2, esp. 112–13, 118–19 (*KD* III/1:132–33, 139–40). Barth acknowledges that Brunner made a positive step in breaking the existentialist circle, "for there is taken into account not merely a frontier situation but a genuine limit with a real that side and this. There is envisioned a real Other, a real Transcendent, a real Opposite to man." But then the familiar Barth-Brunner disagreement emerges and 1934 is replayed (*CD* III/2:128f. [*KD* III/2:153f.]).
192. Theunissen, *The Other*, 353.

of absolute respect for, love of, and dependence upon human otherness. The archetype of the I-Thou relationship is the divine-human encounter and its spokenness, which is "the happening itself" in Hebrew scripture; an essential part of the encounter is the freedom of both God and God's human covenant partner. Buber thought that Paul (and most Protestant theologians) obscured the freedom to turn to God in their doctrine of grace.[193] The turning Buber advocated was too close to synergism for Brunner and Barth alike.[194] But all three—Buber, Brunner, and Barth—shared the view that the isolated life was sinful. And Gollwitzer thought that Barth's Christian anthropology, more than any other, including Brunner's, realized Buber's idea when it presented, with the greatest attention and intensity, the coexistence and mutual orientation of human with human as the fundamental, not accidental, definition of being human. The interhuman relationship presupposes the mutual appreciation of otherness—irreducible otherness—which Gollwitzer felicitously calls polyphony.[195]

Buber himself, in his "History of the Dialogical Principle," said that Barth took over, "naturally in the manner of genuine independent thinking, our recognition of the fundamental distinction between It and Thou and of the true being of the I in the meeting." Buber finds Barth's appropriation more authentic than Gogarten's "almost naive" attempt at annexation of the idea for Protestantism.[196] (He also thinks Barth overlooks an essential similarity when he finds wanting in Buber the gladness, the "freedom of the heart between human and human" that is the "root and crown of the concept of humanity." Buber wishes he could show Barth how, in its own way, the same is said and lived with joy in the Hasidic world of faith.)[197]

In an intangible way that eludes pinpointing, Buber's I-Thou concept seems to permeate Barth's view of fellow-humanity. In Dieter Becker's study of the ideas that Buber and Barth share, he isolates the presence in Barth of the contrast between I-it and I-Thou and stresses the constitutive nature of the I-Thou encounter. Barth understood Buber thoroughly when he wrote in CD III/2: "Ich bin indem Du bist" (I am in that thou

---

193. It is not surprising that Brunner and Gollwitzer expressed frustration with Buber's unnuanced reading of Paul: see Gollwitzer, "The Significance of Martin Buber," 394.

194. Ibid., 395.

195. Ibid., 386, 397.

196. Buber, "Afterword," 222.

197. Ibid., 223–24.

art).[198] Becker also sees as integral to Barth's doctrine of the image of God Buber's conception of the dimension in human existence of "being in relation to God" (*Sein in der Beziehung zu Gott*); one's dialogical human existence is founded in the double movement of one's being to God and to cohumanity (*Mitmenschen*)—Barth would find an analogy here in Christology.[199] Barth turned his attention to Buber's work in an essay of 1944—the same in which he referred to Buber as the visitor from another planet in a time of great need. He thought "the greatness and service" of Buber consisted in "the inexorable clarity and consequences of his pointing (in opposition to all idealists and mystics but also the great majority of Christian theologians) to the I-Thou relation as the essential in humanness and just thereby pointing to the essence [or paragon: *Inbegriff*] of that which God wills." And the foundation of Buber's theme was the clear opposition (*Entgegenstellung*) and connecting (*Verbindung*) of God and the human being. "He made an impression then and does so still today."[200]

Barth's dissatisfactions with Buber remain. He thinks that Buber's conception of revelation lacks a sense of historical particularity, of concreteness, of the cumulative and decisive meaning (Barth sometimes called this the once-for-all) in the sequence of God-events in scripture. He also criticizes Buber's excessive attention to the "I" in the I-Thou relationship in both its human-divine form and its inter-human form.[201] When Buber describes the dialogue between God and the human being as a free partnership "in a conversation between heaven and earth whose speech in address and answer is the happening itself, the happening from above and the happening from below,"[202] the problem for Barth is its inappropriate symmetry. Becker rightly notes that the criticism may not be entirely accurate for Buber. However, Barth felt a disparity, which may have further obscured for him some of their real commonality.

Two concepts in Buber may have been of special importance for Barth: the sphere of "the between" and "presence." The idea of the between (*das Zwischen*) serves to convey the compelling reality in I-Thou encounter. The between is that which is created by the I and Thou as

198. Becker, *Karl Barth and Martin Buber*, 30ff., 110f., 124ff., and passim. It is interesting that Becker's extensive study originated as a dissertation under Albrecht Peters, who has studied Luther and Barth. (Barth's statement is in *CD* III/2:248 [*KD* III/2:296].)

199. Becker, *Karl Barth and Martin Buber*, 188–89.

200. Ibid., 20–21.

201. Ibid., 25–27.

202. Buber, "Afterword," 213.

they meet and open themselves to each other in dialogue. It is neither the one nor the other, nor a combination of them, nor an encompassing of them. Created in confrontation, it is something real only to them and yet essential to their very existence.[203] And the idea of presentness or presence (*Gegenwart*) may be the most important contribution of Buber's—or the most important shared idea. *Presentness*, in contrast to what occurs in the I-it realm, means the absolute openness of the I to the Thou; it is the renunciation of any preconception of what the Thou will say, the relinquishing of any predecided limitation on the effects and implications on the self of what the Thou says. This ensures both the integrity of the other and the absolute historicity or event-nature of what happens between the I and the Thou. There is only a past in the I-it experience, and, rather than relationship, there is use of objects. "Presence is not what is evanescent and passes but what confronts us, waiting and enduring."[204] The event-nature of encounter is, of course, analogous to Barth's reading of scripture as word-event; it is what foregrounds listening in the I-Thou encounter. It is a measure of the trust between I and Thou, and it is based on valuation, on treasuring the otherness of the Thou.[205] This is a countertruth to Lacan's true thesis that the other is the signifier's treasure: in the I-Thou relation, the other is you or I or some other real being.

It may be the case that Barth tampered with Buber's idea and weakened his own argument for cohumanity when he stipulated that the other should be of opposite sex. He is sometimes ambiguous on whether the cohumanity of male and female (and more specifically, of husband and wife) is a paradigm or a qualitatively better dyad. He insists on defining the I-Thou image as male and female when he is differentiating his doctrine from alternative versions. I think he does this (aside from the simple need for originality) to stress otherness. The ambiguity, as well as the weight and fluid pattern of his discussions as they move to other kinds of relationships and to unspecified kinds of relationships, argue for paradigm status. In either case, however, Barth saw the irreducibility of otherness as integrity.

203. See Maurice Friedman, *Martin Buber: The Life of Dialogue*, 3rd ed. (Chicago: University of Chicago Press, 1976), chaps. 10–14, 19.
204. Buber, *I and Thou*, trans. Walter Kaufmann (New York: Touchstone/Charles Scribner's Sons, 1970), 64. For Buber it is also the site of freedom: "The world of the You [Thou] is not locked up. Whoever proceeds toward it, concentrating his whole being, with his power to relate resurrected, beholds his freedom" (107).
205. Ibid., 168.

5. Gender and the Image of God

Carving Out a New Doctrine

Barth does not mention Brunner in *CD* III/1. In III/2, he criticizes
Brunner's inconsistency on the *imago* in maintaining both "the concept
of man constituted by the Word of God and the idea of a neutral
capacity [to reject God] in man."[206] He does not mention Gogarten in the
Dogmatics after I/1. The two doctrines of the *imago* that Barth finds
closest to the text in Genesis are those of Dietrich Bonhoeffer and
Wilhelm Vischer. It is Bonhoeffer who brings together two basic ideas:
the I-Thou constitution of humanity and the I-Thou relationship as the
image of God. The phrase *analogia relationis* is Bonhoeffer's, as Barth
notes when he adopts it; it is from his *Creation and Fall*, two studies on
Genesis published in 1933.[207] Vischer was an Old Testament scholar
whose christological interpretation in *Christuszeugnis* (translated as *The
Old Testament Witness to Christ*) reflected Barth's approach to scripture.
His work on the I-Thou relation of God and humanity was worked out in
articles published from 1927 through 1931; the first volume of his book
on Old Testament witness was published in 1934, one year after Bonhoeffer's *Creation and Fall*. His contribution to Barth's *imago* doctrine
was to understand all of God's creation in reference to the I-Thou
relationship of God and humanity.

Vischer was also a close friend of Barth who, after being forced to
leave Germany, became Barth's colleague, pastor of his church, and
neighbor from 1936 onward.[208] In his preface to *CD* II/2 (Whitsuntide
1942), Barth referred to the unity of purpose and content between his
work and that of his two friends: Eduard Thurneysen's *Jacobsbrief in
Predigten* and the second volume of Wilhelm Vischer's *Christuszeugnis*,
both of which had appeared in the past half year. He found this unity
welcome amid "these evil times." To Barth, Bonhoeffer was the young
Lutheran colleague at Bonn and active member of the Confessing Church
who visited him several times in Basel to discuss theology as well as the
political crisis.[209]

206. *CD* III/2:130–31 (*KD* III/2:155–57).
207. Barth on the phrase: III/1:195-96 (*KD* III/1:218–19).
208. Busch, *Karl Barth*, 196, 269, 307.
209. Their letters (including those von Kirschbaum wrote in Barth's stead) and an
account by Eberhard Bethge are in Dietrich Bonhoeffer, *Schweizer Korrespondenz
1941–42. Im Gespräch mit Karl Barth*, ed. Eberhard Bethge (Theologische Existenz heute
214 [Munich: Chr. Kaiser Verlag, 1982]).

Bonhoeffer absorbed Barth's stress on the personal, decisive nature of encounter with the divine that places us under the divine command. He went on to reject the traditional view of the *imago* as the soul, or reason, and instead saw it as personal, loving relationship involving the whole person.[210] Besides the major idea of the *analogia relationis* and of the image of God as this analogy, Bonhoeffer took the important step (from the perspective of Barth's work) of incorporating the duality of the male/female relationship into the doctrine of the *imago*. However, Barth and Bonhoeffer do not interpret the significance of the male/female relationship in the same way.

To Bonhoeffer, "Male and female He created them" points to sociality as the foundational, defining characteristic of humanity.[211] Umidi suggests that Bonhoeffer's Lutheranism is reflected in his understanding of sin as *cor curvum in se*. Certainly Barth shared this understanding, and Bonhoeffer may have decisively reinforced it. In contrast to Bonhoeffer, however, Barth sees male and female gender differences as essential. One implication of this divergence is that relationality for Barth, even when extended to other I-Thou relationships, may remain dyadic rather than communal, however much he sees the original human unit as the prerequisite to communal, societal life. Umidi suggests that Bonhoeffer's Lutheran conception of *communicatio idiomatum* may facilitate continuity among all human relationships and between the divine-human encounter and communal life, while the atomistic quality in Barth's stress on the decisive act of encounter itself (as well as the dyadic *humanum*) reflects a Calvinism that stresses the separation of human and divine.[212]

One may not need this historical explanation of their difference. In the years in Münster, Martin Rade said of dialectical theology that it was too one-sided, that "it speaks to my soul but not to a community, in which I live with my soul."[213] I think it remains a problem in dialogical personalism, whether gender-prescriptive or not, that the only social units it conceives and formulates are the dyadic and the communal, and the latter tend to be abstract collectivities, such as a church, a geographical

210. Umidi, "Imaging God Together," 134, 220ff.
211. Umidi cites Moltmann's appreciation of the "profound this-sided Christianity" in Bonhoeffer's *imago* doctrine, in which "we encounter the Thou of God in the concrete Thou of social life. Men become the likeness of God through the impact of their fellow men" (169).
212. Ibid., 164, 169–71.
213. Quoted in Neuser, *Karl Barth in Münster*, 34–35.

unit, or all of humankind.[214] But one can find countertexts in Barth. One of these is in *CD* IV/2, in which Barth praises Bonhoeffer's *Cost of Discipleship* superlatively.[215]

Von Kirschbaum was also well acquainted with the work of Bonhoeffer and Vischer (and with them as friends); she speaks of Vischer's work in her correspondence with Visser't Hooft Boddaert.[216] However, it is Barth who writes about Bonhoeffer and Vischer in relation to the *imago*. Barth immediately adopts Bonhoeffer's term *analogia relationis*, and he uses the concept of relational analogy in opposition to essentialist and structuralist conceptions of the image.[217] Or as von Kirschbaum states, the *imago* is not in a predicate of the individual human or a quality or an achievement, but it is exactly the createdness and encounter of the unlike (*ungleich*) duality of male and female.[218] In Barth's summary, "God is in relationship, and so too is the man created by Him. This is his divine likeness."[219] Perhaps to emphasize the indirectness in the *analogia relationis* (and its difference from the method of correlation), Barth defines a *"tertium comparationis,"* a feature "common to both likeness and reality, to both copy and original." It consists "in both cases, between man and his fellow man on the one hand and God and man on the other, in an indestructible connection and fellowship between two subjects which are indestructibly distinct." The point of comparison is that "on both sides there is a firm and genuine covenant. . . . Apart from this common feature everything is different."[220]

Barth values in Vischer the idea that God created in the human "the real counterpart to whom He could reveal Himself. . . . 'the eye of the whole body of creation which God will cause to see His glory.'" Indeed, all of creation, like the totality of scripture, "aims at the confrontation of God and man and the inconvertible I-Thou relationship between Creator

214. Thus one could miss the recognition of differently and variously composed encounter units, such as working groups that draw upon individual differences or resolutely leaderless feminist groups. Catherine Keller in *From a Broken Web* points to another dimension of communal existence: its fluid, changing constitution as groups form and as they die, and as the individual self adapts to these shifts. In a similar vein Umidi ("Imaging God Together") stresses Bonhoeffer's sense of the polyphony of life.

215. *CD* IV/2:533f., 540f. (*KD* IV/2:604, 612f.). Noted by Umidi, "Imaging God Together," 223.

216. vK to HVH, 18 December 1942. (Visser't Hooft Boddaert drew upon Vischer prominently in "Eve, Where Art Thou?" 213.)

217. *CD* III/1:194ff. (*KD* III/1:218ff.) and as conclusion of par. 45 in *CD* III/2:324 (*KD* III/2:391).

218. *WF*, 8 (Shepherd:56).

219. *CD* III/2:324 (*KD* III/2:391).

220. *CD* III/2:320 (*KD* III/2:386).

and creature."²²¹ In Bonhoeffer, he values the conception of the image as the reflection of God's freedom for his creature. Freedom in itself is meaningless and godless; to provide the human creature with real freedom for an other, freedom in relationship, God created the human as man and woman. So Barth finds Bonhoeffer closer to the text than Vischer: Bonhoeffer saw in Genesis 1:27 and again in Genesis 5:1–2, "Male and female created He them," that "the image and likeness of the being created by God signifies existence in confrontation."²²² In Bonhoeffer's spirit, cohumanity is more than living with another and is different from helping another. It is mutual determination.²²³ It is total orientation to another. Neither the illusion of self-sufficiency nor "the waste of isolation" is permitted: one must always be aware of one's need for the other "as a fish needs water."²²⁴ But the need is not for a missing part, a specific lack or deficit: I escape the other if I depend on the other. We must each be unique and irreplaceable for each other. Neither one is the property of the other, nor the other's rescuer.²²⁵

The I-Thou relationship is, in Barth's most characteristic phrase, the freedom of the heart for the other. In such a relationship, the I and the Thou think and live only referentially to each other, and only in this way are they human. Von Kirschbaum says that in love, "the existence of the other is allowed to become the condition for one's own existence."²²⁶ The most direct model for cohumanity is the man Jesus Christ, who is also the Son of God begotten before all worlds. As human beings we are not free to disavow the freedom of the heart for the other because to do so would be to renounce our humanity. The existence that God willed for Godself, God also willed for us, in covenant. The I and Thou reflect the divine election in that they have elected each other. The absence of coercion or any external necessity in cohumanity, as in the divine plurality, is reflected in the gladness with which it is carried forth.

Barth maintains that he has "supplemented and focused" the theses of Vischer and Bonhoeffer.²²⁷ What he finds missing in Vischer and Bonhoeffer is, first, recognition of the significance of the divine plural in

221. *CD* III/1:194 (*KD* III/1:218).
222. Ibid., 195 (*KD* III/1:219).
223. *CD* III/2:268 (*KD* III/2:322).
224. Ibid., 263, and repeated on 264, 273 (*KD* III/2:315, 317, 329). Note that the phrase is "Wüste dieser Einsamkeit" (cf. Barth on Hell as *Einsamkeit*). See also the lengthy excursus on Nietzsche: ibid., 213–42 (*KD* III/2:276–90).
225. Ibid., 270–71 (*KD* III/2:324–25).
226. "zur eigenen Existenzbedingung werden" (*WF*, 18 [Shepherd:69]).
227. *CD* III/1:197 (*KD* III/1:221).

verse 26 ("Let us . . ."). Thus they miss the trinitarian connection and its perichoretic nature, "the plurality in the divine being plainly attested in this passage, the differentiation and relationship, the loving co-existence and co-operation, the I and Thou, which first take place in God Himself." "Is it not palpable," Barth asks, "that we have to do with a clear and simple correspondence, an *analogia relationis*, between this mark [the grammatical shift] of the divine being, namely, that it includes an I and a Thou, and the being of man, male and female?"[228] Barth demonstrates the dynamic nature of this plurality when he refers to "the relationship between the summoning I in God's being and this summoned divine Thou."[229] Or in von Kirschbaum's words: "God created 'man' [*der Mensch*] in the unlike duality of male and female 'man' [*die ungleiche Zweiheit des männlichen und weiblichen Menschen*]. Thus we see that God did not create 'man' as solitary but as one who is a counterpart, that is, in correspondence to God's own not-aloneness [*Nichteinsamkeit*]."[230]

Second, despite Bonhoeffer's attention to the creation of the human person as male and female, both Vischer and Bonhoeffer miss the exact significance for the *imago* of male/female differentiation. Barth makes much of the shift from the singular to plural in Genesis 1:27—"In the image of God He created him, male and female He created them"—and its parallelism to the divine "Let us" just before it, in verse 26.[231] His basic discussion of the *imago* proceeds from and refers to verse 27. Barth's exegesis (or exposition, as he calls it) has had a major impact on Old Testament scholarship on Genesis and the *imago*. It has also been challenged: Phyllis A. Bird argues alternatively that the latter part of verse 27 should be read as separate from the *imago* reference and, rather, as preparatory to the next verse, "And God blessed them, and God said to them, 'Be fruitful and multiply.'"[232]

228. *CD* III/1:196 (*KD* III/1:220). I have corrected the English translation of the second sentence (which says the opposite of the original text). German: "Oder ist es nicht greifbar dass wir es zwischen jenem Merkmal des Wesens *Gottes*: das er ein Ich und ein Du in sich schliesst, und dem Wesen des Menschen: dass er Mann und Frau ist, mit einer nun wirklich einfachen und klaren Entsprechung, und zwar eben mit einer *analogia relationis* zu tun haben?"

229. *CD* III/1:196 (*KD* III/1:220).

230. "Gott schuf also den Menschen nicht einsam, sondern in diesem Gegenüber" (*WF*, 8 [Shepherd:56]).

231. The primary exegeses are *CD* III/1:184ff., 196f. (prefaced by a history of the exegesis from the early church to his own time, 192ff.), and 288. (*KD* III/1:206ff., 220f., 329). Barth refers to and continues these in III/2:323–24 (*KD* III/2:390–91) and III/4:116f. (*KD* III/4:127f.).

232. See Jónsson, *The Image of God*, 65ff., and Phyllis A. Bird, "Sexual Differentiation and Divine Image in the Genesis Creation Texts," in Børreson, *Image of God and Gender*

Shared Vision with Variants

It is Barth's exposition of Genesis 1:26 in *CD* III/1 that von Kirschbaum
cites on the first page of her first lecture, "Jesus Christus und die
Gemeinde—Mann und Frau."[233] His exposition, not constrained by
format, is more extensive and contains material not in von Kirschbaum's
lecture—for example, he looks at the parallel pairs of days within the six
days of creation. But in striking ways—in key phrases, exegetical steps,
and theological interpolations—von Kirschbaum's presentation reads
like a condensed version of Barth's.[234] Both begin with reflections on
God's inner soliloquy (*Selbstbespräch*) after the creation of the first man,
in which God considered his own non-aloneness.[235] Both take care to
point out that God's freely made internal consultation demonstrates
God's true nonsolitariness yet does not violate the unity and integrity
of God.[236]

The identification of the *imago* with the male/female relationship
(which Barth also calls human fellowship or the *humanum*) follows and
is intimately related to his doctrine of election; in *CD* (III/1) it is first
introduced in paragraph 41, Creation and Covenant, sections 2 (Creation
as the external basis of the covenant) and 3 (Covenant as the internal
basis of creation). The male/female *humanum* is a copy of the Creator
and also "a type of the history of the covenant and salvation which will
take place between him and his Creator."[237] Or as von Kirschbaum says,
the unlike duality that is the truly human reflects both the creation of
humankind in God's image and the human creature whom God elected
to be God's *Gegenüber*. This human creature will be addressed by God as
Du and be as *Du* to God.[238] But it must be noted that it is human
interrelatedness in I-Thou fellowship, not the specification of the two

---

Models, 11–34, esp. nn. 3 and 19. Bird regrets that Barth's reading reinforces the texts on
male/female ordering in the Epistles, which conservatives (she includes Barth) take as
normative.

233. See esp. *WF*, 7–12 (Shepherd:56–62). Her reference: "cf. on this whole connection [she is referring to the biblical saga of God's creation of the human being and the
human's createdness in God's image] Barth, *KD* III/1 (par. 41):197ff. [=*CD* III/1:176ff.]."

234. We must remember the dialogical role of von Kirschbaum in Barth's work: the
braid suggested above could describe their collaboration here.

235. *Nichteinsamkeit* in von Kirschbaum, *WF*, 7–8 (Shepherd:56–57); the Barth text
uses *Nicht-Einsamkeit* [*KD* III/1:204].

236. Barth, *CD* III/1:183 (*KD* III/1:204–5); von Kirschbaum, *WF*, 8 (Shepherd:56).

237. *CD* III/1:186–87 (*KD* III/1:208–9).

238. *WF*, 8 (Shepherd:57).

humans as male and female, that follows necessarily from the doctrine of election. That specification is distinctly another matter, which Barth sees as his second supplement to the *imago* doctrine. That humankind has two sexes, like other animals, is a mark of its creatureliness. But the sexual *identity* of male and female is part of the *humanum*; the perfect fellowship of the I-Thou *humanum* is founded on it.[239] Von Kirschbaum says that the sexual differentiation that we share with the animal world does not constitute animal nature (*das Tierische*) inasmuch as God has designated that differentiation, in humans, for the *imago*.

In his somewhat muddy and belabored explication of this significance, Barth contrasts the unique relationship between man and woman to the "different groups and species" within all other creatures—the plants and animals of land, air, and water. These groupings were made by God, who created them "according to their kind" (Gen. 1:24–25) on the different days of creation. But for humankind God made only one distinction, and made it very deliberately: that between man and woman.[240] In von Kirschbaum's words, "It is the glory of man and woman that they are addressed as such by God."[241] The distinction of sexes found in humankind is "the only genuine distinction between man and man, in correspondence to the fact that the I-Thou relationship is the only genuine distinction in the one divine being."[242]

Barth's insistence on the irreducibility and importance of gender difference is certainly related to his impatience with feminism. The measure of his impatience is set forth in the peremptory "A-B" formula in III/4: "Man and woman are not an A and a second A whose being and relationship can be described like the two halves of an hourglass, which are obviously two, but absolutely equal and therefore interchangeable. Man and woman are an A and a B, and cannot, therefore, be equated." Yes, the A and the B "are fully equal before God." But "the fact remains" that God has sanctified them as man and woman "and therefore in such a way that A is not B but A, and B is not another A but B."[243]

This insistence also places Barth in opposition to the fairly common concept in depth psychology of bisexuality. Well into volume III of the Dogmatics, in a discussion of the mutual completion that male and female offer to one another (and immediately preceding his discussion

239. *CD* III/1:196 (*KD* III/1:220).
240. *CD* III/1:196 (*KD* III/1:220–21).
241. *WF*, 116 (Shepherd:195).
242. *CD* III/1:196 (*KD* III/1:221).
243. *CD* III/4:169 (*KD* III/4:188).

of Simone de Beauvoir), Barth feels constrained to vehemently reject the concept of bisexuality in Berdyaev as well as Plato, Jacob Böhme, Bachhofen, Freud, and Ludwig Klages: "There is a point at which the good work of mutual completion ceases to be good if it becomes the representation of a myth which has its foundation neither in the will of the Creator nor in the reality of His creature, and therefore has no foundation at all, except to warn us against the sin of *hybris*, of wanting to be the whole either individually or together." The "criterion" for defining the "limit" of mutuality is consciousness of being the man or woman that God created and being glad of this identity.[244]

If there is some strong psychic energy fueling and sometimes forcing Barth's elaboration of the importance of gender difference, his steady, serious insistence that we hear him out suggests the presence of still other concerns. There is indeed something else. Barth contrasts this "genuine dualism," "the duality of male and female which cannot be resolved in a higher synthesis,"[245] to other distinctions that have no scriptural foundation. In Genesis, "man is not said to be created or to exist in groups and species, in races and peoples, etc." And again: "[n]othing is said about groups and species (i.e., races, nations, etc.) in the account of man's creation, but an eloquent silence is maintained."[246]

In 1945 Barth is wonderfully right to reject specious distinctions within humankind. As so often in his life, Barth's theological concerns and perceptions reflect the problems in his historical world. He is writing an alternative to the Nazi polarization of Aryan and Jew. Four years later von Kirschbaum too referenced her conception of duality in encounter to Nazism. The woman is not the only embodiment of "other," she tells us. The *Führerkult* had its own exclusionary myth.[247] This important point, however, is made just once and less centrally than in Barth—I think because it is less immediate in 1949 and because von Kirschbaum's engagement with the subject of the male/female relationship long predates the war. With regard to the *imago*, one might say that

244. *CD* III/4:158–59 (*KD* III/4:176–77). He might have included Jung in his list too: See Keller, *From a Broken Web*, 110, or Ellenberger, *Discovery of the Unconscious*, 798–9. Johan Jakob Bachofen (1815–87) was another well-known, though earlier, citizen of Basel whose *Mutterrecht und Urreligion* (1861) introduced the idea of matriarchy (see Ellenberger, 219–20). Von Kirschbaum cites Bachofen's observation (in *Mutterrecht*) that Paul's hierarchicalism is contrary to mythological thought, which proceeds from the female to the male (*WF*, 44 [Shepherd:103]).

245. *CD* III/2:289 (*KD* III/2:349).

246. *CD* III/1:186 (*KD* III/1:208); ibid., 179 (*KD* III/1:200).

247. *WF*, 92 (Shepherd:166).

the phenomenon of Nazism offered her supporting material, whereas for Barth it was a trigger to think an old doctrine anew. The "genuine dualism of male and female" itself contains prejudicial assumptions and implications—and in relation to the I-Thou concept, a later reader might also argue that it is unnecessary. But it is necessary to Barth from multiple viewpoints. It is part of his rejection of abstraction to maintain that "there is no being of man above the being of male and female," and Barth also contrasts his confirmation of duality to "identity-mysticism."[248]

I have noted that Barth does not always sustain the identification of the sexual relationship with the *imago*. He and von Kirschbaum agree (in exposition of the Genesis creation stories) that whatever a man or woman does, he or she does it as man or woman.[249] Sometimes the sexual relationship is presented as the one true *humanum*, and sometimes as the paradigm for other human relationships of I-Thou form. Barth will speak of the reflection of "man's determination as the covenant partner of God in the perfect fellowship of man and woman," and it is in reference to this reflection that he prefers the term *partner* (*Partner* also in German) to *helpmeet* in Genesis 2:18.[250] Barth (like von Kirschbaum) also uses the term *counterpart*[251]—it should be remembered that friends of Barth and von Kirschbaum referred to von Kirschbaum as Barth's *Gegenüber* (which was, as they would have realized, the language of dialogical personalism). Recurrently in Barth, the first significance of the man and women for each other is actually gender-free: it is as fellow human being (he says fellowman) who is, at the same time, different.

It is in Barth's description of encounter between man and woman that we see the significance of their sexual differentiation. To Bonhoeffer, as we have seen, the human being is created in two forms to ensure the relationality and sociality that reflects God's willed non-aloneness. To Barth (as in Buber's I-Thou concept) it is precisely the *otherness* in the two forms that makes the relationality of the human species in itself

---

248. *CD* III/2:268 (*KD* III/2:322).
249. Kirschbaum: *WF*, 8 (Shepherd:57); Barth: *CD* III/1:186 (*KD* III/1:209).
250. *CD* III/4:143 (*KD* III/4:159); *CD* III/1:290 (*KD* III/1:331). For the truly fundamental identification of partner-being with the *imago*, see Wolf Krötke, "Gott und Mensch als 'Partner.' Zur Bedeutung einer zentralen Kategorien in Karl Barths Kirchlicher Dogmatik," in *Theologie als Christologie: Zum Werk und Leben Karl Barths. Ein Symposium*, ed. Heidelore Köckert and Wolf Krötke (Berlin: Evangelische Verlagsanstalt, 1988), 106–20.
251. The first extensive explication of *Gegenüber* is in *CD* III/1:290 (*KD* III/1:331f.); Barth says, "*Partner* is perhaps the best modern rendering for the term 'helpmeet.'" Von Kirschbaum, *WF*, e.g., 8, 30, 31 (Shepherd:57, 85, 87).

positive: "In humanity it is not a question of the removal and dissolution but the confirmation and exercise of duality as such."[252]

The radical otherness that exists within the human species is reflected in Adam's startled, fascinated recognition of Eve as both "of him" and different from him, like and unlike. Von Kirschbaum focuses as much as Barth on the recognition by Adam of the woman as finally— "Diese nun endlich!"—the one he could call *Du*.[253] It is in this recognition of the woman who was like and yet unlike himself that he truly first became *zum Manne*. Von Kirschbaum comments additionally in this exegetical context on the equality of rights (*Gleichberechtigung*) or, as "we prefer to say, equality of grace [*Gleichbegnadigung*] conferred upon man and woman in their createdness by God and on the parallel between their I-Thou relationship and the covenantal relationship."[254]

Both Barth and von Kirschbaum also introduce a concept that is consonant with the Weberian distinction between *Gesellschaft* and *Gemeinschaft*: they maintain that the woman was encountered by the first man as fellow human, *Mitmenschen*, thereby creating a community or *Mitwelt*.[255] In Barth, this is contrasted to Adam's detached naming of the other creatures objectified into the environment, the *Umwelt*.[256] In von Kirschbaum's version, although these creatures satisfied some of the man's needs, he found none among them to address as *Du*; they remained for him objectified into the *Umwelt*. The *Mitwelt* first appeared to him in the woman.[257] In Barth, the man's cry of recognition was a completely new kind of name-giving: "There takes place here something which could not take place between [humans] and animals. Association gives way to fellowship."[258] Von Kirschbaum extends this chain of ideas to conclude that the male/female relationship is the basic form of human community (*Gemeinschaft*).[259] Barth says in his exegesis that in

252. *CD* III/2:268 (*KD* III/2:322).
253. *WF*, 9 (Shepherd:58–59).
254. *WF*, 10 (Shepherd:59).
255. Maurice Friedman has suggested (in *Martin Buber*, 274 n. 1) that Karl Löwith was an influence on Barth: Friedman refers to Löwith's *Das Individuum in der Rolle der Mitmenschen: ein Beitrag zur anthropologischen Grundlegung der ethischen Probleme*. Löwith's name does not appear in the index of *CD* (or in Busch's highly detailed biography), but Buber ("Afterword," 217–18) and Becker refer to him. It is certainly plausible as an indirect influence.
256. *CD* III/1:304f., 290–91, 301 (*KD* III/1:348f., 332–33, 344).
257. *WF*, 9 (Shepherd:58).
258. "Es kommt zu dem, wozu es zwischen Mensch und Tier nicht kommen konnte: die Umwelt wird zur menschlichen Mitwelt" (*CD* III/1:300 [*KD* III/1:342–43]).
259. *WF*, 8 (Shepherd:57).

being-in-encounter, man (Adam) receives and will always have a neighbor (*Nächsten*).[260] He further defines *Gemeinde* in III/2, when he presents Jesus, the *imago Dei*, as "Neighbor and Saviour of men in time" and establishes this identity as "something ontological, . . . not accidental, external or subsequent but primary, internal and necessary." What Jesus is for us, in "the narrower circle of the disciples and community [*Gemeinde*], he is, obviously, through the ministry of this narrower circle" for all the world.[261] From a different perspective, the normative pattern of Christ and community is not something to be followed but to be uncovered (by the analogy of faith) in and throughout our own lives.

Like the human eye that Vischer evoked, the eye that finds and glories in God in his created world, being-in-encounter begins when two human beings, male and female, meet and find each other as the Thou for each I. In a phenomenological description, Barth evokes four elements of the encounter: immediate meeting of the eyes, mutual openness in speaking and hearing, mutual helping or (because it is not an aggregation of deeds) supplementing, and the gladness of the freedom of the heart for the other.[262] The elements are not strictly separate: for example, Barth's explication of mutual speaking and hearing is about a form of mutual supplementing. Recalling Buber's concept of presence, this example seems also of importance in understanding Barth's relationship with von Kirschbaum, the one he called his helper. Each, he tells us, must assist the other and accept the assistance of the other in expressing his or her self. Only in this way does one avoid the embarrassment of uncertainty and distortion in mere self-declaration. And just because "I am not Thou, nor Thou I," we can each offer to the other "something new and strange and different."[263]

Ultimately, the elements are only approximations: the real "living center of the whole" eludes further description. We can only say that there is "a discovery, the mutual recognition that each is essential to the other. There is thus enacted the paradox that the one is unique and irreplaceable for the other." Barth describes the I-Thou relationship as a mutual electing and election in which each confirms the other "as the being with which he wants to be and cannot be without."[264] Von Kirschbaum says that the affirmation of the woman by the man is his

260. *CD* III/1:300 (*KD* III/1:343).
261. *CD* III/2:210, 213 (*KD* III/2:251, 255).
262. *CD* III/2:250ff. (*KD* III/2:299ff.).
263. *CD* III/2:254–55, 256 (*KD* III/2:304–5, 306–7).
264. *CD* III/2:271–72 (*KD* III/2:321–22).

acceptance of a mysterious yet trusted otherness—an *Andersheit*.[265] The man's saying Yes (*Bejahung*) to what God has done, as he slept, is also the man's free decision and the recognition that the woman given by God is the offering of his grace.[266] Barth too speaks of creation as the act of the grace of God and likens the man saying Yes to the woman (*"er sie bejaht"*) to saying Yes to God; this affirmation changes the passivity represented by his sleep during the woman's creation.[267] The two are in agreement on the great mystery of the creation of woman as the prefiguring of the covenant—which is the whole secret or inner basis of creation. Barth stresses that the saga concerns the mystery of the one not only created but brought to the man by God. "It is God's relationship to man, His mercy toward him, which brings about this completion of his creation, giving meaning to the existence of woman and disclosing her secret."[268]

Barth and von Kirschbaum include another dimension in their commentary on the creation of the woman who then confronts the man: that it was not without suffering that the man moved from aloneness to community. Barth sees in the anthropomorphic saga a fourfold dialectic: that the man sees the woman as unlike himself yet like himself (God created her from his rib); that he can neither produce her nor separate himself from her (passive in the creation, he was in deep, life-threatening sleep and was deprived of something); that while he suffered a loss, he is still whole (God preserved him and left him woundless); and finally, that the part taken from him has its own autonomous structure (as God made the man from the dust of the earth, he again made the new from the old in fashioning woman from part of the already existing male).[269] Von Kirschbaum states this dialectic of loss and gain succinctly: "This does not occur without suffering, that is, without seizing and assaulting this solitary man. The sage's words describe here how God claims and uses the man just in order to help him. He inflicts on him a mortal wound, he takes a rib from him and out of it makes woman."[270] It may be

265. *WF*, 9 (Shepherd:58).
266. Ibid., 9–10 (Shepherd:59).
267. *CD* III/1:185, 300, 295 (*KD* III/1:207–8, 343, 336–37).
268. *CD* III/1:298 (*KD* III/1:340).
269. *CD* III/1:296–97, 299, and in summary on 302 (*KD* III/1:338–39, 342, 345).
270. "Das geschieht nicht ohne Leiden, d.h. ohne Zugriff und Angriff auf den einsamen Menschen. Die Sage schildert hier in ihrer Sprache, wie Gott den Menschen selber beansprucht und braucht, um ihm zu helfen. Er fügt ihm eine tödliche Wunde bei, er entnimmt ihm eine Rippe und baut daraus die Frau" (*WF*, 9 [Shepherd:58]—a more didactic rendering).

the case that the theme of suffering in the creation of the woman from the man and by extension in all male/female relationships is more characteristic of von Kirschbaum than of Barth, and its recurring importance in *CD* III may derive largely from her. The theme appears prominently in her correspondence with Visser't Hooft Boddaert in 1941 on the subject of male/female encounter (*Begegnung*). A genuine encounter "implies *suffering* [*Leiden*] which, since we [women] are as we are and since the man is as he is, we cannot avoid and even do not *want* to avoid, if we remember that Christ fulfilled our destiny through his suffering and dying."[271]

To Barth and von Kirschbaum alike, it is Christology that does not allow a theologian to treat the human being in isolation; in its light an isolated human being is a fiction.[272] In the man Jesus, the New Testament witness gives "a kind of incomparable picture of human life and character. What emerges in it is a supreme I wholly determined by and to the Thou." We see that Jesus "stands under a twofold determination"— he is for man and he is for God; he is for man *as* he is for God, and he is for God *as* he is for man.[273]

Barth's Christology is self-consciously trinitarian: "The resolve and will of God was and is and will be: 'Christ and the community.' And for this reason [the New Testament] says of the humanity of man that it is *this* mystery; that it is the concealed and declared content, undisclosed without the Word and the Spirit and faith but disclosed by the Word, in the Spirit and for faith, of the reality 'Christ and the community.'"[274] And most specifically: humanity is modeled on "the man Jesus and His being for others," and "the man Jesus is modeled on God." Although one in essence, God is not alone but "primarily and properly He is in connection and fellowship. It is inevitable that we should recall the triune being of God at this point. . . . As the Father of the Son and the Son of the Father He is Himself I and Thou, confronting Himself and yet always one and the same in the Holy Ghost."[275] The human I and Thou cannot repeat the original love of Christ:

271. vK to HVH, 20 November 1941. In this comment one may hear the deaconess in von Kirschbaum that Frederick Herzog commented on and one may think of her personal situation in the Barth household.
272. *WF*, 85 (Shepherd:158), and also a theme in the correspondence with Visser't Hooft Boddaert; a running theme in *CD* III/2: e.g., 243ff., 264–65, 273, 323 (*KD* III/2:290ff., 317–18, 329, 389).
273. *CD* III/2:216 (*KD* III/2:257).
274. *CD* III/2:317 (*KD* III/2:383).
275. *CD* III/2:324 (*KD* III/2:390).

But even less can there be any question of living in the light of this original without accepting the summons to a relative imitation and reflection of this original. This once-for-all and unique light does not shine into the void but into a sphere of men and therefore of males and females, i.e., into the sphere described in Gen. 2, where it is decided that it is not good for man to be alone, where he is to recognize himself in another and another in himself, where humanity relentlessly means fellow-humanity, where the body or existence of woman is the same to man as his body or existence, where the I is not just unreal but impossible without the Thou, and where all the willing and longing of the I—on the far side of all egoism and altruism—must be the willing and longing of the Thou. This is the humanity of man which in the community is set in the unique and once-for-all light of the love of Christ.[276]

We can hear within this insistence the Barth who dreaded aloneness and perhaps the Barth who was attracted to socialism. But those are matters of reinforcement only.

Some observations are in order. It is not immediately clear how male and female *as such* uniquely supplement each other—though we must remember the self-evident value of otherness for a generation schooled in dialogical personalism.[277] And the link between the *imago* as male/female fellowship and the doctrine of the Trinity or triune being of God seems strained. We have seen that the trinitarian referent in the I-Thou relationship and the *imago* is the divine coexistence within God—the plurality of the divine being. That the human I-Thou relationship, the *imago*, and the triunity of God are not precisely analogous—that they are a mismatch—is suggested by the slippage in Barth's referencing from God's triunity to the fellowship of Father and Son and the cohumanity of Jesus Christ.[278] There is, of course, difference in the two sides of an analogy, but at a different level than the structural. The cohumanity of Jesus Christ *is* analogous for the human I-Thou. But to isolate the fellowship of Father and Son is to violate Barth's perichoretic and Chalcedonian theology. And to refer to the triune God may elide the

276. Ibid., 315 (*KD* III/2:380).
277. And, one might add, historicism.
278. Such "slippage" does not occur in von Kirschbaum; she references God's non-aloneness to his existence in the duality of Father and Son consistently. See, for example, *WF*, 84 (Shepherd:157).

essential duality, the betweenness of I-Thou encounter. The I-Thou concept is part of a stream in Barth that includes the dialectical theology of *Romans*, the theology of the human creature in relation to the absolute Other, which continued as an undercurrent in the "mature" Barth of the *analogia fidei*. I think one effect of the new doctrine of the *imago* is to strengthen that current.

In the *CD* III/4 treatment of the ethics of marriage, Barth describes the sexual encounter of male and female—"this natural dualism"—as a "truly breath-taking dialectic . . . the dialectic of difference and affinity, of real dualism and equally real unity, of utter self-recollection and utter transport beyond the bounds of self into union with another"—and this description leads into the cautionary reminder of the absolute Other with whom there can be no merging whatsoever.[279] In the same pattern, Schleiermacher, whose ideas about the feminine appealed to Barth, is praised for his "precise knowledge of the dialectic of the relationship of male and female" and for his inclusion therein of "the sensual and spiritual," "the earthly and the heavenly." He is then censured for depicting male and female in encounter as not merely undivided "but actually identical" and, further, as losing themselves (delusively) in divinization.[280] That Barth's theology for so many decades was worked out in dialogue with von Kirschbaum probably contributed to the persistence of duality.

The theme of gladness in the free electing of and election by the other is a major emphasis in Barth's version of the *imago*. Barth frequently invests the gladness or joy of mutuality with an aura of awe and mystery—that great mystery in the Epistles. The gladness in the freedom of the heart is akin to another Barthian motif—the joy of theology. And it has another face, that of worldly joy, of true *Eros*. Here Barth sees a positive contribution in the Hellenism that he so often opposes. We must recognize within the Greek *eros*, even if distorted in daemonism and hybris, an affirmation of the being of humankind as "free, radically open, willing, spontaneous, joyful, cheerful, and gregarious." The Greeks could live together in freedom as friends and, most important, "as citizens."[281] This "downward connection in the direction of the world of Greek *eros*" informed Paul in his hymns of Christian love.[282]

279. *CD* III/4:119–20 (*KD* III/4:131–32).
280. *CD* III/4:122 (*KD* III/4:134).
281. *CD* III/2:283 (*KD* III/2:341).
282. Ibid., 283–84 (*KD* III/2:341–42). Barth also thinks that to reject Hellenism entirely and violently would only lead to a counterinsurgence of "the Greek danger."

It is characteristic of Barth to heighten the intensity of two sides of an important matter alternately. Even in recognition of the correspondences in the *humanum* to the divine love in God's triune existence, he guards and maintains the absolute difference between human and divine. He distinguishes between the I-Thou love or summoning within Godself and the I-Thou love or summoning in the *humanum*, and between the I-Thou love in God's covenant with God's people and the I-Thou love within the *humanum*.[283] Yet all these relationships are covenantal—they are lasting connections between two subjects that are everlastingly distinct.[284] Human awareness of the existence of these relationships depends on God's disclosing of them as such in and by the Word and Spirit. The human being, created as man or woman, thus and only thus discovers that God has marked his or her nature as the one who lives with and for his or her fellow human, and this is the sign of the divine covenant: "This sign and likeness, this reality full of declaration, the mystery of his [and her] own reality, is no longer dumb but eloquent."[285] Von Kirschbaum, too, often tries to present the difference as well as the connection between the image of God in humanity and in Jesus Christ. While we can only point or refer to Jesus Christ (*"immer nur hinweisen"*) we can, as it were, become this reference—and being human we will have to become it ever anew (*"zu diesen Hinweis immer wieder werden"*).[286]

Within the *humanum*, the male and female who hear one another are engaged in dialogue—a dialogue that is not two monologues.[287] Barth also uses the concepts and language of existentialism, which is sometimes the language of the 1920s. The I and the Thou are subjects, not objects, to each other. They are free. Of course the human being as a creature posited by God is object. But he and she are subjects too, as they are responsible before God, as they know and obey and seek after God and thus posit themselves. The human being "is the one creature which God in creating calls to free personal responsibility before Him, and thus treats as a self, a free being." To speak in any way of the human being is to "allude to man in his freedom, to man who is active subject in

283. *CD* III/1:196 (*KD* III/1:220); *CD* III/2:320 (*KD* III/2:386).
284. *CD* III/2:320–21 (*KD* III/2:388).
285. *CD* III/2:322 (*KD* III/2:388–89).
286. *WF*, 45 (Shepherd:104). The context of this formulation is discussion of male-female ordering in analogy to Christ and community. I have abstracted the dynamic common to both.
287. *CD* III/2:259 (*KD* III/2:310). This contrast is an important motif in Buber (see Friedman, *Martin Buber's Life and Work*, 68, 312).

responsibility before God."²⁸⁸ But we are talking about "real man" and that means about man in encounter with fellow man, human in encounter with fellow human. Barth provides "the basic formula" for encounter: "I am as Thou art." The "human style is always to be I for the self and Thou for the other." "Nor is this human being static, but dynamic and active. It is not an *esse* but an *existere*. To say man is to say history."²⁸⁹ Our historical, temporal existence becomes further important as such when we look to Jesus, the true image of God and the Lord of time, who in his time lives not only with, but for God, and not only with, but for humanity.²⁹⁰ In their otherness to each other, the male and female each confronts the other with "an unfathomable abyss." Yet they meet and create an indestructible bridge when they recognize and summon each other as human subjects in genuine dialogue.²⁹¹

As in Buber's idea of the "between," the meeting of I and Thou is immediate. The I-Thou encounter is as absorbing and in its own way as overwhelming as the encounter between God and his people Israel, and it should be similarly determinative. In the "true plurality of male and female," humans "are all that this differentiation and relationship includes in its whole dialectic . . . of gift and task, of need and satisfaction, of lack and fulfillment, of antithesis and union, of superiority and subjection."²⁹² But, again, the male/female encounter is paradigmatic for all encounters: this can be the case because "each fellow-man is a whole world."²⁹³

In its continuing, lived nature, the I-Thou encounter of the *humanum* is further like the covenantal relation of God and the human creature. Barth tells us "we are not created the covenant-partners of God, but to be His covenant-partners, to be His partners in the history which is the goal of His creation and in which His work as Creator finds its continuation and fulfillment. That this is achieved, that we fulfill this determination, that this history is in train and moves steadily to its goal, is a matter of the free grace with which God deals in sovereignty with His creature."²⁹⁴ Why is it certain that the *imago Dei* persists after the

288. *CD* III/2:194–95 (*KD* III/2:232).
289. *CD* III/2:248 (*KD* III/2:296).
290. *CD* III/2, Par. 47: Man in His Time, Sec. I, Jesus, Lord of Time: 437ff. (*KD* III/2:524ff.).
291. *CD* III/2:194ff., esp. 194–95; 248, 286 (*KD* III/2:230–31, 296, 344–45).
292. *CD* III/1:187 (*KD* III/1:209).
293. *CD* III/2:258 (*KD* III/2:309 ["Eine ganze Welt ist ja schliesslich jeder Mitmensch . . ."]).
294. *CD* III/2:320; similar to III/1:197 (*KD* III/2:385–86; *KD* III/1:221).

Fall? Because "[w]hat man does not possess he can neither bequeath nor forfeit."[295] This is the theology of one who could not rest in temporal solutions to social problems that claimed completeness and sufficiency. It has another side in analogy to Jesus Christ as the Truth and the Life. Following Eduard Schweizer, Barth takes the Johannine passages "in which Jesus describes himself as the Light, the Door, the Bread, the Shepherd, the Vine and the resurrection [to] point to pure process, to a being which is caught up in its products, so that it is impossible to distinguish between this being in itself or apart from these products, but only in them."[296]

We can now see more clearly the eschatological dimension in this doctrine of the *imago Dei*. The I-Thou existence of the *humanum* is a preparation for the realization of covenant partnership with God. What the human being is in relationship with the fellow-human, he or she is "in hope of the being and action of the One who is his [and her] original in this relationship."[297] And in von Kirschbaum: "from the beginning" Adam recognized Eve as fellow human and so recognized that he was not alone "but existed in encounter and just in this way is prepared for the encounter with God."[298] Theological anthropology in Barth and von Kirschbaum has both ecclesiological and eschatological dimensions.

Barth, self-consciously following Paul, reads the *imago* from Jesus.[299] He sees Jesus in the three ways that are separate paragraphs in chapter 10 of III/2: Jesus as Man for God (par. 44), Man for other men (par. 45), and Whole man (par. 46). Cohumanity involves obedience that is free acceptance of God's determination of one's existence; cohumanity requires a self undivided into soul and body just as it is undivided in its response to a human Thou or to the divine. Thus it is the case that the *humanum* is the embodied love of male and female.

The sexual aspect of the male/female duality presents and connotes total acceptance and union. Each—male and female—is a totality of body and soul that becomes part of a greater totality. The marriage relationship situates "the freedom of the heart" of I and Thou for each other. It is holistic and erotic: here, indeed, "the Bible thinks and speaks far more seriously 'erotically' than all Hellenism."[300] The sexual relation-

295. *CD* III/1:200 (*KD* III/1:225).
296. *CD* III/2:56 (*KD* III/2:65).
297. Ibid., 324 (*KD* III/2:391).
298. *WF*, 45 (Shepherd:103–4).
299. *CD* III/1:202f. (*KD* III/1:228f.).
300. *CD* III/2:293 (*KD* III/2:354).

ship in marriage is absolutely distinct from family and procreation. In his exegeses of Genesis 1:27f. and Genesis 2:18, 21f., Barth calls and recalls our attention to the fact that the text refers to "man and woman in their relationship as such, not to fatherhood and motherhood or the establishment of the family." The relationship has its own reality and dignity and is "the basic relationship involving all others."[301]

Barth's and von Kirschbaum's exegeses of the Song of Songs are commentaries on the human wholeness in the *imago*. The eroticism of the Song of Songs is not an allegory: the Song is exactly what its words proclaim, a poem of uninhibited love between a man and a woman. If Genesis 2:18–25 is "the first Magna Carta of humanity," the Song of Songs is "almost a second."[302] Genesis 2 and Song of Songs are the two halves of the anthropology of Hebrew scripture. After Genesis 2 and throughout the Old Testament, the covenantal relationship between Yahweh and Yahweh's people is described as a marriage in which God keeps his pledge of faith despite Israel's transgressions.[303] (One notes in this analogy that the fault for a bad marriage lies with the wife.) Then comes the astonishing voice of the Song.[304] The Song of Songs shows us what Genesis 2, in a different way, declares: that although marriage in the Old Testament looks always to the birth of a messiah (and it is for this reason that marriage must be considered sacred),[305] procreation is not the essence of the male/female relationship. It tells us beyond any doubt that embodied, sexual love in marriage does not exist in a separate, "merely" erotic sphere outside the *humanum*; rather, sexual love is part of what von Kirschbaum and Barth consider the witness of marriage, the true affirmation, the *Bejahung*, of the Thou.[306] To Barth, the Song tells us of human love "in a form which is almost terrifyingly strong and unequivocal. . . . It is almost incredible that this should be found so unreservedly in the Bible."[307] And the Song is of one piece with Genesis 2. Its substance, like that of Genesis 2:25, is "the *eros* for which there is no such thing as shame"; the lovers are fulfilling the covenant for the sake of which God created man as male and female. "The Song of

301. Ibid.
302. *CD* III/2:291, 293–94 (*KD* III/2:351, 354–55).
303. This is Barth's reading from his earliest lectures on the Bible (collected in *The Word of God and the Word of Man* in 1924) onward.
304. *WF*, 11 (Shepherd:61).
305. *CD* III/1:312 (*KD* III/1:357).
306. Von Kirschbaum, *WF*, 18, 22 (Shepherd:70, 75); Barth, *CD* III/2:306–7 (*KD* III/2:370). This is a recurring motif.
307. *CD* III/1:312–13 (*KD* III/1:358).

Songs is one long description of the rapture, the unquenchable yearning [*unstillbaren Sehnsucht*] and the restless willingness and readiness,
with which both partners in this covenant hasten towards encounter.
Gen. 2 is even more radical in its great brevity. It tells us that only male
and female together are man."[308] Barth asks us to look at and absorb the
dialogue of ecstasy of man and woman in the Song, the immediacy and
physicality of which are highlighted by depiction against a background
"of day and night, of the passing seasons, of the plants and animals of
the Palestinian scene."[309] As noteworthy as the eroticism, and necessary
for it, is what Barth and von Kirschbaum recognize as a new voice—the
voice of the woman, whose feelings and words are absolutely parallel to
those of the man.[310] Von Kirschbaum hears that voice "above all."[311] We
shall return to Barth's development of the concept of inversion from this
parallelism.

The occurrence of the Song toward the end of the Old Testament,
separated from Genesis by a territory of sin, infamy, and shame dominated by the Law "and especially the danger and prohibition of adultery,"
is significant. The beginning and the end, "the origin and goal, both
between Yahweh and Israel and between man and woman, are as
depicted in Genesis 2 and the Song of Songs. In retrospect of creation
and prospect of the new creation of the last time, we can and may and
must speak of man and woman as is done in these texts."[312] Von Kirschbaum does speak of man and woman and the Song of Songs as Barth
does, if less extensively. She highlights the expression in the *Hohelied* of
unquenchable yearning (*unstillbare Sehnsucht*) and unconditional
union (*vorbehaltlose Vereinigung*) and connects it as Barth does to
Genesis 2: "Here again appears the central theme of I-Thou encounter
in Gen. 2:18."[313]

Barth and von Kirschbaum have a strong, deep theology of marriage
as embodied love, an integrated view of the male/female sexual relationship though in the context of a very Calvinistic view of sin, of the
mortal sickness in historical existence, the *aber* that goes with the *ja*.[314]

308. Ibid., 313 (*KD* III/1:358–59).
309. *CD* III/2:294 (*KD* III/2:355).
310. Barth in *CD* III/1:313 (*KD* III/1:358); von Kirschbaum, *WF*, 11–12 (Shepherd:61–62).
311. Von Kirschbaum, *WF*, 12 (Shepherd:61).
312. *CD* III/2:294 (*KD* III/2:355).
313. *WF*, 11–12 (Shepherd:61).
314. First articulated by Barth in "Theologie und Kirche" (1923) in *Gesammelte Vorträge* 2, to which my attention was called by E. Busch.

They both oppose strongly those who would use Galatians 3:28 to negate sex or gender differences.[315] Barth writes on human sexuality more extensively than von Kirschbaum, a reflection perhaps of experience, but certainly of his freedom as a married male to speak on the subject in the middle decades of the twentieth century in Europe. The *CD* III/4 context of a Protestant ethic of marriage, as distinct from von Kirschbaum's contribution toward a Protestant doctrine of women, further requires him to give it more attention. It seems also to reflect greater theological interest in the subject. Nevertheless, von Kirschbaum too insists on the wholeness of male/female encounter. From it she abstracts the equality of the woman's participation in the encounter; with reference to her relationship with Barth, one may also wonder if this core of wholeness is a countertext to her rejection of divorce. Paul knew, she states, that embodied love is essential in marriage; without it the union of male and female would be as meaningless as the fornication he condemned in 1 Corinthians 6. It is "the whole human being, the human being as soul and body, who is addressed by the Word of God."[316]

Barth and von Kirschbaum both maintain that knowledge of the New Testament covenant of Christ with his church is needed to shed the light that *enables* us to see marriage in the Old Testament as analogous to the relationship of Yahweh and Israel.[317] The prophetic background of the Old Testament is a stream flowing from Genesis, parallel to the stream connecting Genesis and the Song of Songs, that sets the framework within which to read the Song. The Song in this light is neither allegorical nor literal alone. Both streams are about Israel and Yahweh, as the New Testament finally makes clear. Von Kirschbaum evokes Eve as "Mother of All Living" and bearer of hope for Israel and humankind. The Song presents and re-presents the covenant of Israel and God: "the eschatological connection in the representation of the regal splendor of Solomon" wherein "the covenant stands out, no longer in the shadow of Israel's infidelity [*Untreu*] but in the light of the faithfulness of God which covers that infidelity."[318] Furthermore, Genesis and the Song of Songs *and* Ephesians 5 are the real "unit" about the male/female relationship.

---

315. *CD* III/2:294–96 (*KD* III/2:356); von Kirschbaum, "The Role of Women," 114 (Shepherd:193).
316. *WF*, 33–34 (Shepherd:90).
317. Von Kirschbaum: *WF*, 18 (Shepherd:70); Barth: *CD* III/2:298–99 (*KD* III/2:360–61).
318. *WF*, 12 (Shepherd:61).

Despite the theological clarity that unites Old and New Testaments such that "we are forced to affirm convergence rather than divergence," despite the great mystery of correspondence asserted in Ephesians 5,[319] there is room for some ambiguity in Barth and von Kirschbaum about the status of Old Testament knowledge independent of the New Testament. Barth argues at some length that it is the very imperfections of Israel in the covenant with Yahweh that enable Israel to comprehend God's true, everlasting commitment. The descriptions by the prophets of "the alliance between Yahweh and Israel" in terms of love and marriage have as their context the ungratefulness, unfaithfulness, and shame, the harlotry and adultery and prostitution in which Yahweh finds Israel.[320] Some conclusions can be drawn immediately. That Yahweh is an incomparable husband that no earthly man can imitate indicates that we have here an analogy, not an identity. That Israel is an inescapably human wife verifies that marriage is never to be understood in an "ideal" sense or one in which the erotic has no place.[321] Barth goes a step further in III/2. The Old Testament, he tells us, shows "an amazing knowledge" about the ultimate, covenantal meaning of the relationship of man and woman; without such a knowledge, it would have been "intolerable to see this inter-creaturely relationship in the holy relationship between Yahweh and Israel." Then, something that is not vertical from above: "Again, without a knowledge of the menacing and shattering of the relationship between man and woman the Old Testament could not have such a terribly plastic view of the devastation of the relationship between Yahweh and Israel."[322]

Human sexuality is uniquely holy and dangerous in its potential for love and for transgression. In the frailty and imperfection of the *humanum*, it exists on a razor's edge, in a delicate, precarious balance within the totality of life. Reference has been made to Barth's program of demythologizing, de-demonizing, and decentering of the sexual relationship in marriage. It is just because the sexual relationship of male and female, of I and Thou, is "a vital, nervous, crucial point of their being" that it must not be isolated and regarded as either determinative or

---

319. *CD* III/1:320–21 (*KD* III/1:366–67).
320. Ibid., 315–16 (*KD* III/1:360–61).
321. *CD* III/1:318–20 (*KD* III/1:364–66).
322. *CD* III/2:298 (*KD* III/1:360). Von Kirschbaum may allude to this distinctive idea when she tells us that "the man who wrote of the Fall was an Israelite who had before his eyes the Israel whose unfaithfulness God had ever again to confront" but to whom God still remained true (*WF*, 11 [Shepherd:60]).

extraneous.[323] It was "the genius of sin," or again "the awful genius of sin," to attack the *humanum* at just this point, corrupting the human judgment of good and evil in "this most intimate sphere of humanity and human glory and freedom." Here the human judgment "stumbled" and "first discovered shame . . . here first it conceived it to be its duty to frame moral codes, thus causing and introducing corruption and shame. Where, from the standpoint of God's creation, everything is pure and holy and harmless, there the impure eye of disobedient man sees nothing but impurity, unholiness and temptation, and in so doing defiles, dishonours and destroys everything."[324]

From *The Epistle to the Romans* onward, Barth opposed the traditional dualism of matter and spirit: he meant something very different by his human-divine dualism.[325] He took pains in his introduction of the mature doctrine of the *imago* to repudiate a Greek dualism that would see a spirit imprisoned in a material body: the human being created by God is *not* a soul within a transient, "accidental" body.[326] The insistent holism of the doctrine of the *imago* is consistent with the Barth of *Romans*, and the reception of that work may have reinforced, if it did not create, his awareness that he had always to reassert and clarify his criticism and opposition to spirit/flesh dualism. One may witness this holism in set pieces of high elegance, in Barth's unique style, in his commentary on male/female encounter in Genesis and Song of Songs—for example, the question and answer sets in III/1:321 and in III/2:299f. These also bespeak an internalization of the I-Thou idea beyond extraneous assimilation.[327]

Barth's doctrine of the *imago Dei* had many implications. In its light the history of humanity after the Fall displays two basic forms of sexual disorder: "an evil eroticism and an evil absence of eroticism," or the "demonic and bourgeois views of love and marriage."[328] Here is another instance of Barth's radical middle.

---

323. *CD* III/4:131 (*KD* III/4:144).
324. *CD* III/1:311 (*KD* III/1:356); *CD* III/2:292 (*KD* III/2:352–53).
325. See extensive discussion of this point in W. Lowe, "Barth as Critic of Dualism" and *Theology and Difference*.
326. *CD* III/1:243 (*KD* III/1:276).
327. It should be clear that I agree with but modify George Hunsinger's distinction between doctrinally derived and assimilated ideas in Barth (*How to Read Karl Barth*, 62).
328. *CD* III/1:310 (*KD* III/1:355). In this historical sketch, Barth includes what he sees as the abstract, sexless, and therefore anemic and soulless ideals of man and woman in the movement for female liberation and the blind male dominion to which this women's movement reacted so jealously. See below, pages 169–72, regarding Barth's and von Kirschbaum's discussion of Simone de Beauvoir.

Shared Hierarchicalism

Because it is at the heart of the I-Thou relationship for man and woman to continually but never finally discover themselves as such, because the *imago* is relational rather than a set of qualities or properties, Barth and von Kirschbaum can reject the stereotyping of male and female "natures," the phenomenologies or typologies of the sexes. They consider but reject various attempts at "psychologizing," or they see "half-truths" in these attempts that should be avoided because they lure the uncritical.[329] Male and female should rely on "the divine command," which will permit them to "discover their specific sexual nature, and to be faithful to it . . . without being enslaved to any preconceived opinions." Then, "in every situation, in face of every task and in every conversation, their functions and possibilities . . . will be distinctive and diverse, and will never be interchangeable." And, Barth assures us (defensively, I think), "life is richer, and above all the command of God is more manifold, than might appear from preconceived opinions."[330]

The male/female relationship is almost a perfect example of present-ness. However, one of the major reasons that the male/female "freedom of community" is a type, the basic form for all to follow, is that it is coordinated.[331] And Barth, it seems, cannot imagine a nonhierarchical coordination. So it is not enough to say that the "reciprocity of the sexes, and therefore that which they have in common, must take absolute precedence of the difference in their modes of interrelation."[332]

Barth and von Kirschbaum have not escaped the habit of stereo-typing. Their great inconsistency is that, while their doctrine prescribes mutual subordination, while it glories in mutual coordination, they consider it natural (as well as scripturally correct) for woman to subor-dinate herself to man. In Barth's words, this is "not problematical but self-evident."[333] While it is true that "real men and real women" are too complex to be categorized by such assumption as outward and objective versus inward and subjective, it nevertheless "cannot be contested that both physiologically and biblically a certain strength and corresponding

---

329. *CD* III/4:152ff. (*KD* III/4:169ff.) on E. Brunner; *CD* III/2:287 (*KD* III/2:346–67) on psychologizing; von Kirschbaum, *WF*, 88 (Shepherd:161).

330. *CD* III/4:153–54 (*KD* III/4:170–71).

331. *CD* III/4:164 (*KD* III/4:182–83).

332. Ibid. Elizabeth Frykberg (*Karl Barth's Theological Anthropology*) correctly sees that the superordination-subordination hierarchy vitiates the perichoretic nature of the male-female relationship.

333. *CD* III/1:303 (*KD* III/1:346–47).

precedence are a very general characteristic of man, and a weakness and corresponding subsequence of women." He goes on to state that "in what the strength and precedence consist on the one side, and the weakness and subsequence on the other . . . is something which is better left unresolved in a general statement."[334]

General statements can, of course, say a lot. Barth's views on the natural subordination of women are inextricably tied with his Romantic notions about women. From this viewpoint one can revisit the story of the creation of Eve. Barth speaks several times in III/1 of "the mystery of woman."[335] Theologically, the mystery surrounding a particular woman is twice seen by Barth as noetic: the Virgin Birth and Eve's creation are both signs of God's incomprehensibility to human ways of knowing.[336] It is true that later in III/4 Barth maintains that both man and woman are a mystery to each other—their ultimate incomprehensibility is essential to their otherness.[337] However, the dominant note in III/1 is the awe of Adam before "the mystery of [Eve's] being and the mystery of her creation"; this mystery stands before him "in all its concreteness."[338] And she will always be present, inescapably present, for the man. She is his "incomprehensible honor," his "strange glory."[339] Her presence is also threatening. We have seen that Adam was not merely passive in the creation of Eve: somehow he allowed it. The "mortal wound" that he suffered "entailed sacrifice, pain and mortal peril as God marched to the climax of His work. God spared him, and yet this strange mixture of the perfect joy of finding and the never-absent pain of deprivation in his relationship to woman is the constant reminder of that from which he was spared."[340]

We can infer that Barth's attitude toward the Pauline injunction of silence for women in the church was also shaped by this Romantic view of the feminine and its association with ineffability. Concluding the sole reference to the New Testament injunction on silence in *CD* III/1 is this characterization: "The *arcana revelatio* which man perceives [in the Gen. 2 account] is this still, quiet, soft and silent message of the work furnished and presented by God. Woman created by God and brought to

334. *CD* III/2:287 (*KD* III/2:346–47).
335. *CD* III/1:298–99, 302–3 (*KD* III/2:341–42, 345–46).
336. On Mary, see above, page 101; on the noetic basis of the creation of Eve: *CD* III/1:298 (*KD* III/1:340).
337. *CD* III/4:167 (*KD* III/4:186).
338. *CD* III/1:299 (*KD* III/1:342).
339. *CD* III/1:302 (*KD* III/1:345–46).
340. Ibid.

man reveals herself by her existence. She convinces by her presence. She cannot be mistaken, but can be recognized without any effort on her part."[341] It is natural and positive that women have been assigned the role of representing the listening church. Barth's lack of extensive consideration of the problem of women and silence in the church—in contrast to von Kirschbaum, as we will see—is the effect of not really seeing it *as* a problem.[342]

The story of the creation of woman is distinguished from that of man not only by the aura—and implicit threat—of mystery that surrounds her. In sharpest contrast to the man, *she* does not find *him* threatening; her mandated coexistence with him is "self-evident":

> For as God has made her out of and for man, as man has to confirm this by his choice and explanation, she is this, and in her case the question of choice or explanation does not arise. She would not be woman if she had even a single possibility apart from being man's helpmeet. She chooses that for which God has chosen her. She thus chooses herself by refraining from choice; by finding herself surrounded and sustained by the joyful choice of the man, as his elect.[343]

The mutual election of man and women is less mutual for the woman at closer look.

Barth is consistent in his attribution of creativity to the male. He speaks (most often in III/4) of male initiative in relation to which "the task and function of woman" is to follow. "Properly speaking," he assures his reader, "the business of woman, her task and function, is to actualize the fellowship in which man can only precede her, stimulating, leading and inspiring."[344] He repeats the assignment to the woman to "follow up the initiative which is assigned to him [the man]"; this includes the assumption that she will "be the answer to his question" and "give effect to his inspiration."[345] Is Barth approximating von Kirschbaum on the

---

341. Ibid., 327 (*KD* III/1:374). One might well think of Gerda in *Buddenbrooks*.

342. To him the only problem that follows from 1 Corinthians 14:34–35 is what feminists have made of it. They have failed to read verse 33, which explains that God is the author of peace, not confusion. And peace in the church is preserved by proper order, not talking (*CD* III/2:309–10 [*KD* III/2:372–74]; *CD* III/4:156 [*KD* III/4:172–73]).

343. *CD* III/1:303 (*KD* III/1:346–47). See also discussion above, Part 1, on von Kirschbaum's options.

344. *CD* III/4:171 (*KD* III/4:189–90).

345. Ibid., 175 (*KD* III/4:195).

creativity of women, on the constructive building of community by women? No, though he and von Kirschbaum come within negotiating range in their delineation of spheres. The unambiguous context of this passage is the assurance to woman that acceptance of her subordination to man is not demeaning. Fellowship is actualized by woman's acceptance of her place in the order designed by God.

Von Kirschbaum allows the attribution of male initiative in the context of women as representatives of the church vis-à-vis Christ.[346] What she does not allow in the responsiveness of woman is an active/passive dichotomy for the male and female or the denial of creativity in women. And she argues that male/female differentiation guarantees the independence of each.[347] So she can finally offer a vista of the *wirkliche Frau* that seems both biblically derived and contemporary. More problematically she talks of the natural quality of dependency in women that makes them the ideal witness of the church vis-à-vis Christ, while a woman's corresponding subordination to the male enables her to be free from the lifelong anxieties of the weak.[348]

Von Kirschbaum knows more acutely than Barth that she is in an awkward position on the subordination of women. Her denials that subordination is problematic, in what seems the form of negation, are more extensive. She is also more honest in attempting to confront scriptural problems for women in the twentieth century.[349] Only when Barth focuses more closely on *applicatio* (the last step of his threefold exegetical formula, *explicatio, meditatio, applicatio*)[350] do we see another view of woman that is scripturally based in a freer way. Only when von Kirschbaum draws on her experience as a woman and among women, does she allow *meditatio* to more fully inform *applicatio*. But these final fruits are hard to see amid the hierarchicalism of male/female ordering. Is the ordering a thicket that obscures or a fault line that threatens an entire theology?

Barth sometimes describes male/female fellowship as mutual election. However in his exegesis of Genesis 2:18, he describes woman, the help-

346. *WF*, 22 (Shepherd:75).
347. It is "precisely the differentiation that guarantees the independence of each and also their equality of birth as counterparts to each other" ("The Role of Women," 115–16 [Shepherd:194]).
348. "Frei sein von der Lebensangst des Schwächeren" (*WF*, 33, 43 [Shepherd:89, 101]).
349. On 1 Timothy 2:8ff.: Barth does not deal with it extensively; von Kirschbaum says this is a tough text (*schwierig*) and works on it (*WF*, 53 [Shepherd:114]).
350. See *CD* I/2:722–40.

meet or (in his preferred term) partner, created after the male, as "the elect of man."[351] And in correspondence to the covenant, the male is "primarily and properly Yahweh" and the female "primarily and properly Israel."[352] The order in the relationship of husband and wife, and by extension in all male/female relationships, is treated at length, and sometimes defensively, by both von Kirschbaum and Barth. Their thinking on the subject provides an informative vista on early European feminism. Their discussions are guided by their understanding of key scriptural texts, especially 1 Corinthians 11:3 and Ephesians 5:22–33, in the light of Christology. One observes that the strict equality of the image of God in male and female in *CD* III/1 is displaced by equivalence in its later explication in III/2.

For both, it is true in both absolute and relative senses that the male is superordinate to the female and the female subordinate to the male, and that this order was established in creation and is not merely chronological.[353] The first point they would note is the last one: that ultimately we are speaking of a mystery, of Christ and the community (Eph. 5:32).[354] In III/1, Barth has also begun to pay closer attention to the various meanings of *dominion*. Consonant with his rejection of the *analogia entis* and all abstract and substantialist categories in regard to the *imago*, he firmly rejects the traditional inclusion of *dominium terrae* in the *imago*. It is true, he grants, that Genesis brings together the image and dominion over the earth, but not in a necessary or "technical connection." *Dominium terrae* is simply "allotted" to the human creature who is already distinguished by the *imago*.[355] Barth asks whether those who insist that dominion over the earth is part of the *imago* are not "really more

351. *CD* III/1:303 (*KD* III/1:347).
352. *CD* III/2:297 (*KD* III/2:358). Barth's phrase is "zuerst und eigentlich."
353. *CD* III/1:301ff. (*KD* III/1:344ff.)
354. Barth: *CD* III/2:315–16 (*KD* III/2:380–81); von Kirschbaum: *WF*, 20–21 (Shepherd: 73–74).
355. Barth is certain that dominion over the earth means primarily that the earth, not the heavens, is humanity's dwelling place. Genesis does not give us license to blast tunnels through mountains or to dry up or divert rivers—it is not, in fact, concerned with such questions. Genesis does inform us that we have lordship over the animals because we, not they, were created in God's image. This means that we have special dignity within creation. We have (with animals) peaceful use of the superfluities of the plant kingdom for sustenance. Only with the Fall does the breach of peace and the killing of animals for food begin. Repeatedly in the exposition of Gen. 1:26–30, Barth reminds us that we have lordship *in* creation, not *of* or *over* it; that our power is only relative compared to God's power; and that much of it is actually a curse—we will reap its bitter fruits following the Fall (*CD* III/1:205ff. [*KD* III/1:231ff.]).

interested in a Greek and modern concept of humanity than an Old Testament" one.[356]

The superordination and subordination represent—and are needed to completely represent—the fullness of the divine economy. The male who (as we have seen) leaves father and mother to cleave to his wife, "without whom he himself could not be a man and could not be saved,"[357] is superordinate for two purposes. First, his superordination affirms the total order of God's creation, or "the order which embraces them both." Second, in his superordination he imitates the archetypal love and salvific headship—Barth presents them as inseparable—of Christ for all humankind. No one can repeat "the original" of the love of Christ for his community. Christ's headship was and is his alone, and it is important in every way to note that the man "is not the Christ of the woman."[358] However, the male can be a copy and reflection or imitator of Jesus Christ, the effectuator and archetype. The male's superordination in relation to woman "cannot mean more for man than to be first, the leader, the initiator [again], the representative of the order which embraces them both, and for woman *not* to be head in relation to man cannot mean less than to be the second, the led, the one who [again] must follow up the initiative, standing in the order represented by him."[359] Following Ephesians 5:24, the woman represents the church or community, which is an order within the order of creation; it is also Israel. The woman is "the type of the community listening to Christ and the apostolic admonition," the one of whom it can be said that all hearing and obedience are "represented in her hearing and obedience."[360] The woman also imitates the scriptural role of discipleship. "Man may and should precede her in imitation of the attitude of Jesus Christ, as she does in imitation of the attitude of the community and therefore discipleship."[361] Or in von Kirschbaum's words, Jesus Christ "is the image and honor of God, to which the human male, as head of the woman, can only point. But he should and may ever again become this reference; he may . . . become its reflection [*Abglanz*] . . . while the woman should and may become the image of the community [*Abbild der Gemeinde*] and thus be to the honor of the male as the community is to the honor of Christ."[362]

356. *CD* III/1:194 (*KD* III/1:218).
357. *CD* III/4:175 (*KD* III/4:195).
358. *CD* III/2:311, 315, and III/4:173, 175 (*KD* III/2:374–75, 380; *KD* III/4:193, 195).
359. *CD* III/4:173–74 (*KD* III/4:193–94).
360. *CD* III/2:314 (*KD* III/2:379).
361. *CD* III/4:175 (*KD* III/4:195–96).
362. *WF*, 45 (Shepherd:104).

6. Traces of Input, Signs of Exchange, Abiding Differences

Von Kirschbaum cites several authorities in her exegesis of 1 Corinthians 11:3, but Barth is not one of these. It should be recalled that von Kirschbaum told Henriette Visser't Hooft in 1941 that her work essentially centered around and proceeded from 1 Corinthians 11, "the place where the New Testament speaks most fundamentally on the question of man/woman ordering."[363] Yet the closeness and concord in Barth's and von Kirschbaum's later thinking is nowhere as apparent as in this difficult, charged subject matter. So too is the interweaving and cross-fertilizing of ideas in their collaboration.

It is in a source note in *CD* III/4, preceding an exposition of 1 Corinthians 11, that Barth cites a page in *Die wirkliche Frau* (in lecture III on the role of women in proclamation) and a page in his own work in III/2.[364] When one looks at each of those pages, one finds the following: a sketch of the situation that Paul addresses in Corinth, Paul's consequent need to place the ordered relationship of male and female in relation to the supraordination and subordination embodied in Jesus Christ, and then attention to the *Reihenfolge*, the sequence of statements in verse 3 that places the anthropological statement—that the man is head of the woman—between two christological statements. In von Kirschbaum's concentrated distillation, "Jesus Christ thereby establishes and relativizes all earthly power." In Barth's eloquent summation,

"The head of the woman is the man." So little does this ascribe to man or refer to woman! So sharply and clearly is it determined and limited on both sides by what is primarily and properly the affair of Christ! His is the superordination and His the subordination. His is the place of man and His the place of woman. And what place is there to speak of little or much?[365]

<hr>

363. "Meine Arbeit geht im wesentlichen um 1.Kor.11 als der Stelle, in der am grundsätzlichsten das Wort zu der Frage der Ordnung Mann/Frau in der hl. Schrift gesprochen ist, resp.im Neuen Testament. Aber zunächst führt das in so viele Einzeluntersuchungen, dass ich noch nicht sehe, zu welchem Ergebnis ich kommen werde" (vK to HVH, 20 November 1941).

364. *CD* III/4:173 (*KD* III/4:193), citing *WF*, 42–43 (Shepherd:100–101). The exegesis reference is for *CD* III/2:309–11 (*KD* III/2:372f.).

365. *CD* III/2:311 (*KD* III/2:375).

Von Kirschbaum and Barth alike oppose not only the threat of anarchy in the rejection of any earthly power, but the common misinterpretation of verse 3 to justify the male assumption of a scale (*Skala* in Barth) or ladder (*Stufenleiter* in von Kirschbaum) that he can ascend and also use to bar direct relationship between the female and Christ. The source reference in III/4 is to the same text in two voices. Whose set of ideas is it? As I think Barth is saying, he and von Kirschbaum *both* own it. As I think von Kirschbaum is saying, she is responsible for the fact that they both own it. Somewhat like the sermons Barth and Thurneysen copublished without individual attribution of their parts (the difference is that both were credited with authorship) and like the collaboration von Kirschbaum described on the visit to Union Theological Seminary in 1962, both have authored the chain of ideas, both have nurtured it, and at various phases they hammered it out together in theological dialogue.

The reach and insistent reality of the male/female order is enormous: all ethical decisions must be made in its light. Every man and every woman, in marriage and outside it, is placed at a crossroads by the fact that God's command uncompromisingly requires of them the observance of divine order in their relationships.[366] From the exegesis of the creation story in III/1, we know the essential nature of male priority and female inferiority *and* we understand that *inferior* is not used pejoratively.[367] The *imago Dei* is the related and differentiated creation and existence of male and female. But subsequentness is not always the exact meaning of the created order. In the III/4 version of the exegesis, immediately following a strong, holistic affirmation of the mutuality of the male/female relationship, Barth posts one of his "Everything depends on this" signs with regard to "the concrete subordination of woman to man." This is "the whole point of the text" in Paul.[368] "Everything depends on this" because Paul's exhortation to women to obey, to be subordinate to their husbands, is the archetype of exhortation to the community, to men and women and all its members.

Is the concrete subordination of women the whole point of Barth too? Is this why he uses words like *subversion* and *confusion* for the effects of the unrest in the church in Corinth?[369] It seems probable that he is reflecting the normal anxieties set off by the likelihood of real change in power structures in which one has an advantaged position. In

366. *CD* III/4:176 (*KD* III/4:196).
367. *CD* III/1:301ff. (*KD* III/1:344ff.).
368. *CD* III/4:175 (*KD* III/4:196).
369. Ibid., 174 (*KD* III/4:194).

this regard the post–World War II years were a more intense replay of the previous postwar time. Barth marshals the female support of von Kirschbaum in his exegesis. And throughout *Die wirkliche Frau*, Von Kirschbaum gives him the vigorous and wholehearted defense of Paul that he needs and that she thinks her audience needs—and, in the process, she appropriates some rhetorical cues from Barth. For von Kirschbaum, the fact that women in the New Testament all follow Jesus indicates that they are in a different world than that proposed by the movement for women's emancipation; the fact that the natural existence of women is realized in their Christian existence in the community of Christ shows Christianity to be "the most revolutionary event in the history of women."[370]

Why this nonnegotiable stance in both on male/female order? Most immediately because it is being challenged by early feminism, just as (in their association) Paul's epistle was directed to the inappropriate enthusiasm with which women in Corinth greeted the new gospel and mistakenly tried to apply what they had learned of Christian freedom. In a belabored way, Barth characterizes the women of Corinth and the *Frauenfrage* as part of "the old aeon"—that is, a specious progressivism that ignores the inwardly necessary, not merely conventional, nature of the male/female order.[371] An essential part of von Kirschbaum's and Barth's exegesis of 1 Corinthians 11:3 is affirmation of its compatibility with Galatians 3:28— the ultimate absolute versus the human and relative, the locus for an obedience that is freely chosen.[372]

Practically speaking, what would be lost if the male/female order were set aside? The proper functioning of the I-Thou relationship would be lost. What seems most important for Barth is to establish a stabilizing framework that will allow and assure the continuance of the male/female relationship. For von Kirschbaum, it is a framework that will guarantee recognition (which men have been loathe to give) and protection of the gifts that the female, as well as the male, contributes to their relationship and—this is essential to her—to the church. On the one hand, these gifts are limited to those that serve the Christian community, the body of Christ, the actual church. This is a bottom line in von Kirschbaum,

---

370. *WF*, 30 (Shepherd:86): in "Die Frau in der Lebensordnung der Gemeinde des neuen Bundes." Cf. Barth on Genesis 2:18ff. and the Song of Songs as the first and second Magna Carta of humanity (above, page 153).

371. *CD* III/2:312 (*KD* III/2:376).

372. Barth: *CD* III/2:294–95, 309 (*KD* III/2:356, 373); von Kirschbaum: *WF*, 15 (Shepherd:66).

though she does not always construe it in the same way. In its most extreme form, a woman should refrain from using gifts that do not support her God-given role in the church. On the other hand, the gifts she brings to the male/female relationship and to the church are uniquely feminine and in this sense can be exerted and are recognizable apart from the male/female relationship.[373] For von Kirschbaum, the main reason one should welcome this order (and the reason God created it) is that it makes it possible to realize—to actualize—the richness of male/female differences.[374]

The Pauline conception of the gifts of the Spirit is a pervasive part of von Kirschbaum's conceptual vocabulary; it underlies her long-standing conviction—which she discussed with Visser't Hooft Boddaert—that male and female differences must be maintained and valued for their potential contribution to the church. In contrast, Barth does not weave the theme of the gifts into the discourse of *CD*. In II/2 he spoke emphatically of unity *amid* the many different gifts of grace. The relevance of the gifts to ministry and the church becomes a subject of some close attention only in IV/2 (1955) and IV/3.2 (1960).[375] There is one exception during the writing of *CD* III though separate from it. In 1947 Barth was called upon to write a preconference working paper for the founding meeting of the World Council of Churches (WCC) in September 1948. He also published the paper, "Die Kirche—die lebendige Gemeinde des lebendigen Herrn Jesus Christus" (The Church—the Living Community of the Living Lord Jesus Christ), as the second part of *Die Schrift und die Kirche*; and he told a friend it was his first precise and detailed formulation of a congregationalist model, in contrast to the episcopal and synodal forms, for the church.[376] This idea followed from the basic and characteristically Barthian conception of the church as a dynamic reality, an *Ereignis* rather than an institution.[377] In such a church "one speaks of service, not of offices," and the service will take different forms according to the different gifts of the many members.[378]

---

373. "The Role of Women," 111, 109 (Shepherd:190, 188).

374. *WF*, 38–39 (Shepherd:95–96); "The Role of Women," 115–16 (Shepherd:194–95).

375. See *CD* IV/2:321 and IV/3.2:856–63. He refers to the gifts of the Spirit in the section on Vocation in III/4.

376. Published as *Theologische Studien*, 22 (1947), 38ff. For his comment on the paper, see Busch, *Karl Barth*, 343.

377. Early in the paper, Barth used the words "Das Sein der Kirche ist das Ereignis" to open successive paragraphs from shifting perspectives (with powerful rhetorical effect) (ibid., 22–25).

378. Ibid., 38.

This very congregationalist conception is also von Kirschbaum's understanding of the church. One wonders if this first important use of the gifts idea by Barth is a fruit of discussion with von Kirschbaum, discussion in which one of her favorite topics resonated with his most fundamental theology of the church and gave direction to further development of that theology for the WCC paper. That this may be a prime instance of their collaboration is also suggested by von Kirschbaum's citation of the paper in her 1951 lecture, "The Role of Women in the Proclamation of the Word." Barth does not supply any material on male and female differences there. But von Kirschbaum can draw upon an earlier passage in the paper for theological support on the counterintuitive idea of servanthood in the New Testament.[379] Here we seem to have exchange in the very best sense.

The distinctness of von Kirschbaum's and Barth's voices within harmony continues in their exegeses of 1 Corinthians 11:5 (the exhortation to women to cover their heads in church), following upon their commentary on verse 3. They ask why Paul attached so much importance to an apparently minor (Barth says "liturgical") matter. They say it is because the women of Corinth had a false and dangerous understanding of Christian freedom: they characterize this with the word *enthusiasm*, a Barthian negative.[380] They say that Paul had to enforce the rule in order to assert and protect his apostolic authority. They agree on the elusive significance of verse 10 on angels: the angels were grieved by the violation of the male/female order.[381] Von Kirschbaum engages more of the exegetical tradition (for example, Tertullian) and church history. She can refer approvingly to their contemporary Schlier's characterization of the Corinthian church as an essentially "enthusiastic church" and his reading of the theological subject of the epistle in that light.[382] A few pages earlier she drew on Harnack on the history of the early church, and she draws on Cullmann for the foundation of her argument about the maintaining of silence in the church and by implication for all signs of the male/female order in church. In the early church the Eucharist and preaching *together* constituted one great act of celebration, and in this act men and women participated equally. The silence enjoined therein was part of a privilege. The seeming limitations Paul enjoins cannot be understood apart from this wider context.[383]

379. She does this in her exegesis of Luke 22:27 and Mark 10:43–45. See below, page 174.
380. Von Kirschbaum: *WF*, 41 (Shepherd:99); Barth: *CD* III/2:310 (*KD* III/2:373).
381. Barth: *CD* III/2:310 (*KD* III/2:374); von Kirschbaum: *WF*, 46–47 (Shepherd:105–6).
382. *WF*, 41 (Shepherd:99).
383. Ibid., 51–52 (Shepherd: 111–13).

Von Kirschbaum points out (in her lecture on the role of women in proclamation!) that Paul, in 1 Corinthians 11:5, does not criticize the *what* of women "in prayer and prophesy" but the *how*.[384] This affirmation is the important thing for us women, and the matter of church form, while necessary, is secondary to Paul's inclusiveness. We must also bear in mind the nature of the apostolic authority that Paul is asserting: it is further defined in the epistle as love. The church he established at Corinth (the first one on classical Greek soil) was "as his beloved child."[385] Paul asserts his authority as father and apostle. Von Kirschbaum reminds her audience of one of her key themes: the equal birthright of male and female before God.[386]

Barth's point of departure—that in the Pauline texts on woman's relation to man "everything depends on the correct translation"[387]—is not entirely comprehensive. The dominant tone and focus of attention in his argument is on Paul's need to guard against the reversal at Corinth of the relationship between the apostle and the community: "And it may be gathered from 12:29 that the slogan 'We are all apostles' was only just round the corner.'"[388] It is the opening of the floodgates. It is not Paul who was being legalistic; the women of Corinth were—they, with their "general, liberal, non-christological concept of humanity," attacked Paul's and God's order as if they were apostles and as if apostles were geniuses.[389] It is just as true, however, that Paul is arguing that "without Christ's commission and Spirit there was no apostolic word, but without the apostolic word there was no Christian hearing, no hearing of the Word of Christ, no life in the Holy Spirit."[390] Within the right structure, we are free in ways beyond all our words.

Barth and von Kirschbaum comment at length on another text, Simone de Beauvoir's *Le deuxième sexe*. In her first lecture, Von Kirschbaum distinguishes the concerns of modern feminism from what she sees as the real *Frauenfrage*. The new European feminism (since the middle of the nineteenth century), like the workers' movement with which it is concurrent, is a response to changed conditions of existence

---

384. Ibid., 40 (Shepherd:98).
385. Ibid. ("als sein liebes Kind").
386. (*Ebenbürtigkeit*): ibid., 47 (Shepherd:106–7). Similarly, cf. *Gleichbegnadigung*—the term she says she prefers to *Gleichberechtigung*—of male and female, pp. 10 and 36 (Shepherd: 59, 94).
387. *CD* III/4:172 (*KD* III/4:192).
388. *CD* III/2:309 (*KD* III/2:373).
389. Ibid., 312 (*KD* III/2:377).
390. Ibid., 309 (*KD* III/2:373).

and only secondarily to the question of the existence of the woman as such. Worse, modern feminism sees the latter question as part of a myth created by *le mâle*. But to von Kirschbaum, the *Frauenfrage* is a particular and necessary way of approaching "the question of the humanity of the human being."[391] Von Kirschbaum followed the literature of feminism, and visitors noted books and pamphlets from the movement on her desk.[392] She grapples extensively with Simone de Beauvoir's work—with volume 1 of *Le deuxième sexe*, published in 1949 by Gallimard—in chapter 5 of *Die wirkliche Frau*, along with the approach to women of Catholic Mariology represented by Gertrud von Le Fort in *Die ewige Frau* (Germany, 1934; Switzerland, 1947). She opposes her Protestant doctrine of women to both of these. Barth discusses Beauvoir's work in a two-page section in small print in III/4: he cites, perhaps as a small sign of independence, "the two volumes of her *Le deuxième sexe* (1949)."[393]

Von Kirschbaum gives a detailed summary of Beauvoir's work—of her argument that sexual identity as male or female is secondary to human existence and must be transcended in the realization of human freedom; that women have been and still are decisively burdened by the domestic identity and dependency that men, in their own interest, have imposed upon them; that the appearance of progress in the working world and in law is delusive, for it covers a painful split between the public and private life of women. She presents Beauvoir's argument that the female situation is not inevitable: for example, childbearing itself may be replaceable by some other model found in nature, such as parthenogenesis. She summarizes Beauvoir's analysis of women in myth that includes the creation story in Genesis and the modern myth of woman as provider of a haven for man from his harsh encounters with nature and his fellowmen. And she tells us, in textual examples and then with overt recognition, what impresses her in Beauvoir. Von Kirschbaum finds Beauvoir's analysis of the situation of women applicable and instructive.[394] Furthermore, she finds formal parallels in Christianity to important themes in Beauvoir: in the scriptural view of the person who over and over again "becomes" in act what he or she has decided upon;[395] in the totalistic response of the human being to God's call, which includes (as Charlotte knew well) taking risks and leaving behind the

391. *WF*, 7 (Shepherd:55–56).
392. Reported by John Hesselink in personal conversation.
393. *CD* III/4:161–62 (*KD* III/4:179–80).
394. *WF*, 95 (Shepherd:169).
395. "Der Mensch je und je im Akt seiner Entscheidung 'wird'": *WF*, 94 (Shepherd:169).

familiar and comfortable; in the historicity and nonabstractness of scripture. But along with her rejection of abstraction, Beauvoir maintains that there are no eternal truths, and she maintains throughout her book that the sexual differentiation of humans is not an essential part of their life in the world. In contrast, an evangelical doctrine of woman must recognize and affirm the biblical witness of man and woman as the basic form of humanity, and it can only reject the existentialist view of that freedom to which human beings are condemned in a godless world—and its optimistic directive to humanity to attain that freedom. Von Kirschbaum's highest compliment to Beauvoir is to argue (with some negation perhaps) that the Christian "is most certainly not a quietist": with "the same zeal as the existentialist's striving for freedom, the Christian will realize [*wahr machen*] his and her God-given freedom in concrete life decisions."[396]

Von Kirschbaum (and Barth) rightly felt more threatened by, and defensive vis-à-vis, the challenge to their view of women in contemporary feminism than in Catholic Mariology. There is some evidence that von Kirschbaum wrote to or corresponded with Beauvoir—Markus Barth told Renate Köbler there was such a correspondence—though Hinrich Stoevesandt thinks this is not the case.[397] I think it is clear in any event that von Kirschbaum preferred the company of Beauvoir's writings to that of Catholic Mariology.

Barth turns to Beauvoir in the context of an attack on the ideas of bisexuality or sexless identity, beginning with a scathing discussion of Berdyaev on bisexuality and androgyny. Simone de Beauvoir is included "in the category of the flight from one's own sex," which to Barth (as to von Kirschbaum) is a flight from God.[398] He summarizes de Beauvoir more selectively and in less detail than von Kirschbaum, and it is clear that he has read Beauvoir as well as von Kirschbaum's summary. He includes many of the details that von Kirschbaum includes: the idea that female procreation might be replaced by something analogous to parthenogenesis, the idea that the male is the creator in history, even of the myths by which he dominates the woman.[399] He includes one quotation from volume 2 of *Le deuxième sexe*: "On ne nâit pas femme, on le devient"; it is the first sentence of the opening chapter. After his summary,

396. *WF*, 94–96 (Shepherd:169–71).
397. Köbler, *In the Shadow*, 60; Hinrich Stoevesandt in personal communication, 14 August 1996.
398. *CD* III/4:161 (*KD* III/4:179).
399. Ibid., 161–62 (*KD* III/4:179–80).

he asks the rhetorical question: "Was sollen wir dazu sagen?" which happens to mirror von Kirschbaum's "Was haben wir gehört?" at the beginning of her discussion of von Le Fort, three pages before the presentation of Beauvoir.[400] Barth is uncommonly, perhaps chivalrously, generous in his appreciation of Beauvoir's unmasking of the ways in which man has made himself master of woman—it is worthy of attention "especially on the part of men and not least Christian theologians."[401]

Unfortunately, he says, Beauvoir offers only another myth in place of the one she exposes. To urge all humankind to overcome masculinity or femininity to achieve human freedom on a higher plane is impossible—and it betrays a male model as its basis. A few pages earlier he has argued that male and female identity is so important that nothing is indifferent to it.[402] The accusation that feminists are sexless or masculine is not isolated in Barth (and many of his contemporaries). He sees their sexlessness as a measure of their wrongheaded rebelliousness, and it irritates him and often provokes a response of gratuitous sniping.[403] Barth has alluded to the existentialist themes that he criticizes elsewhere at length. Here his conclusion is abrupt and lame: what we all need is sexual identity and grace.[404]

Von Kirschbaum's context—charting a path between Roman Catholic and contemporary feminist thought on women—provides more scope for admiration, and she listens to all of Beauvoir, not bracketing, as Barth seems to do, the existentialism that both point out is stamped by Sartre's.[405] Nevertheless, their readings are unified by a passionate conviction and the felt need to defend that conviction against a formidable challenge. To Barth and von Kirschbaum, male and female identity—in scripturally based ordering—is not merely a biological matter and is not secondary. I think Barth virtually placed a set piece by von Kirschbaum, with editing for context, into his own work, with only the minor (and announced) change that includes the second volume of Beauvoir. Von Kirschbaum "found" the material for him or, more accurately, for their theological dialogue. That she did this seems exactly right—just as the reverse so often seems the case: for example, for much of the Old Testament exegesis.

400. Ibid., 162 (*KD* III/4:180).
401. Ibid., 162 (*KD* III/4:180).
402. Ibid., 155 (*KD* III/4:172).
403. Ibid., 156–59 (*KD* III/4:173–77).
404. Ibid., 159 (*KD* III/4:177).
405. Ibid., 161 (*KD* III/4:179); von Kirschbaum, *WF*, 94 (Shepherd:168).

Von Kirschbaum's real openness to Beauvoir suggests that a different yet equally critical feminism, such as the "second wave" that evolved in the 1970s and 1980s, especially in France and the United States, affirming maleness and femaleness, each with its distinctive way of knowing, as innate, would have elicited a different reaction from her. Feminists today can build on two foundations, draw from two streams. Sometimes in tension and looking dialectical in their unfolding, the two phases are also options: we can variously *combine* cultural construction of gender and essentialism. Von Kirschbaum did not have these choices. Her reading of Beauvoir is understandable because European feminism before the late 1960s was, in the Enlightenment tradition, dominated by the thesis of cultural construction. And that feminism would be sharply alien in the German Women's Movement in the early twentieth century. In a milieu with alternatives, von Kirschbaum might have been able to reject hierarchy for complementarity—and just might have brought Barth along with her.[406]

Barth's distinctive understanding of the relative nature of male/female order is in his concept of inversion—*Umkehrung*—and von Kirschbaum agrees with it fundamentally and vitally in her own theology. *Inversion* has several meanings, the most important of which we have encountered in Barth's and von Kirschbaum's exegeses of 1 Corinthians 11:3. Inversion occurs when we understand the ordered male/female relationship christologically through the analogy of faith. Von Kirschbaum declares that Jesus Christ establishes and relativizes the place of the man and the place of the woman. Barth describes the relativizing when he declares that the woman "is surpassed in inferiority by the same Lord who surpasses the superiority of man."[407] Just this superiority and inferiority, this "unity

406. See Hester Eisenstein, *Contemporary Feminist Thought* (Boston: G. K. Hall, 1983), for a good survey of first- and second-wave feminism. Many German feminists today are understandably wary of a feminism that shares any core ideas (on the nature of women) with the *"Alten Frauenbewegung"* of the nineteenth and early twentieth centuries (see Almut Witt, "Anna Paulsen—Lebensbild einer Theologin," in *Querdenken*, 286–87). Witt and others are in step with "third wave" feminism. On this development as a convergence of postmodernist pluralism and anti-essentialism with critical voices on the determinisms of race and class, see Susan Bordo, "Feminism, Postmodernism, and Gender-Scepticism," in *Feminism/Postmodernism*, ed. Linda J. Nicholson (New York: Routledge, 1990), 133–56. Bordo herself counters with a cogent defense and reconstruction of second-wave gender analysis: when held responsibly and with consciousness that it is but one perspective, that it is a hypothesis, such analysis continues to illumine anew realities long taken for granted and continues to create communities of interest among women despite differences. (My remarks about von Kirschbaum and an alternative feminist tradition would also hold for Henriette Visser't Hooft Boddaert.)

407. Von Kirschbaum: *WF*, 42 (Shepherd:101); Barth: *CD* III/2:311 (*KD* III/2:375) and III/4:173 (*KD* III/4:193).

between the deity and humanity, the sovereignty and service, the majesty and humility" in Jesus Christ, defines and limits the male/female order.[408] In both the III/2 and III/4 versions, Barth's elegant, intricate, and impassioned presentation combines negation and conviction. Thus he sees "the advantage of the wife" in representing, reflecting, and attesting the community—the whole church community, young and old, master and slave, male and female, the Apostle himself—that is addressed by the Lord.[409]

Von Kirschbaum makes the same point with the same reference to Galatians 3:28. What is interesting in Ephesians is not the subordination of women but what that means for the sake of witness.[410] Women represent the actuality of the whole community, men and women, old and young, masters and slaves. "So what seems a disadvantage in the world is actually a distinction for women." This is followed by the remark that, in the subordination of man and women in obedience to Christ, men have to assume the subordination, but it is natural to women.[411] However, von Kirschbaum takes another theologically interesting step. In her discussion of the role of women in proclamation, she points to the transvaluation by Jesus of the idea of service (*diakonia*) in the New Testament (Luke 22:27 and Mark 10:43–45), commenting also on the counterintuitive nature of the self-sacrifice and suffering that service may require: "This path from above downward is an absolute contrast to the natural human way of life."[412] She cites not *CD* but Barth's WCC preconference paper, calling upon its eloquent description of the life of the church, a life that *must* be in the world, that is at work for the world even when it goes counter to the world's comprehension. We have seen that Barth does not discuss male and female in that text; nor does he include the subject in his exegesis of the same New Testament texts in *CD*.[413]

To Barth and von Kirschbaum, *mutual* subordination is inherent in the *imago*. The male is concurrently dominant and subordinate; male dominance (like female subordination) demonstrates acquiescence in created order, an order in which the male and female, oriented in their

408. *CD* III/4:173 (*KD* III/4:193).
409. *CD* III/2:314 (*KD* III/2:378–79).
410. *WF*, 13 (Shepherd:63).
411. Ibid., 13 (Shepherd:63–64).
412. "The Role of Women," 95–96 (Shepherd:176).
413. Barth, *Die Schrift und die Kirche*, 25–26; *CD* III/2:215–16 (*KD* III/2:257) on Mark 10:44. Cf. again *CD* III/4:476–77, 661–62, on the foot washing in John and on John 12:26 (*KD* III/4:545–46, 761–62).

I-Thou relationship, in life with each other and for each other, are engaged in mutual subordination. In III/1, Barth presents Genesis 2:24 ("Therefore a man leaves his father and his mother and cleaves to his wife, and they become one flesh") as a major illustration of inversion, in which all is visibly topsy-turvy—*alles umgekehrt*. A man uproots himself and leaves his parents to become one with his wife. He will experience this event as humiliation. But it is "only in the fact that—as the one who seeks, desires, sacrifices and is referred to her—he confronts the woman as the weaker partner" that he can be "her lord and stronger than she."[414] The goal of the whole supremacy of man is his subordination to the arrangement in which he is superordinate.[415] Again in III/2: because the woman "is so utterly for [the man], he must be utterly for her; because she can only follow him in order that he should not be alone he must also follow her not to be alone; because he the first and stronger can only be one and strong in relationship to her he must accept and treat her, the second and weaker, as his first and stronger."[416] It is in such inversion that all human possibilities, positive and negative, are developed in reality. Its vital nature (as well as Barth's inclusion of the political and the sexual-political in his sphere of attention) is made clear in his cryptic remark that, in this ordering of human existence in superordinate and subordinate forms, "there exists the possibility of man in isolation, but also of all androcracy and gynocracy."[417]

That Barth has embraced the new version of the *imago* as genuinely as von Kirschbaum is no wonder: he is always the dialectical theologian, and the doctrine of the *imago* is profoundly dialectical. One can see Hegel's master/slave dialectic in his exposition. To Barth, in his exegesis of Ephesians 5, because "woman especially is invited to subordinate herself" in God's order, there is "a kind of primacy of woman" in relation to *all* Christians; it is "she and not man who is the type of all those who have in [Christ] their Head."[418] This is "the *particula veri* in the strange view of Schleiermacher"—the wish that he had been a woman.[419] Inversion with regard to husband and wife is conditional and emphatically so for the wife: "If she does not break but respects the true relationship to

414. *CD* III/1:306 (*KD* III/1:350).
415. Ibid. Cf. also III/2:313 (*KD* III/2:377–78); von Kirschbaum: *WF*, 41f. (Shepherd:100).
416. *CD* III/2:292 (*KD* III/2:352).
417. Ibid.
418. *CD* III/4:174–75 (*KD* III/4:195).
419. Ibid., 175 (*KD* III/4:195). Also in III/2:314 (*KD* III/2:379). Barth also says of Schleiermacher (in III/4:155 [*KD* III/4:171]), that, in light of his emphasis on dependence, one might wonder whether he was sufficiently aware of his male existence.

her husband, the wife is not less but greater than her husband in the community. She is not the second but the first. In a qualified sense she is the community. . . . She and not her husband is the type of the community listening to Christ and the apostolic admonition."[420]

Inversion has further meaning. *Within* the relation of male and female there is a fluidity and reversing of roles of male and female relative to each other. As Barth explicates this idea in III/2, it consists of each willing him or herself only as he or she wills the other. He reminds us that this inversion occurs in the Song of Songs,[421] describing it as mutual love in the sense of the love of the church community for Christ and of Christ for the community; he goes on to reiterate the hierarchical theme of male/female order. But it is his presentation of the startling, dazzling equality of feelings and expression in the male and female in the Song of Songs that we have been asked to remember amid the discussion of superordination and subordination. The Song is a major and dramatic instance of inversion of the male/female order pronounced in Genesis. To Barth, the Shulamite woman is an exact counterpart to Solomon. She is "now portrayed in the same rapture—one might almost say with the same eager: 'This is now'—in relation to man."[422] Barth is alluding to his exposition of Adam's cry of recognition: "This is now bone of my bones, and flesh of my flesh."[423] She "now answers just as loudly and expressly as she is addressed by him." She now praises him no less than he praises her. "It is she who now seeks him with pain and finds him with joy. The famous inversion is now found on her lips: 'My beloved is mine, and I am his' (Song 2:26); 'I am my beloved's, and my beloved is mine' (Song 6:3)."[424] Barth's subject is the encounter of the man and woman as a new creation in itself. In his second exegesis of the Song, he simply expands upon the startling impact of the new voice with its echoing of the creation saga: "This is the voice of the woman, to whom the man looks and moves with no less pain and joy than she to him, and who finds him with no less freedom—only the 'This' of Genesis is lacking—than she is found. Implicitly, of course, this voice is to be heard in Genesis as well. But it now finds expression in words. And what words!"[425]

420. *CD* III/2:314 (*KD* III/2:379).
421. Ibid., 316 (*KD* III/2:381).
422. *CD* III/1:313 (*KD* III/1:358).
423. Ibid., 300 (*KD* III/1:342).
424. Ibid., 313 (*KD* III/1:358). (Barth references the Song as *"Hohelied"* and discusses it—as von Kirschbaum does—by the name *"Lied der Lieder."*)
425. *CD* III/2:294 (*KD* III/2:355). There is some resemblance between this idea of inversion and the aspect of romantic love in Schleiermacher (in his discussion of Schlegel's

Though far less expansively, von Kirschbaum likewise interprets the Song of Songs as a dramatic, intentionally startling statement and an essential part of scriptural anthropology.[426] "The encounter described in Gen. 2:18f. of the man and woman, the fulfillment of their counterpart roles as 'I' and 'Thou' appears here again as the central theme, except that here, now, and above all, the voice of the woman resounds [*erklingt*]." It is also "the love and fidelity of Jahwah to Israel that is sung," the divine promise that enables us to see what is hidden in the shadow of the faithlessness of God's people.[427] The Song is a transforming completion of Genesis 2. Against this background, von Kirschbaum (like Barth) proceeds to the discussion of Ephesians 5. Here and in other instances, she is back in line at the end, but it is after a fruitful journey that affects her discussion of hierarchy.

One could say that von Kirschbaum mainstreams her discussions of gender and that she has used Barth to get beyond Barth. In contrast, Barth in many ways insulates—which means he segregates—his discussions of gender from the rest of his theology. It seems noteworthy that the final section in *CD* III, the section titled "Honor," at the end of III/4 (Par. 56, Freedom in Limitation), contains some of his most strikingly exclusive thinking. The section proceeds from John 12:26 ("If any man serves me, him will my Father honor"). One of its principal themes is that the honor of the world and of God are different and separate but not always incompatible. For example, worldly power can be serviceable to the Lord—on this, Barth dissents from Kierkegaard.[428] His final point (developed at some length) is that turning the other cheek is not the only appropriate response to disparagements to one's honor. In some situations, Christians will be justified and even required to defend themselves.[429] The discussion here is not inclusive, nor is it strictly gender-neutral. The single reference to women per se is chivalrous: men should respect them.[430] Barth's use of *man* frequently seems not to be about humankind but about manhood. Following the light of the Lord will not *necessarily* lead to "dishonor,

---

"Lucinde") that Barth finds impressive (*CD* III/4:122 [*KD* III/4:134]). In the end, however, Barth requires that the basic duality of male-female be protected and returned to. Inversion is an exhilerating transitory experience rather than a transforming experience.

427. *WF*, 11–12, 19 (Shepherd:61–62, 70).
427. Ibid., 11–12 (Shepherd:61–62).
428. *CD* III/4:671; the theme also appears on 672, 676, 677, 679 (*KD* III/4:772–73, 778, 779, 781–82).
429. Ibid., 680f. (*KD* III/4:783–84).
430. Ibid., 685 (*KD* III/4:788).

disgrace, shame, the gutter."[431] It is true that both "collective and individual concepts of honor" exhibit wide variations and degrees of refinement
in history, yet they tend to have some general agreement, and "from the
Christian standpoint there is no objection to the fact that there are such
concepts." In fact, we need them in order to live, "whether in isolation or
in company with others."[432] At the end of the vast tracts of CD III, Barth
is unselfconsciously in the vicinity of the ordinances of creation.

7. Two Voices

I want to return now to the historical reality of Karl Barth and Charlotte
von Kirschbaum by way of their theology of historical existence. I have
suggested that the theme or refrain of the mortal sickness in the male/
female relationship, which enters into every discussion of the *imago Dei*
in Barth and von Kirschbaum, has an identity of its own. We recognize
and declare God's glory and mercy when we say that the image abides
even in all the creaturely limitations of male/female fellowship. Von
Kirschbaum says that man and woman will live together in their destroyed
relationship, just as the Old Testament covenant of God and faithless
Israel remains always. She thinks there would be fewer divorces if
husband and wife understood that their attempt to live together in I-
Thou relationship, in the pattern of Christ's love, inevitably will differ
from that pattern "in this earthly, sinful realm."[433] Typically she speaks of
"the domain of the relations of man and woman that is so shattered and
sick" yet can be illuminated by the light of Christ to show forth features
"of its original God-willed determination."[434]

To Barth, the image persists in lives that deny it and that in denying
it evoke their mortal sickness.[435] Only the divine can penetrate the
darkness of the marriage relationship, the disorders and corruptions, the
tensions and friction, the complex, almost hopeless problems with
which the love of husband and wife is burdened.[436] Only a marriage ethic

431. Ibid., 671 (*KD* III/4:772).
432. Ibid., 669 (*KD* III/4:770).
433. *WF*, 19–20 (Shepherd:70–72).
434. Ibid., 22, again on 31 (Shepherd:76, 86).
435. *CD* III/1:191 (*KD* III/1:214).
436. Ibid., 311, 313–14 (*KD* III/1:356, 359).

that proceeds from this inevitability may dissuade the disillusioned from divorce.[437] Barth says that in the resurrection marriage will not continue but male/female differences will, that (citing Augustine) we will be freed not from nature but the violation of nature. It seems clear that by marriage he means sexual relationship in historical reality, and that it applies to any male/female relationship of intimacy.[438] The foremost characteristic of male/female fellowship in comparison to the divine original is limitation.[439]

The image of God, it will be recalled, is twice-removed from the divine and from accessibility in humankind: first in its created form as a reflection; then, as broken by sin. The two states of the *imago*, both in the *humanum* and in historical reality, are related not only as higher and degenerate form. The "ultimate incomprehensibility of male and female to each other" is at the core of the centrifugal forces in marital discord *and* it is fundamental in the I-Thou relationship of two othernesses.[440] The tension that separates is the tension that can bind. There is explosive power in mutual attraction. The tension and danger in the male/female relationship is the counterpart of productivity and potential in this relationship; "this subterranean motive" exists in all male/female forms of fellowship. Not only in the sphere of the sexual love of a married couple, where it is "fully and properly" achieved, but in "the wider circle around the narrower . . . in the relationship of fathers and daughters, mothers and sons, brothers and sisters, and in similar relationships it plays its fruitful but perhaps disturbing and even dangerous role in the whole sphere of education and instruction and the life of churches of all confessions." And it extends to "the innumerable ways in which it finds compensation or sublimation in friendships between man and man or woman and woman."[441] Thus for all its pain and danger, the sexual relationship serves a purpose: "To know nothing of this sphere is to know nothing of the I and Thou and their encounter, and therefore of the human."[442] Let us now recall Barth's idea that the Old Testament writers could not have repeatedly used the metaphor of marriage for Yahweh and Israel if they had not known something of the ultimate meaning of the relationship of man and woman, nor could they have

437. *CD* III/4:195ff. (*KD* III/4:218ff.).
438. *CD* III/2:295–96 (*KD* III/2:357).
439. *CD* III/4:129 (*KD* III/4:142–43); also, *CD* III/2:320 (*KD* III/2:385–86).
440. *CD* III/4:191 (*KD* III/4:214).
441. *CD* III/2:288 (*KD* III/2:347–48).
442. Ibid., 289 (*KD* III/2:348–49).

comprehended the devastation in the relationship between Yahweh and Israel without their knowledge of the vulnerability in human marriage.[443]

Unequivocally the *imago* persists even in this life. Barth's comments on the reach of male/female attraction have obvious relevance to the Barth–von Kirschbaum relationship. Observers of this relationship must note that Barth's theologically accurate insistence that we accept the imperfection, tension, and disorders in marriage is also self-exculpating. One must rejoice in the guidance of the impossibly strict command, "[b]ut we must add that he keeps the command who allows it to be said of himself that in any event he is at fault in relation to it, that he is its transgressor and an adulterer in the strict biblical sense [as in Mt. 5:28] of the term, certainly in his own individual way, certainly not equally consciously and flagrantly at every point and in every dimension of the command, yet clearly and indisputably in face of the absoluteness, unity and totality of its requirement."[444] Certainly Barth maintains that we have to keep working at marriage in this life; that one must bear witness for "the new, sinless, pure and holy man [who] does not bear his name but the name of Jesus Christ" in face of "the old creature and his life and kingdom."[445] However, the reader of this text on marriage and adultery cannot ignore the theologian's personal situation, and must long for some distinctions within his generalized lament over human frailty. One also wonders at the hypocrisy in his extensive defense of monogamy, of marriage as "an exclusive life-partnership" that "does not know any third party, male or female, in the mystery of that element of life and joy which forms the center of the whole, in relation to the task and the work which is to be done by the couple, in the dialectic of freedom, fellowship and order which it is the destiny of these two and these two alone to experience and suffer and in some way master." Two pages later he repeats the point: "In every dimension a third party, whether male or female, can only *eo ipso* disturb and destroy full life-partnership."[446] We envision Karl Barth dictating to Charlotte von Kirschbaum, and we remember the triangle, with all its forces, of Karl, Lollo, and Nelly.

Barth and von Kirschbaum sometimes look beyond male/female order to political power and talk as if their arguments apply to all power relations by extension—they also use the vocabulary of politics for the domestic and ecclesial realms. Barth was able to use the concept of

---

443. Ibid., 298 (*KD* III/2:360).
444. *CD* III/4:231–32, 234 (*KD* III/4:260, 262).
445. Ibid., 238 (*KD* III/4:266–67).
446. Ibid., 195, 197 (*KD* III/4:218, 220).

inversion in a view of power that reflects, in its love and responsibility for those subordinated to it, the majesty and lowliness of Christ the Lord.[447] He is well aware that men frequently abuse and exploit their power over women for their own ends.[448] He twice warns against the dangers of androcracy and the gynocracy to which it might give way in reaction. These forms of domination can never be "necessary," in contrast to the super- and subordination of male and female in Christian existence.[449] In III/4 (par. 55, Freedom for Life) he considers ethical issues in the wider social community and touches on political responsibility and on human power per se, juxtaposing the views of Nietzsche and Burckhardt and arguing for a third possibility, a power understood as strength loaned to "man" by God, to which one could truly say Yes.[450]

But in Barth's discussions of super- and subordination in the *imago*, he focuses on the dangers inherent in female protest against male abuse. Although it is understandable for woman to protest and rebel against male offense, she herself, even if "a thousand times in the right," is threatening the divine order by her stand. After many assertions that protest alone is wrong, Barth's only real prescription is "the way of the woman who refuses to let herself be corrupted and made disobedient by [the offending man's] disobedience, but who in spite of his disobedience maintains her place in the order all the more firmly."[451] Barth's association of androcracy and gynocracy contains some accuracy. Women who assume power, whether political or economic, have sometimes internalized the ideology of patriarchy. But Barth chooses not to further analyze the relationship between gynocracy and androcracy. The question of order in male/female fellowship is a charged one for Barth, and his confrontations with the question can be wildly short-circuited.

The equivalent in *CD* to von Kirschbaum's writing on women seems flat even when it is clear that Barth has seen and understood some of the noxious effects of the male myths of femininity. It is good clean fun to hear him speak out against the co-conspiracy or vicious circle in which a woman becomes the "pliable kitten," the "flattering mirror" of her husband.[452] But his condemnation of coquettishness is laced through

---

447. *CD* III/2:314–15 (*KD* III/2:379–80).
448. *CD* III/4:170 (*KD* III/4:190).
449. *CD* III/2:292, 315 (*KD* III/2:352, 379).
450. *CD* III/4:391–93 (*KD* III/4:446–48).
451. Ibid., 171–72 (*KD* III/4:190–91).
452. Ibid., 178, 180 (*KD* III/4:198f.). Barth cites no authorities for this view, but it was long familiar to him from a source identified by von Kirschbaum. She cited (in "The Role of Women," 112–13 [Shepherd:191–92]) Fritz Barth's idea that men create dependency in

with the sexism of chivalry. A woman should respond to male transgressions by "quietly restricting herself" and thus appealing "to the kindness of man."[453] Barth himself named and demonstrated the problem in
his thinking on gender when he defined "the strong man" as the one
who "is vigilant for the interests of both sexes. This is what is intended
and tenable in the otherwise doubtful idea of chivalry."[454]

Markus and Rose Marie Barth agreed that von Kirschbaum tempered
Karl Barth's writing on women such that it was less sexist than it would
otherwise have been.[455] It also seems likely that von Kirschbaum's
intense interest in the significance of the woman's role in the community
prompted Barth to think more about human power, in order to devise a
complementary male role, as early as III/2. But his imagination for the
possible is limited. In a commentary on the Christ/community analogy
for husband and wife, Barth stresses that the male reflects, can only
reflect, and must reflect the role of Christ in relation to the community.
To this end, it is peculiarly the case that more has to be said to husbands
than to wives "because in respect of the life of the community, more has
to be said about the being and action of Christ than the being and action
of [the members of the community] concerned."[456] Male abuse of power
is a problem, and the solution to this problem is male restraint and male
responsibility.

Von Kirschbaum agrees with this as part of the solution. In her
exegesis of 1 Corinthians 11:3 (among other places), she reminds her
audience that Paul confronted the male, who is the bearer of earthly
power (*Machtträger*), with the Lord "who has power over all" and whose
power is "the foundation and limit" of all other power, whether the
bearer of power knows it or not.[457] In contrast to Barth, however, von
Kirschbaum is able to separate female listening from obeying and see a
positive, substantive role for women in listening; and she draws important
conclusions from the recurrent misuse of power by males for a new

women by displaying them as ornaments in society while relegating them to the home as
their natural place.

453. *CD* III/4:180–81 (*KD* III/4:201–2).

454. The counterpart of the strong man, "the mature woman," is the one who desires
"nothing better than that this order should be in force" because her own interests, including independence and dignity, are "best secured within it" (*CD* III/4:177 [*KD* III/4:197]).
Von Kirschbaum, as we have seen, agreed with the last point.

455. Per Bruce McCormack's report on conversation with them, in personal communication, 7 March 1994.

456. *CD* III/2:315 (*KD* III/2:379–80).

457. *WF*, 42 (Shepherd:85–86).

theology in which female power can supplement and correct that of the male. Barth's views on women are freed from his prejudices only when he focuses on male/female encounter itself. There the theologian seems to find his own voice.

Charlotte von Kirschbaum had a message to proclaim to her audience. First, just as women and men share equality in birth and equality in grace, each has direct and independent access to Jesus Christ, the only mediator: the woman's access is not mediated by the man.[458] Second, the gifts that women and men *as* women and men can bring to the church are of equal importance. The New Testament knew of no radical distinctions among the different kinds of service, *diakonia*, that contribute to the edification of the church.[459] Finally, men and women have to *use* their gifts. Von Kirschbaum is extremely bothered by the passiveness of contemporary churches. And she is concerned that the habitual passivity of women, based on a misunderstanding of Christian subordination that husbands and male proclaimers of the Word do nothing to correct, is increasingly harmful to the whole church—to men and women alike.[460] We hear this concern as she situates herself between passive Evangelical women on the one hand and radical feminists on the other. Von Kirschbaum sounds far more like a feminist in this *Sitz im Leben* than in her juxtaposition of Roman Catholic Mariology and radical feminism.

In her two lectures on the role of women in proclamation of the Word (Lecture III in the Bièvres series and in greater detail in the separate lecture at Basel in 1951), she describes the nonmutuality of minister and congregation or church community, and intentionally contrasts it to the overenthusiasm addressed by Paul at Corinth.[461] "The man who has studied theology and passed his examinations" now presides "in loneliness over against the congregation [women *and* men] who at least outwardly are almost totally passive. The fullness of voices is silenced, the work of the Holy Spirit—at most—is done by one voice."[462]

Barth agreed with her on the excessive silence in the churches, and he was theologically ready for her positive prescripts. In *CD* I/2 of 1939, in his doctrine of the church that teaches and hears, he too rejected the idea that the congregation was an assembly of spectators: "The truth is

458. "The Role of Women," 109 (Shepherd:188).
459. *WF*, 38; "The Role of Women," 104 (Shepherd:96, 183–84).
460. "The Role of Women," 114; *WF*, 52 (Shepherd:193, 113).
461. *WF*, 52; "The Role of Women," 118–19 (Shepherd:113–14, 197–98).
462. "The Role of Women," 118–19 (Shepherd:197). She draws on the work of E. Schweizer and F. Leenhardt for support.

that theologians cannot teach except as the mouthpiece of the congregation of Jesus Christ which does not in any sense consist of listeners only, but of those who, as listeners, are themselves teachers."[463] In the 1947 preconference paper for the WCC, he envisioned a church constituted by the coming together of its congregation and said that the church needed the service of all its members, not the offices of a few. In his not totally marginalized preface to CD III/4, in which he speaks of church ministry as "the decisive part of what can be done by human effort" in Christendom, he further observes that "in the future" this work "will no doubt be performed even more than in the past through the cooperation of ministers with as many other members of the parish as possible."[464]

What does the fullness of voices, insofar as it includes women, mean to von Kirschbaum? She thought that women in particular pose the question of the nature of humanity.[465] With regard to ecclesiology—and this is a development from the same foundation that is laid in CD I/2—women are "the listening church to which the teaching church must over and over again return."[466] Indeed, the silence enjoined by Paul points to the limits of everyone's speech. But the present character of our public worship allows no room for the traditional sign of silence.[467] The immediate function of women remains representational; it is to serve as a model—or, more accurately, as models. This role is carried out by responding to the Word, with due silent reverence *and* in service, to edify the community. And the edifying and building up (*Erbauung*) of the community is, in the end, the aim of all proclamation.[468]

Representationality also means informing the understanding of the minister who is the vehicle of the Word in address to the people. Women have long responded to the calling to serve the church, and the emergency situations of World War II created the possibility for extending the usual forms of female *diakonia* to the pulpit itself. Women are creative and constructive. Women who are called today can respond in two directions: out into the community, bearing witness of a living Word, and in—this is an "in" that refuses to be "up"—to the pulpit.[469] Women who earnestly

463. *CD* I/2:798.
464. *CD* III/4:xi (*KD* III/4:vii).
465. Stated near the beginning of her first lecture: *WF*, 7 (Shepherd:55–56).
466. Ibid., 51 (Shepherd:112).
467. "die Gestalt unserer heutigen Gottesdienst" (ibid., 51–52 [Shepherd:112–13]).
468. Ibid., 43, 49 (Shepherd:102, 109).
469. "The Role of Women," 119–20 (Shepherd:199–200).

listen to the whole of scripture will think and speak about the edification of the community and earnestly engage in dialogue with men who think and speak of the same.[470]

Furthermore, men should not declare that women must always hear the Word from males only.[471] Von Kirschbaum's concern is not the claiming of equal time, and it is more than the adding of a neglected voice. Women have a voice that is needed in the church, and this may include the pulpit. For there is something *wrong* with the male voice in the pulpit and it needs correcting. The silence of the listening church is eloquent testimony to "the limits of all human speech."[472] But the male minister has not listened to this testimony and has abused his power. He has forgotten that he is but a vessel for the Holy Spirit, and he has separated his office from the community. It is time to ask

> whether women as ministers of the word can make an essential contribution to the necessary transformation of this "office." By their natural position women are less likely to claim authority and thus as ministers of the divine word are less tempted to an authoritarian view of their ministry. . . . [T]hey would be less tempted than men are to obscure the authority of the word through the authority of their person. We have heard [in the Epistles] that their natural position corresponds to that of the church, and so they are advised to perform their ministry in obedience, even as servants of the word, standing not above, but in the midst of their congregation. They will work, therefore, not at a distance but in their person to bring the office and the congregation together, without detracting in the least from the authority of the ministry that has been entrusted to them. It is then that the authority of the word, and not of the person, will be evident.[473]

Von Kirschbaum cites an article by Franz Leenhardt to support this idea. Leenhardt wondered "to what extent" ministry has "suffered because of the exclusive preponderance of the male nature." (Barth mentions Leenhardt twice [in *CD* III/4]. In neither case is it about this point, and the idea that von Kirschbaum is presenting simply does not

470. *WF*, 56 (Shepherd:119).
471. Ibid. (Shepherd:118).
472. "The Role of Women," 111 (Shepherd: 190).
473. Ibid., 120–21 (Shepherd:199–200).

appear in his discussion.)[474] She approvingly notes Eduard Schweizer's opinion that "the striking prominence of the preacher has misled us to see the entire life of the church of Jesus as consisting of talking." In contrast, a woman who does proclaim the word will be informed by the deeds of the community and by the various voices of its less educated and less articulate members. Von Kirschbaum thinks that such women will, not as a matter of indifference, "probably find their own style in the externals (perhaps even giving up the robes of office!)."[475] In such ways (to be worked out in the appropriate time and place) these women can demonstrate their solidarity with the church community "and help overcome the division that has developed between the church officials and the congregation." How will this come about? Individual congregations must make the decision to summon women to the ministry of the word, but women should not just wait passively. "As active members of the church they are part of the process of helping to make the decision."[476]

In her third lecture at Bièvres, and even more in the lecture at Basel in 1951, von Kirschbaum's tongue has been set free for proclamation and in proclamation. At Bièvres the greater part of the lecture on proclamation is devoted to the tempering of impulses toward total freedom from constraints, on the one hand, and total passivity on the other, with a call to feminine action. Two years later, at the address in Basel, she focuses on and intensifies her criticism of male authority in the pulpit and extends her vision for transforming the church. It is also an early feminist vision that sustains gender inequality at the same time that it presents a view that would undermine inequality. The view is perichoretic more than, and rather than, hierarchical. It anticipates the insistence of one of our feminisms today that female autonomy, power, and peace will be won and grounded in fidelity to female nature—and the same for and by men if freed from sexist obscurations.

Charlotte von Kirschbaum speaks the language of the German Women's Movement with a different, almost foreign accent. The first thing she sees in motherhood is creativity. She advocates nonseparatism. The interaction she envisions is not so much complementarity as cross-fertilization. She sees, in her study of possible roles of women in proclamation, altogether good transgressions. The prophetic role of women in Hebrew Scripture is as important as the New Testament witness of the

474. Ibid., 121 (Shepherd:200); *CD* III/4:172, 173 (*KD* III/4:191, 193).
475. Ibid., 122 (Shepherd:201).
476. Ibid., 122–23 (Shepherd:201–2).

women who chose to follow Jesus. If we look more closely at her postwar "Address for the Movement 'Free Germany'" we see an orientation and a purpose different from that of the traditional *Frauenbewegung*. Von Kirschbaum's orientation is *in* the world, and it is not a world that is indiscriminately a hospital of the sick and guilty, but a world in which distinctions must be made and Germany told and convinced that it has a special, urgent task. The purpose of those sewing and mending circles she recommends is to relieve some immediate suffering *and* demonstrate concern to make "this people once again responsible for their own lives."[477]

Von Kirschbaum's thinking seems akin to the feminism of Elisabeth Moltmann-Wendel. While recognizing the contribution of the nursing work of the German deaconesses to the *Frauenbewegung*, Moltmann-Wendel thinks it is "time to de-mythologize this 'motherhood-ideology,' to enlighten and inform people as well as to heal them," and "not only to bind up their wounds but also to prevent them."

Work by and for women—and perhaps this is a new idea for us—will always include liberation and social change. We should not abandon our traditions of inner values, a realistic view of people, and the sober realization of the limitations of our society, but rather we must shift the emphases. The world is not only a hospital; it already reflects the reality of the Kingdom of God. Human rights are not merely to be laid down in constitutions; they can and must be implemented. Justification of the sinner is not the only way in which God acts with us; there is an urgent need to heal and liberate the whole of [humankind].[478]

As Karl Barth dictates his material, he is looking at Charlotte von Kirschbaum; as they discuss the subject of his choice, he is listening to her words and observing, reading, their relationship. In the I-Thou relationship of male and female wherein each will "consciously, wholly and openly affirm their specific sexuality," each "is for the other a horizon and focus . . . a center and source."[479] In the I-Thou relationship of male and female, "openness to the opposite is not an incidental and dispensable attribute; . . . it constitutes its very essence."[480] The differentiation and

477. Von Kirschbaum, "Address," 92.
478. Moltmann-Wendel, "The Women's Movement in Germany," 129–30.
479. *CD* III/4:149, 163 (*KD* III/4:165, 181).
480. Ibid., 163 (*KD* III/4:181).

relationship of male and female is dialectical.[481] Barth makes it clear that von Kirschbaum's importance to him as dialogue partner was functional as much as supplemental. In his elaborations on the male/female encounter, one feels that one is reading two texts: a compelling, mature theology of relationality that reaches back to the commentary on Romans, and a description of the dialogue of Barth and von Kirschbaum.

At one level the Thou is necessary to fill the lacunae in the I—to bring to the I views that are new and strange and different to it.[482] But there is more. The address of an I to a Thou "is coming to another with one's being, and knocking and asking to be admitted." In Barth's phenomenological account in III/2, "As I address [the other], I allow myself to unsettle and disturb him/her by drawing attention to the fact that I am there too."[483] In greater detail in III/4, each sex must realize

> that it is questioned by the other. The puzzle [*Rätsel*] which the opposite sex implies for it is not theoretical but practical, not optional but obligatory. . . . It is the great human puzzle which as man and woman they put to one another in their mutual confrontation. . . . Man is unsettled by woman and woman by man. There is always this unsettlement by the opposite sex where there is the encounter of man and woman. Each is asked by the opposite sex: Why, *quo jure*, are you *de facto* so utterly different from myself? Can and will you guarantee that your mode of life which disconcerts me is also human?[484]

The asking is not always verbal; there is "a silent but severe criticism which tacitly but persistently and in all conceivable forms passes between man and women." We have seen that each stands in relationship to the other in "a certain tension," that there is tension and danger in all male/female relationships, even professional relationships in school and church, even between friends.[485] No one who wishes to live humanly "can escape this unsettlement, this criticism and tension."[486] (As an example of the possible fruit of this awareness, Barth suggests that a state decision to go

481. *CD* III/1:186 (*KD* III/1:208).
482. *CD* III/2:254–55 (*KD* III/2:304–5). (Barth is talking specifically about the understanding that the I and Thou have of each other.)
483. Ibid., 256 (*KD* III/2:307).
484. *CD* III/4:167 (*KD* III/4:186).
485. Ibid.; *CD* III/2:288 (*KD* III/2:347–48).
486. *CD* III/4:167 (*KD* III/4:186).

to war might be made less lightly if female viewpoints were considered.)[487] The placing of the question about the *humanum* echoes von Kirschbaum's statement that woman in particular ways poses the question of the humanity of the human being, though she does not develop it further. Here is an instance in which (again) we cannot know who initiated the idea, but we see that it was more interesting to one than the other.

In his description of the interaction of male and female, Barth is using the conceptual vocabulary of the commentary on Romans, the vocabulary that persists in *CD* when he evokes the God who is not genial and affirming but radically questioning and abrogating of the certainties of human existence.[488] It is the vocabulary of decentering, of the overwhelming encounter with the wholly Other. It is the vocabulary of the actions of God as light that pierces, and of *Krisis* as crossroads. It is the vocabulary of the ultimate incomprehensibility of two who are locked in encounter. Perhaps the most important of the questions of Charlotte von Kirschbaum are those she asked, those she posed to Barth. Barth wrote a job description for her when he described the role or function of man and woman as man and woman in dialogue. In this sense it is accurate to say that her job was to be a woman. Just as God created men and women to exist in relationship, men and women should not seek to systematically define themselves or each other; rather, accepting and being faithful to their male or female existence, they will discover it in everything they do and think and see and hear in their orientation to each other.[489] This is the mutual orientation in which each is "a horizon and focus" for the other and which constitutes the being of each. "It is always in relationship to their opposite that man and woman are what they are in themselves."[490]

Von Kirschbaum's job was to be freely herself for Barth—a perfect realization of I-Thou relationship. And she did choose it—it was her calling; it was Barth's work to which she said "That's it!" But Barth did not see as *his* job or life or calling to be himself for her. That is the unfreedom in their relationship, a Proustian captivity made by Barth and modern, post-Cartesian culture combined. The job description—the assignment of roles—served, I think, to contain and channel—and harness—the explosiveness in their relationship. It functioned as a model for both of them, and as such it had healthy and unhealthy, positive as

487. Ibid., 168 (*KD* III/4:187).
488. *CD* I/1:386 (*KD* I/1:407).
489. *CD* III/4:153 (*KD* III/4:170).
490. Ibid., 163 (*KD* III/4:182).

well as deceptive and self-deceptive, aspects. Its one-sidedness (while I assume she discussed her lecture series with him and used material from their discussions, they were, with that exception, working on his assignments) made it exploitative, as did its manipulative deflection from other possible responses to the tensions in their relationship. Part of the exploitiveness was that von Kirschbaum was confined by cultural boundaries, whereas Barth could experiment in his role-casting as he wished. But in the most genuine way, their relationship *was* theology. And the perplexing questions raised by their personal situation must always be viewed in the light of this theology, though not exclusively in its light.

Walter Lowe has underlined the importance of Barth's conception of difference. Barth "revised" Kierkegaard's notion of the infinite qualitative distinction by removing the predicate *infinite* so that it was not inherently oppositional and we, no longer at the opposite pole from the Other, are no longer "in line" with it. A difference rendered "simple" in this way is preserved *as* different from the self.[491] So it was that Barth could read the gospel (through Romans) as the announcement of "the limitation of the known world by another that is unknown. . . . The Gospel is not a truth among other truths" but the one that "sets a question-mark against all other truths." In "being completely different," God's power is "the KRISIS of all power." So it is that the gospel can dissolve and establish "the whole concrete world."[492] Lowe connects this reading with Derrida's conception of "certain possibilities foreign to a linguistic system" that neither negate that system nor leave it undisturbed but elicit within it "a certain trembling, a certain decentering."[493] In Barth's description of male/female encounter, the alterity of the Thou erupts into the life of the I as another world. From this perspective we can see that von Kirschbaum, as a woman, offered and posed to Barth an alterity that neither Thurneysen nor any other of Barth's dialogue partners could offer—or perhaps we must say, an alterity that Barth could not find in the Thurneysens of his world.

Barth seems very careful to state that woman *and* man render each other human in the I-Thou relationship. Is the otherness of the woman for the man, which is so precisely analogous within the human sphere to the otherness of God, the same as the otherness of the man for the

491. Lowe, *Theology and Difference*, chap. 2, pp. 33–48 (esp. 34–35, 43–44).
492. Barth, *Epistle to the Romans*, 35–36; discussed by Lowe, *Theology and Difference*, 36.
493. Lowe, *Theology and Difference*, 36.

woman? No. Barth retained the Romantic view of woman as mystery, the nineteenth-century fascination with the one who at some level was either angelic or demonic or both. I think this undermines his valuation of alterity. The mystery of woman is distinct from the Christian mystery of the community of Christ. It is the configuration (to use Alice Jardine's term) that lurks behind evocations of the shadow side, the original mother, the dark, cool, quiet cave so far away from progressive, frenetic, loud, glaring civilization. It is the watering place at which to drink and be whole again, and the manifold other forms of otherness that male selves—selves designed by men in post-Cartesian patriarchal culture— have believed in and feared and yearned for, and the magnetic, fascinating, seductive forces they have believed in and feared and yearned for. Simone de Beauvoir still tells us, as she told von Kirschbaum and Barth, that man "feminizes the ideal he sets up before him as the essential Other, because woman is the material representative of alterity."[494]

Jardine has discussed the extent to which Otherness in post–World War II discourse is "always already" in the (male) self; it is "the signifier's treasure" (Lacan). In French psychoanalytic theory, Otherness reflects the subject's never-completed break away from the holistic space and rhythm of the maternal body.[495] Kristeva has pointed out the linguistic perpetuation of the ultimate equation of Other and other sex such that space "outside of the conscious subject has always connoted the feminine in the history of Western thought—and any movement into alterity is a movement into that female space; any attempt to give a place to that alterity within discourse involves a putting into discourse of 'woman.'"[496]

In his rejection of Liberal Protestantism, Barth was condemning, besides its optimism, a leveling and superficial view of human nature. Beneath his own intellectualism and his constant sociality, there seems to have been an extraordinarily ambivalent attitude toward women. We have encountered Wolfgang Schildmann's analysis of Barth's recurring dream (in 1920, 1928, and again in the 1950s) of being buried alive by his mother even as she professed her benevolence. We know from psychology that at some level his mother abided as *Urbild* in his image of women and his seeing and hearing of women. I think she abided, not so much threateningly or benignly, but being both, as the mystery of women— reinforcing the common set of notions we have reviewed. I suggested in

---

494. Simone de Beauvoir, *The Second Sex*, trans. and ed. H. M. Parshley (New York: Modern Library, 1968), 179.
495. Jardine, *Gynesis*, 106–7.
496. Quoted in Jardine, *Gynesis*, 114f.

Part 1 of this study that Barth's incorporation of von Kirschbaum into his household was (in contrast to earlier attempts) a successful defiance of his mother's wishes for him. But I also have often had the sense that Barth infantilized himself in relation to von Kirschbaum—that he engendered a dependence on her that went beyond the mutuality of I and Thou. Partly he did this to justify, to himself as well as to her and all others, his request that she move into and remain in the household because he *needed* her there, constantly, for the work that, they both agreed, had to be done.

Barth's radically imperfect relationship with his mother may also have created the almost incurable loneliness of this widely revered and convivial theologian. Schildmann also looks at the dream in 1967 that Barth recounted to Eberhard Busch, the dream of that *steineinsam* figure in hell, "an endless waste," that chilled and terrified him and gripped him with the final words: "Und das droht dir" (this threatens you).[497] Hell was loneliness. There is more than the absence of real mother-love in the dream, but that absence may have been palpable in more ways than Barth knew and that we know.

Did Barth listen to von Kirschbaum? Of course—and probably even on the subject of listening. In 1951 he seemed to glance at von Kirschbaum's point about women's potential contribution to proclamation when he alluded to a future in which ministry might move away from the predominance of a single authoritative voice. Though still in an ungendered version, in 1963 he said he believed

> that the time of long lectures, when someone spoke for an hour and the audience was condemned to sit and listen to whatever they were given, is . . . perhaps over—not just for me but for everyone. What we need in theology and in the church is . . . [to] talk together and try to arrive at answers together, instead of someone trying to present something to other people as though the Holy Spirit had dictated it to him in person.[498]

Remember, though, that Barth's respect and attention to difference goes back to *Romans* and before—to the "Strange New World within the

---

497. Busch, *Glaubensheiterkeit: Karl Barth: Erfahrungen und Begegnungen* (Neukirchen-Vluyn: Neukirchener Verlag, 1985), 85 [inter alia]; Schildmann, *Was sind das für Zeichen?* chap. 11: "Ein Traum des alten Karl Barth," 168–83.

498. From a recorded conversation with the Württemberg brotherhood in July 1963, quoted in Busch, *Karl Barth*, 463–64.

Bible." It is part of his criticism of "official" ecumenism too: he thought it self-suppressing and impoverishing to work toward common denominators on important matters. This respect does balance the Barth who went for the jugular in combat with Brunner and others over theological differences.

I will end with a phrase from Luther and an image, both concerning relatedness, but of two different kinds. The phrase is *fides ex auditu*, and it points to openness. Barth listened and learned well, as so many have testified. The image is of Barth at work. Karl Barth worked in a controlled environment of signs: over his desk, a picture of his father and, above that, Grünewald's John pointing to the crucified Christ; the portraits of Calvin and Mozart on adjacent walls at the same level; and, as horizon and focus, the presence of Charlotte von Kirschbaum.

Bibliography

Adler, Renata. *Toward a Radical Middle: Fourteen Pieces of Reporting and Criticism.* New York: Random House, 1970.

Antwort. Karl Barth zum siebzigsten Geburtstag am 10. Mai 1956. Edited by Charlotte von Kirschbaum and Ernst Wolf. Zollikon-Zurich: Evangelischer Verlag, 1956.

Arendt, Hannah, and Karl Jaspers. *Hannah Arendt/Karl Jaspers: Correspondence 1926–1969.* Edited by Lotte Kohler and Hans Saner. Translated by Robert and Rita Kimber. New York: Harcourt Brace Jovanovich, 1992.

Atkinson, Clarissa W., Constance H. Buchanan, and Margaret Miles, eds. *Immaculate and Powerful: The Female in Sacred Image and Social Reality.* Boston: Beacon Press, 1985.

Baas, Marga, and Heleen Zordranger. "Freiheit aus zweiter Hand: Feministischer Anfrage an die Stellung der Frau in Karl Barths Theologie." *Zeitschrift für dialektische Theologie* 3 (1987): 131–51.

Baker, Howard S., and Margaret N. Baker. "Heinz Kohut's Self-Psychology: An Overview." *American Journal of Psychiatry* 144 (January 1987): 1–9.

Banks, Olive. *Faces of Feminism: A Study of Feminism as a Social Movement.* New York: St. Martin's Press, 1981.

Barth, Karl. *Die christliche Dogmatik im Entwurf.* 1927. Zurich: Theologischer Verlag, 1982.

———. *Church Dogmatics.* See *Kirchliche Dogmatik.*

———. *The Epistle to the Romans.* 6th ed. (based on 2nd ed., 1922). Translated by Edwyn C. Hoskyns. London: Oxford University Press, 1933; Oxford University Press paperback, 1968.

———. "Das erste Gebot als theologische Axiom." Lecture in Copenhagen and Aarhus, March 1933. In *Theologische Fragen und Antworten*, Gesammelte Vorträge 3, 127–43. Zollikon-Zurich: Evangelischer Verlag, 1957.

———. *The Göttingen Dogmatics: Instruction in the Christian Religion.* 1924–25. Vol. 1. Translated by Geoffrey W. Bromiley. Edited by Hannelotte Reiffen. Grand Rapids, Mich.: Wm. B. Eerdmans, 1991.

———. *The Holy Ghost and the Christian Life.* Lecture at Elberfeld, 1929. Translated by R. Birch Hoyle. London: F. Muller, 1938.

———. *How I Changed My Mind.* Prepared by John D. Godsey from *Christian Century* series, "How My Mind Has Changed." Richmond, Va.: John Knox Press, 1966.

———. *The Humanity of God.* 1956. Translated by John N. Thomas. Richmond, Va.: John Knox Press, 1960.

———. *Karl Barth: Letters 1961–1968.* Edited by Jürgen Fangmeier and Hinrich Stoevesandt. Translated by G. W. Bromiley. Grand Rapids, Mich.: Wm. B. Eerdmans, 1981.

————. *Karl Barth's Table Talk.* (*Scottish Journal of Theology Occasional Papers* 10.) Recorded and edited by John D. Godsey. Edinburgh: Oliver and Boyd, 1963.

————. "Die Kirche—die lebendige Gemeinde des lebendigen Herrn Jesus Christus." In *Die Schrift und die Kirche*, 21–44.

————. *Kirchliche Dogmatik.* Zollikon-Zurich: Evangelischer Verlag, 1932–70. ET: *Church Dogmatics.* Translated by G. W. Bromiley et al. Edited by G. W. Bromiley and T. F. Torrance. Edinburgh: T. & T. Clark, 1936–69.

————. "Nachwort." In *Schleiermacher-Auswahl. Mit einem Nachwort von Karl Barth*, edited by Heinz Bolli, 290–312. Munich: Siebenstern Taschenbuch, 1968.

————. *Protestant Theology in the Nineteenth Century: Its Background and History.* 1947 (based on lectures in 1932–33). Translated by B. Cozens and J. Bowden. London: SCM, 1972.

————. *Die Schrift und die Kirche.* Theologische Studien 22. Zollikon-Zurich: Evangelischer Verlag, 1947.

————. "The Strange New World Within the Bible." Address in Leutwil, 1916. In *The Word of God and the Word of Man*, translated by Douglas Horton, 28–50. [Boston, Chicago]: Pilgrim Press, 1928.

Barth, Karl, and Emil Brunner. *Natural Theology, Comprising "Nature and Grace" by Prof. Dr. Emil Brunner and the Reply "No!" by Dr. Karl Barth.* 1934. Translated by Peter Fraenkel. London: Geoffrey Bles/Centenary Press, 1946.

Barth, Karl, and Eduard Thurneysen. *Revolutionary Theology in the Making: Barth-Thurneysen Correspondence, 1914–1925.* Translated by James D. Smart. Richmond, Va.: John Knox Press, 1964.

————. *Karl Barth-Eduard Thurneysen Briefwechsel: 1921–30.* (Karl Barth, *Gesamtausgabe V: Briefe*, 2.) Edited by Eduard Thurneysen. Zurich: Theologischer Verlag, 1974.

Barth, Markus. *Ephesians: Introduction, Translation, and Commentary.* (Anchor Bible, vols. 34–34A.) Garden City, N.Y.: Doubleday, 1974.

Baxter, John. *The Cinema of Josef von Sternberg.* International Film Guide Series. London: A. Zwemmer, 1971.

Beauvoir, Simone de. *The Second Sex.* 1949. Translated and edited by H. M. Parshley. New York: Modern Library, 1968.

Becker, Dieter. *Karl Barth und Martin Buber—Denker in dialogischer Nachbarschaft? Zur Bedeutung Martin Bübers für die Anthropologie Karl Barths.* Göttingen: Vandenhoeck & Ruprecht, 1986.

Bergmann, Karl Hans. *Die Bewegung "Freies Deutschland" in der Schweiz 1943–1945.* Munich: Carl Hansen Verlag, 1974.

Bieler, Andrea. "Aspekte nationalsozialistischer Frauenpolitik in ihrer Bedeutung für die Theologinnen." In *'Darum wagt es, Schwestern,'* 243–69.

Bird, Phyllis A. "Sexual Differentiation and Divine Image in the Genesis Creation Texts." In *Image of God and Gender Models*, edited by Kari E. Børreson, 11–34. Oslo: Solum Verlag, 1991.

Bonhoeffer, Dietrich. *Schweizer Korrespondenz 1941–42. Im Gespräch mit Karl Barth.* Edited by Eberhard Bethge. Theologische Existenz heute 214. Munich: Chr. Kaiser Verlag, 1982.

Bordo, Susan. "Feminism, Postmodernism, and Gender-Scepticism." In *Feminism/Postmodernism*, edited by Linda J. Nicholson, 133–56. New York: Routledge, 1990.

Børreson, Kari E., ed. *Image of God and Gender Models in Judaeo-Christian Tradition*. Oslo: Solum Verlag, 1991.

Briggs, Sheila. "Images of Women and Jews in Nineteenth- and Twentieth-Century German Theology." In *Immaculate and Powerful*, edited by Atkinson, Buchanan, and Miles, 226–59. Boston: Beacon Press, 1985.

Broembsen, F. von. "The Twinship: A Paradigm Towards Separation and Integration." *American Journal of Psychoanalysis* 48 (1988): 355–65.

Buber, Martin. "Afterword: The History of the Dialogical Principle." In M. Buber, *Between Man and Man*, translated by Maurice Friedman, 209–24. New York: Macmillan, 1965.

———. *I and Thou*. 1923. Translated, with a prologue and notes, by Walter Kaufmann. New York: Touchstone/Charles Scribner's Sons, 1970.

Busch, Eberhard. "Deciding Moments in the Life and Work of Karl Barth." Translated by Martin Rumscheidt and Barbara Rumscheidt. *Grail* 2 (1986): 51–67.

———. "Gelebte theologische Existenz bei Karl Barth." In *Theologie als Christologie: Zum Werk und Leben Karl Barths. Ein Symposium*, edited by Heidelore Köckert and Wolf Krötke, 170–92. Berlin: Evangelische Verlagsanstalt, 1988.

———. *Glaubensheiterkeit: Karl Barth: Erfahrungen und Begegnungen*. Neukirchen-Vluyn: Neukirchener Verlag, 1985.

———. "God Is God: The Meaning of a Controversial Formula and the Fundamental Problem of Speaking About God." Lecture, Princeton Theological Seminary, 28 October 1985. *Princeton Seminary Bulletin* n.s. 7 (1986): 101–13.

———. *Karl Barth: His Life from Letters and Autobiographical Texts*. 2nd ed. Translated by John Bowden. Philadelphia: Fortress Press, 1976.

———. "Lobe den Herrn" [funeral address]. *Karl Barth: 1886–1968*, 13–19.

———. "Memories of Karl Barth." Transcription of interview, November 1985, by Donald McKim. In *How Karl Barth Changed My Mind*, edited by Donald McKim, 9–14. Grand Rapids, Mich.: Wm. B. Eerdmans, 1986.

———. "Theologie und Biographie: das Problem des Verhältnisses der beiden Grössen in Karl Barths Theologie." *Evangelische Theologie* 6 (1986): 325–39.

Calvin, John. *Institutes of the Christian Religion*. 1559. Library of Christian Classics. Translated by Ford Lewis Battles. Edited by John T. McNeill. 2 vols. Philadelphia: Westminster, 1960.

Chopp, Rebecca S. *The Power to Speak: Feminism, Language, God*. New York: Crossroad, 1991.

Clark, Elizabeth, and Herbert Richardson, eds. *Women and Religion: A Feminist Sourcebook of Christian Thought*. New York: Harper & Row, 1977.

'*Darum wagt es, Schwestern . . .': zur Geschichte evangelischer Theologinnen in Deutschland*. Frauenforschungsprojekt zur Geschichte der Theologinnen, Göttingen. Neukirchen-Vluyn: Neukirchener Verlag, 1994.

Douglas, Ann. *The Feminization of American Culture*. 1977. New York: Double-day/ Anchor, 1988. [first ed. 1977].

Douglass, Jane Dempsey. "The Image of God in Women as Seen by Luther and Calvin." In *Image of God and Gender Models*, edited by Kari E. Børreson, 228–56. Oslo: Solum Verlag, 1991.

Eisenstein, Hester. *Contemporary Feminist Thought*. Boston: G. K. Hall, 1983.

Eksteins, Modris. *Rites of Spring: The Great War and the Birth of the Modern Age*. Boston: Houghton Mifflin, 1989.

Ellenberger, Henri. *The Discovery of the Unconscious: The History and Evolution of Dynamic Psychiatry*. New York: Basic Books, 1970.

Erhart, Hannelore. "Der 'Verband evangelischer Theologinnen Deutschlands' zwischen Frauenbewegung und Kirche in der Zeit der Weimarer Republik." In *'Darum wagt es, Schwestern,'* 151–57.

Erhart, Hannelore, and Leonore Siegele-Wenschkewitz. "'Vierfache Stufenleiter abwärts . . . : Gott, Christus, der Mann, das Weib': Karl Barth und die Solidarität und Kritik von Henriette Visser't Hooft." In *Wie Theologen Frauen sehen—von der Macht der Bilder*, edited by Renate Jost and Ursula Kubera, 142–58. Freiburg: Herder, 1993.

Eva, wo bist du? Frauen in internationalen Organisationen der Ökumene: eine Dokumentation. Edited by Gudrun Kaper, Henriette Visser't Hooft et al. Gelnhausen: Burckhardthaus-Laetere Verlag, 1981.

Fiddes, Paul. "The Status of Woman in the Thought of Karl Barth." In *After Eve: Women, Theology and the Christian Tradition*, edited by Janet Martin Soskice, 138–55. London: Marshall Pickering, 1990.

Frei, Hans. "Eberhard Busch's Biography of Karl Barth." In Hans Frei, *Types of Christian Theology*, edited by George Hunsinger and William C. Placher, 147–63. New Haven: Yale University Press, 1992.

Frevert, Ute. *Women in German History: From Bourgeois Emancipation to Sexual Liberation*. 1986. Translated by Stuart McKinnon-Evans. Oxford: Berg Publishers, 1989.

Friedlander, Judith, et al., ed. and trans. *Women in Culture and Politics: A Century of Change*. Bloomington: Indiana University Press, 1986.

Friedman, Maurice. *Martin Buber: The Life of Dialogue*. 3rd ed. Chicago: University of Chicago Press, 1976.

———. *Martin Buber's Life and Work: The Early Years, 1876–1923*. New York: E. P. Dutton, 1981.

Frykberg, Elizabeth. *Karl Barth's Theological Anthropology: An Analogical Critique Regarding Gender Relations*. Studies in Reformed Theology and History. Princeton: Princeton Theological Seminary, 1993.

Gatz, Margaret, et al. "Dementia: Not Just a Search for the Gene." The *Gerontologist* 34:2 (1994): 251–55.

Gay, Peter. *The Bourgeois Experience: Victoria to Freud*, vol. 1, *Education of the Senses*. New York: Oxford University Press, 1984.

———. *Weimar Culture: The Outsider as Insider*. New York: Harper & Row, 1968.

Godsey, John. "Portrait of Barth." In Karl Barth, *How I Changed My Mind*. Richmond, Va.: John Knox Press, 1966.

Gollwitzer, Helmut. "Ansprache" [funeral address]. *Karl Barth: 1886–1968*, 37–40.

———. "Predigt bei der Beerdigung Charlotte von Kirschbaum am 8 Juli 1975, Friedhof am Hörnli, Basel." In *Junge Kirche protestantische Monatshefte* [Bremen] 37 (1976): 33–35.

———. "The Significance of Martin Buber for Protestant Theology." In *Martin Buber: A Centenary Volume*, edited by Haim Gordon and Jochanan Bloch, 385–417. New York: KTAV Publishing House for the Faculty of Humanities and Social Sciences, Ben Gurion University, 1984.

Green, Garrett. *Imagining God: Theology and the Religious Imagination*. San Francisco: Harper & Row, 1989.

Grossmann, Atina. "*Girlkultur* or Thoroughly Rationalized Female: A New Woman in Weimar Germany?" In *Women in Culture and Politics: A Century of Change*, translated from the French and edited by Judith Friedlander et al., 62–80. Bloomington: Indiana University Press, 1986.

Heiler, Friedrich. "The Madonna as Religious Symbol." 1934. In *The Mystic Vision: Papers from the Eranos Yearbooks*, translated by Ralph Manheim, 348–74. Bollingen Series 30, vol. 6. Princeton: Princeton University Press, 1968.

Henze, Dagmar. "Die Anfänge des Frauenstudiums in Deutschland." In *'Darum wagt es, Schwestern,'* 19–40.

———. "Die Konflikte zwischen dem 'Verband evangelischer Theologinnen Deutschlands' und der 'Vereinigung evangelischer Theologinnen' um die Frage des vollten Pfarramtes für die Frau." In *'Darum wagt es, Schwestern,'* 129–50.

———. "Schule als Arbeitsfeld für Theologinnen in der Zeit bis 1933." In *'Darum wagt es, Schwestern,'* 191–209.

Hesselink, John. "The Humanity (*Menschlichkeit*) of Karl Barth." *Reformed Review* 42 (1988): 140–45.

Hunsinger, George. *How to Read Karl Barth: The Shape of His Theology*. New York: Oxford University Press, 1991.

Jackson, Eleanor. See Charlotte von Kirschbaum, *The Question of Woman: The Collected Writings of Charlotte von Kirschbaum*.

Jardine, Alice A. *Gynesis: Configurations of Woman and Modernity*. Ithaca, N.Y.: Cornell University Press, 1985.

Jónsson, Gunnlauger A. *The Image of God: Genesis 1:26–28 in a Century of Old Testament Research*. Stockholm: Almqvist & Wiskell, 1988.

Jung, C. G. "Aion." 1951. In *Psyche & Symbol: A Selection from the Writings of C. G. Jung*, translated by Cary Baynes and F. C. R. Hall, edited by Violet S. de Laszlo, 1–60. New York: Doubleday, 1958.

Karl Barth: 1886–1968: Gedenkfeier im Basler Münster. Zurich: EVZ-Verlag [Evangelischer Verlag], 1969. Also published as Theologische Studien, 100.

Keller, Catherine. *From a Broken Web: Separation, Sexism, and Self*. Boston: Beacon Press, 1986.

Kirschbaum, Charlotte von. "Address for the Movement 'Free Germany.'" 1945. Translated by Keith Crim. In R. Köbler, *In the Shadow of Karl Barth*, 81–92. Louisville: Westminster/John Knox, 1989.

————. "Bibliographia Barthiana." In *Antwort. Karl Barth zum siebzigsten Geburtstag*, 943–60.

————. *The Question of Woman: The Collected Writings of Charlotte von Kirschbaum*. Translated by John Shepherd. Edited and with an Introduction by Eleanor Jackson. Grand Rapids: Wm. B. Eerdmans, 1996.

————. "The Role of Women in the Proclamation of the Word." 1951. Translated by Keith Crim, in R. Köbler, *In the Shadow of Karl Barth*, 93–124. Louisville: Westminster/John Knox, 1989.

————. *Die wirkliche Frau*. Zollikon-Zurich: Evangelischer Verlag, 1949.

Köbler, Renate. *In the Shadow of Karl Barth: Charlotte von Kirschbaum*. Translated by Keith Crim. Louisville, Ky.: Westminster/John Knox, 1989. [Original work: *Schattenarbeit: Charlotte von Kirschbaum. Die Theologin an der Seite Karl Barths*. Cologne: Pahl-Rugenstein Verlag, 1987.]

Köckert, Heidelore, and Wolf Krötke, eds. *Theologie als Christologie: zum Werk und Leben Karl Barths: Ein Symposium*. Berlin: Evangelische Verlagsanstalt, 1988.

Koonz, Claudia. "Some Political Implications of Separatism: German Women Between Democracy and Nazism, 1928–1934." In *Women in Culture and Politics*, edited by Judith Friedlander et al., 268–85. Bloomington: Indiana University Press, 1986.

Krieger, Leonard. *The German Idea of Freedom*. Boston: Beacon Press, 1957.

Krötke, Wolf. "Gott und Mensch als 'Partner.' Zur Bedeutung einer zentralen Kategorien in Karl Barths Kirchlicher Dogmatik." In *Theologie als Christologie: Zum Werk und Leben Karl Barths: Ein Symposium*, edited by Heidelore Köckert and Wolf Krötke, 106–20. Berlin: Evangelische Verlagsanstalt, 1988.

Kupisch, Karl. *Karl Barth in Selbstzeugnissen und Bilddokumenten*. Reinbek bei Hamburg: Rowohlt Taschenbuch Verlag, 1971.

Kurtz, Petra. "Der 'Verband evangelischer Theologinnen Deutschlands' im Spiegel seiner 'Mitteilungen' in der Zeit der Weimarer Republik." In *'Darum wagt es, Schwestern,'* 175–90.

Lowe, Walter. "Barth as Critic of Dualism: Re-reading the *Römerbrief*." *Scottish Journal of Theology* 41 (1988): 377–95.

————. *Theology and Difference: The Wound of Reason*. Bloomington: Indiana University Press, 1993.

McCormack, Bruce L. "Historical Criticism and Dogmatic Interest in Karl Barth's Theological Exegesis of the New Testament." In *Biblical Hermeneutics in Historical Perspective: Studies in Honor of Karlfried Froehlich on His Sixtieth Birthday*, edited by Mark S. Burrows and Paul Rorem, 322–38. Grand Rapids: Wm. B. Eerdmans, 1991.

————. *Karl Barth's Critically Realistic Dialectical Theology: Its Genesis and Development, 1909–1936*. Oxford and New York: Oxford University Press, 1995.

McKelway, Alexander J. "Perichoretic Possibilities in Barth's Doctrine of Male and Female." *Princeton Seminary Bulletin* 7 (1986): 231–43.

McKim, Donald K., ed. *How Karl Barth Changed My Mind*. Grand Rapids, Mich.: Wm. B. Eerdmans, 1986.

Mann, Thomas. *Buddenbrooks*. 1900. Translated by John E. Woods. New York: Alfred A. Knopf, 1993.

———. *The Magic Mountain*. 1924. Translated by H. T. Lowe-Porter. New York: Alfred A. Knopf, 1969.

Moltmann, Jürgen. "Henriette Visser't Hooft." In *Gotteslehrerinnen*, edited by Luise Schottroff and Johannes Thiele, 168–79. Stuttgart: Kreuz Verlag, 1989.

Moltmann-Wendel, Elisabeth. "The Women's Movement in Germany." *Lutheran World* 22 (1975): 121–30.

Neukrantz, Klaus. *Barricades in Berlin*. 1931. [Translator not identified.] Chicago: Banner Press, 1979.

Neuser, W. H. *Karl Barth in Münster, 1925–30*. Theologische Studien 130. Zurich: Theologischer Verlag, 1985.

Nochlin, Linda. "Why Have There Been No Great Women Artists?" In L. Nochlin, *"Women, Art, and Power" and Other Essays*, 145–78. New York: Harper & Row, 1988.

Nützel, Gerdi. "Jugendarbeit als Arbeitsfeld für Theologinnen in der Zeit des Nationalsozialismus." In *'Darum wagt es, Schwestern,'* 421–45.

O'Donovan, Joan. "Man in the Image of God: The Disagreement Between Barth and Brunner Reconsidered." *Scottish Journal of Theology* 39 (1986): 433–59.

Pannenberg, Wolfhart. *Anthropology in Theological Perspective*. Translated by Matthew O'Connell. Philadelphia: Westminster Press, 1985.

Paulsen, Anna. *Geschlecht und Person: das biblische Wort über die Frau*. Hamburg: Furche-Verlag, 1960.

Pope, Barbara Corrado. "Immaculate and Powerful: The Marian Revival in the Nineteenth Century." In *Immaculate and Powerful*, edited by Atkinson, Buchanan, and Miles, 173–200. Boston: Beacon Press, 1985.

Praz, Mario. *The Romantic Agony*. 2nd ed., 1951. Translated by Angus Davidson. New York: Meridian Books, 1956.

Prelinger, Catherine M. *Charity, Challenge, and Change: Religious Dimensions of the Nineteenth-Century Women's Movement in Germany*. Westport, Conn.: Greenwood Press, 1987.

Prelinger, Catherine M., and Rosemary S. Keller. "The Function of Female Bonding: The Restored Diaconessate of the Nineteenth Century." In *Women in New Worlds: Historical Perspectives on the Wesleyan Tradition*, vol. 2, edited by R. S. Keller, Louise Queen, and Hilah F. Thomas, 318–37. Nashville, Tenn.: Abingdon Press, 1982.

Querdenken: Beiträge zur feministisch-befreiungstheologischen Diskussion. 2nd ed. Edited by the Frauenforschungsprojekt zur Geschichte der Theologinnen. Pfaffenweiler: Centaurus-Verlagsgesellschaft, 1993.

Reformierte Kirchenzeitung, 1932, nos. 25, 28, 30. Letters and responses by Gertrud Herrmann, D. W. Rolfhaus, and Karl Barth.

Die Religion in Geschichte und Gegenwart. 3rd ed. Tübingen: J. C. B. Mohr, 1957–65.

Ritschl, Dietrich. "How to Be Most Grateful to Karl Barth Without Remaining a Barthian." In *How Karl Barth Changed My Mind*, edited by Donald K. McKim, 86–93. Grand Rapids, Mich.: Wm. B. Eerdmans, 1986.

Roberts, Mary Louise. "Samson and Delilah Revisited: The Politics of Women's Fashions in 1920s France." *American Historical Review* 98 (1993): 657–83.

Robinson, James M., ed. *The Beginnings of Dialectical Theology.* Translated by Keith Crim and Louis DeGrazia. Richmond, Va.: John Knox Press, 1968.

Romero, Joan. "The Protestant Principle: A Woman's-Eye View of Barth and Tillich." In *Religion and Sexism: Images of Woman in the Jewish and Christian Traditions*, edited by Rosemary Radford Ruether, 314–41. New York: Simon & Schuster, 1974.

Rose, Phyllis. *Parallel Lives: Five Victorian Marriages.* New York: Random House, 1983.

Schildmann, Wolfgang. *Was sind das für Zeichen? Karl Barths Träume im Kontext von Leben und Lehre.* Munich: Chr. Kaiser Verlag, 1991.

Schleiermacher, Friedrich. *Christmas Eve: Dialogue on the Incarnation.* Translated by Terrence N. Tice. Richmond, Va.: John Knox Press, 1967. [Original work: *Weihnachtsfeier*, 2nd ed., Berlin, 1826.]

Smith, Bonnie. *Changing Lives: Women in European History Since 1700.* Lexington, Mass.: D. C. Heath and Co., 1989.

Stephan, Inge. *Das Schicksal der begabten Frau: Im Schatten berühmter Männer.* 6th ed. Stuttgart: Kreuz Verlag, 1991.

Theunissen, Michael. *The Other: Studies in the Social Ontology of Husserl, Heidegger, Sartre, and Buber.* Translated by Christopher Macann. Cambridge, Mass.: MIT Press, 1984.

Umidi, Robert. "Imaging God Together: The Image of God as 'Sociality' in the Thought and Life of Dietrich Bonhoeffer." Ph.D. diss., Drew University, 1993.

Visser't Hooft Boddaert, Henriette. "Eve, Where Art Thou?" 1934. *Student World* (Geneva) 114: 208–20.

———. "Unausweichliche Fragen: Aus dem Briefwechsel mit Karl Barth 1934; Eva, wo bist Du?—Aufsatz von 1934; Briefe an Karl Barth 1941, 1946, 1948." In *Eva, wo bist du? Frauen in internationalen Organisationen der Ökumene. Eine Dokumentation*, chap. 1, pp. 12–36.

Webb, Stephen. *Re-Figuring Theology: The Rhetoric of Karl Barth.* Albany: State University of New York Press, 1991.

Welch, Claude. *Protestant Thought in the Nineteenth Century.* Vol. 2: *1870–1914.* New Haven: Yale University Press, 1985.

Witt, Almut. "Anna Paulsen—Lebensbild einer Theologin." In *Querdenken: Beiträge zur feministisch-befreiungstheologischen Diskussion*, 2nd ed. 268–89. Pfaffenweiler: Centaurus-Verlagsgesellschaft, 1993.

Wyschograd, Michael. "A Jewish Perspective on Karl Barth." In *How Karl Barth Changed My Mind*, edited by Donald McKim, 156–61. Grand Rapids, Mich.: Wm. B. Eerdmans, 1986.

Zuckmayer, Carl. *A Late Friendship: The Letters of Karl Barth and Carl Zuckmayer.* Preface by Hinrich Stoevesandt. Translated by Geoffrey W. Bromiley. Grand Rapids, Mich.: Wm. B. Eerdmans, 1982.

Index

Abegg, Wilhelm, 68
active/passive dichotomy, 103, 161
alter ego function, 54
alterity, 131–32
  Barth and, 134, 189, 190, 192–93
  and gender. *See* encounter, Barth on
  Kristeva on, 191
Althaus, Paul, 56 n. 16
analogy of faith, 118, 145, 150
analogy of relations, 125–26, 135, 137, 139
Arendt, Hannah, 37

Bachofen, Johan Jakob, 142 n. 244
Balthasar, Hans Urs von, 129
Barth, Anna (mother), 6, 7, 35, 191–92.
  See also Barth, Karl, and mother image
Barth, Fritz (father), 35, 92–93, 181 n. 452
Barth, Gertrud (sister), 36
Barth, Heinrich (brother), 7, 57
Barth, Karl
  academic career, 2
  actualism of, 102, 120
  and aloneness, 6, 121, 192
  and cinema, 98 n. 37
  as dean at Münster, 59
  on debt to von Kirschbaum, 1, 42, 81, 82–83, 89
  on male deprivation, 146
  dialogical situation, 26
  and divorce, 7, 8
  and dualism, 122–23, 157
  and feminism, 6, 32, 99–100, 141, 157 n. 328, 160 n. 342, 172, 181
  on God's address to human creature, 85, 130
  on history of theology, 85–87
  on honor, 177–78
  and Jews, 129 n. 181
  on Joseph, 102
  mother image, 18, 191
  and Mozart, 125
  and natural theology, 79–81 passim, 84
  opposition to Nazism, 66–67
  personality, 16–17, 54, 129
  and post–World War II Germany, 69, 70
  and psychoanalysis, 17, 96
  and questioning, 131
  relations with women, 18, 36, 191. *See also* women, nature of, Barth on; marriage, Barth on
  on revelation, 85, 101
  study of Anselm, 79, 84
  Swiss identity, 69
  as teacher, 63
  on his theological development, 78–80, 81
  as university "star," 12–13, 61 n. 32
  weekly schedule, 60–61
Barth, Karl, and Charlotte von Kirschbaum, personal relationship of: *See* Kirschbaum, Charlotte von, and Karl Barth, personal relationship of
Barth, Markus (son), 13, 182
Barth, Nelly (wife), 6, 7, 10
Barth, Rose Marie (wife of Markus), 182
Barth family: interest in women's movement, 35–36, 91
Beauvoir, Simone de, 23, 29, 191
  Barth on, 170, 171–72
  von Kirschbaum on, 170–71
Becker, Dieter, 132–33
Bekennende Kirche. See Confessing Church
Bergli, 4, 7, 12, 27, 32, 36
Berlin, 31–32
Bewegung "Freies Deutschland." See Movement for a Free Germany
biblical exegesis
  Barth, 77–78, 110–13, 116, 139, 164–66, 168–69
  von Kirschbaum, 110–13, 116, 164–67, 168–69
Bird, Phyllis, 139
birth control, 13
bisexuality: Barth on, 141–42, 171
The Blue Angel (movie), 98